The Church and the Culture of Modernity

R. J. Divozzo

ISBN: 1463719450
ISBN-13:978-1463719456

DEDICATION

To my patron, Saint Thomas Aquinas, without whose help this book would not be. And to my beloved wife, Noelle, and my bonny lads and lassies, John-Paul, Anna, Sophie, and Dominic, whose love and affection provide me with that foundation of happiness without which I would, doubtless, do nothing worthwhile in life.

CONTENTS

ACKNOWLEDGMENTS

I would like to thank the many people who read the manuscript and who encouraged me to publish it, especially Dr. Kurt Poterack and Leonard Grotenrath. I am especially grateful to Professor Mark Pestana for his friendly encouragement and for his painstaking editing, for which this book is much the better.

.

Demonstrationis principium' quod quid est'.

St. Thomas Aquinas

The Church lives again the life of Christ. It has its period of obscurity and growth and its period of manifestation, and this is followed by the catastrophe of the Cross and the new birth that springs from failure. And what is most remarkable is that the enemies of the Church—the movements that rend and crucify her—are in a sense her own offspring and derive their dynamic force from her. Islam, the Protestant Reformation, the Liberal Revolution, none of them would have existed apart from Christianity—they are abortive or partial manifestations of the spiritual power which Christianity has brought into history. "I have come to cast fire on the earth and what will I, but that it be kindled."

Christopher Dawson, "Christianity and Contradiction in History"

The conservative response to modernity is to embrace it, but to embrace it critically, in full consciousness that human achievements are rare and precarious, that we have no God-given right to destroy our inheritance, but must always patiently submit to the voice of order, and set an example of orderly living."

T.S. Eliot

Foundations once destroyed, what can the just do?"
The Lord is in his holy temple,
the Lord, whose throne is in heaven. . . .
The Lord is just and loves justice;
the upright shall see his face.

Psalm 11

The Church and the Culture of Modernity

Preface

I might have entitled this book "Ideas Have Consequences", but that title had already been taken. I have written this book only after a long wait for someone else to write it. Doubtless, someone else would have made better work of it. But, although this book is itself a new thing under the sun, what it says has been said and said better already a hundred times over, but not, so far as I know, in the *same* book. Having myself read and been much enlightened by many of the best books that address the subject of modernity directly and indirectly, I have tried in my own book to render for my readers a kind of tapestry of my subject from the various and varied threads drawn from many years of reading and thinking and of discussing these books that have been so instructive to me.

The last seventy years or more have seen a good many critiques of modernity; I have endeavored in this work to appropriate from the best of them the arguments and observations that I think best serve to enlighten my reader to an understanding of the nature of modernity vis-à-vis the

Church. But let the reader beware (or consoled): this book was not written exclusively for Catholic intellectuals. In writing it I have had in view a much wider audience – the educated Catholic who at least takes his religion seriously enough to read a book like this. More than a mere sop to the academic reader, the purpose of the frequent documentation is two-fold: to send my reader to my sources for a more complete treatment of the ideas or arguments presented and, of course, to avoid plagiarizing the many sources to which I clung so closely in the writing. I have considered my task in writing this book to be something more like that of the medieval scribe producing what is essentially the work of others than the modern scholar or essayist whose aim is to produce something original. If the book itself is original, it is original only in the sense that a collage is original: the whole is new but all its parts are borrowed. The bibliography I have provided is a list of those books which have influenced this book and the reader is strongly encouraged to read or, at least, consult them, for together they will enlighten him more than this book could ever do.

I have tried to treat my subject according to the principles of the Catholic intellectual tradition and the perennial mind of the Church. The degree to which I have succeeded is the precise value of this book.

The Feast of St. Francis de Sales, 2010

Introduction

Since the Second Vatican Council and the promulgation of *Gaudium et Spes*, it has been supposed that the Church is to be guided toward a fresh understanding of the modern world and to a rapprochement with its triumphant order by which the Church can speak meaningfully to modern man. At the time of the Council, it seemed to many in the Church that the modern world was a remarkable success. Certainly, it had succeeded in changing profoundly everything – a true *novus ordo saeculorum*. The Church, it was feared, represented the old order that had passed away and become irrelevant in every aspect of civilized life, politics, economics, social organization, for the philosophical principles which were the intellectual foundation of that older civilized order had long since been cast off. It was understood that the problems of the modern world were many, but there was an unshakeable confidence that the solutions could be found only within the scope of modern thought.

Yet in these forty-some years since the Council, both the Church and the modern world have suffered an unprecedented decline. The promised "springtime" for the Church never came, instead she has suffered a winter of discontent that has exceeded her natural capacities to endure it; and the world has sunk morally and spiritually into a seemingly apocalyptic state. Although the generation of the much-vaunted Council will not likely see the renewal that the Council was supposed to precipitate, there are now unmistakable signs that the next generation may enjoy it. But the renewal will not be the fruit of Vatican II. That troubled council can, in my view, be little more than the catalyst for a more prosperous reconsideration of the issues it so wisely took up but less wisely deliberated. But any reconsideration of the issues, the Sacred Liturgy, religious freedom, ecumenism, etc., cannot afford to ignore the counsels of Vatican II, for its success will depend upon a reinterpretation of what the Council declared, which will in turn depend on what Pope Benedict XVI has called the "hermeneutic of continuity". Those who might wish to cannot simply make the Second Vatican Council go away any more than others could make Trent do likewise. By its own admission to being a strictly pastoral council and by its failure to clarify important matters for the Church Vatican II has not merited the tremendous importance attributed to it. But because the council is an historical reality in the Church and because it has been for forty years wrongfully regarded as having almost dogmatic status, it cannot, however much one wishes, be swept under the rug or relegated to the attic. Rather, let us, as is Pope Benedict's intent, welcome the prodigal home. It is my hope that in its very small and oblique way this book will help that effort.

The concern of this book is the relation of the Church to modernity. I do not say to the "modern world" because, in the first place, it is not my intent to try to "fix" the Second Vatican Council's declaration on that matter in *Gaudium et Spes*; and, second, because the Church's fundamental relation to the modern world is the same as it is in every age, that is, the relation of the City of God to the City of Man. Prudential considerations of how exactly to conduct that relationship is a matter for the Church's perennial wisdom. I am only concerned with modernity as distinct from that which is merely modern or up-to-date. The Church does not regard what is modern as inherently bad or necessarily suspect. The Church is necessarily a traditionary institution but she has no animus against innovation as such or against what is new. Modernity is something different. Despite its obsession with the novel and its hostility to tradition, it is itself not of recent vintage. The roots of modernity go back as far as the 14th century, but it is the child of the modern world (historically speaking) brought forth in its peculiar intellectual, social, political, and economic conditions. Those conditions obtained throughout European and American civilization and were given increasingly free reign by the event of, as well as the principles that informed, the French Revolution. While every great historical development needs a catalyst; the French Revolution was the catalyst for the development of modernity, but it was not its formal cause or source. It was rather a nascent modernity that caused the French Revolution.

Every deliberate action begins in thought and, as Pascal said, "to think well is the principle of morality." The source of modernity was bad thinking. And the source of that bad thinking was the abandonment of Aristotelian-Thomistic metaphysics. The profound philosophical errors became the "DNA" that determined the character of the modern world. Metaphysics asks (and answers) questions of the ultimate reasons for existence, of being itself. From the answers to such questions are formed our notions of truth, goodness, and the beautiful. And because metaphysics is the highest wisdom, it makes the most profound mistakes. This book is principally concerned with those mistakes and the inability of the prevailing opinion in the Church (despite Pope Benedict's clarion calls) to take them fully into account in assessing the dangers of modernity to fundamental Catholic principles and all that depends upon the Church's adherence to them.

The failure among Catholics to understand the danger of modernity is primarily the result of two fundamental assumptions about modern civilization; that it is at once superior to all previous civilizations and that the culture of modernity can, like any culture, be Christianized in the same way that classical pagan culture was. The first assumption is hubristic and is based on purely material and technological criteria; it presumes too a moral superiority, a presumption due to an inability to judge fairly and accurately both its own colossal moral and intellectual weakness and the moral and intellectual strengths of its classical and medieval progenitors. The second assumption follows from a failure to understand the nature of culture, that it is fundamentally the expression of man's religious nature and that a secular culture can only be well ordered if it recognizes its religious foundation. Classical pagan culture, for all its hostility to and incomprehension of Christianity, was fundamentally religious and as such had a fundamental affinity to Christianity that modernity lacks. Classical paganism had also through the philosophical tradition of the Platonic and Aristotelian schools a profound *metaphysical* affinity to Christian theology. Modern philosophy's abandonment of what became known as the realist tradition in metaphysics uprooted western thought from that deep affinity. Behind both assumptions lay a still more fundamental failure to understand the culture of modernity as historically and intellectually apostate, that its historical and intellectual development was an ever-deepening rejection of and estrangement from Christianity and Catholicism. These assumptions are not innocent of a deep prejudice in favor of modernity; they reveal an unwillingness as well as an inability to think outside of a modern framework of thought.

The Church and the Culture of Modernity

The Church's relation to the modern world can only be correctly understood as being at a profound level and in certain unavoidable ways antagonistic. The antagonism is fundamentally not a conflict between nature and grace or the sacred and the profane, but a conflict between a spiritual order devoted to transcendent realities and a temporal order devoted exclusively to the mundane realities of material existence. That is to say, it is the perennial conflict between, as St. Augustine conceived them, the City of God and the City of Man. But because modern civilization is a corruption of a Christian one, the conflict between modernity and the Church is more complex and problematic than the conflict between the two "Cities" in Augustine's doctrine. For the Church's evangelical mission to all that was once Christendom is not a perfect stranger to Christianity but a prodigal son. So, now it is a question of the Church's relation to a temporal order in the modern world that is not, as it was in Augustine's time, still virgin soil, that is, still unaffected by Christian influence but one which has for a long, long time progressively effaced, distorted, and opposed that influence. This rejection of grace makes by the modern world make a tremendous difference in the Church's relation to it. The Christianization of the Empire and (eventually) the civilization it encompassed, meant the infusion of grace into the temporal order has been infused with the grace (actual not sanctifying) of Christian truth. With the death of Christian culture, what was a cooperative relationship between the spiritual and the temporal orders is now a hostile one.

The Church and the Culture of Modernity

Even in a Christian civilization the temporal order, so far as it is necessarily determined by original sin, is in need of grace. Now that the specifically Christian culture of old Europe is largely dead that grace no longer obtains in the temporal order. Still it nevertheless operates; otherwise, the Church's mission would be impossible except by miraculous interventions. Modernity, if we understand it as the rejection or exclusion of Christian truth, is neither inevitable nor natural to the temporal order, since modernity often violates the natural order of goods, claiming that no such objective order exists. While the temporal order may recognize the transcendent, it is not naturally oriented to it; hence, the perennial conflict even when there is a formal wish to cooperate as in the conflicts between Church and State in the Middle Ages. Modernity, on the other hand, does not recognize the transcendent order; it does not acknowledge its existence whose reality is independent of man and which lays claim to his devout attention in all that he does. In so far as the first principle of modernity is man's autonomy from any authority above his own, it and Catholicism are not merely in conflict; they are mutually exclusive views of reality. For the first lesson of Christian (or any realist) metaphysics is that man is a *contingent* being. Catholicism and modernity differ in the same way as do a teacher of Thomist metaphysics and a lunatic who thinks he is God.

There are those who reject modernity intellectually, at least in its most discernable tenets, but accept it at the level of culture, insisting that enculturation is the principal means by which the Church can communicate the Gospel. But there is a subtle mistake in this position. It tacitly and uncritically supposes that intellectual ideas have little or no effect on culture or that by the time intellectual ideas filter down to cultural experience they become merely ethical problems which cannot be dealt with intellectually, because they have become part of our subjective experience of reality and must be dealt with as such. Hence, evangelism is more concerned with moral, social, and cultural problems than with the intellectual source of those problems. This is a great mistake because the Church cannot communicate the Gospel to those whose subjective experience of reality is out of kilter with objective reality. It is then not only a question of moral behavior, for example, ending abortion and the social conditions that foster it. More importantly, it is a question of the intellectual principles that make such evils acceptable and commonplace. I do not suggest that evangelism can afford to ignore the subjective experience of the unbeliever, still less his cultural perceptions of reality, nor do I deny that love, as opposed to mere rational argument, is the *modus operandi* of evangelism. But the end to which evangelism aims is not, as in therapeutic psychology, to help the person feel good about himself, but to bring him to an understanding and acceptance of certain objective and eternal truths. To do that one has to disabuse the modern man of his profound misapprehensions of reality, especially the spiritual realities that determine his eternal welfare.

The Church and the Culture of Modernity

While the prospects are dim, for the culture of western civilization has been all but swallowed up by modernity, there remains, for now at least, some distinction between modernity and western culture in so far as the intellectual, moral, and social traditions of the old western culture have not been utterly forgotten or rendered irrelevant. Those traditions, however, grow more tenuous by the day. In so far as the Christian culture that once obtained in the west is still active in Catholic thought and imagination (at very least) and can be articulated in the intellectual disciplines and in art and literature, it need not become a dead letter and may yet be a great attraction to a generation whose culture, they perhaps are beginning to realize, is morally and spiritually starving them.

Many would insist that it is a fear of change that makes one adhere to tradition and that tradition is a kind of worship of the past, which is dead. It is rather the obverse that is true: those who eschew tradition worship the present or, what is worse, the future, which does not exist. The worship of the present is the worship of change; it is the worship of mere sensation. Tradition alone is what makes the past live in the present. To deny the past's participation in the present or refuse to recognize it and have its play in the present is to be scarcely half conscious. Modernity denies the role of tradition because tradition receives, preserves, and passes on what it receives; modernity receives nothing that it does not remake in its own image. Whatever is processed through the modern consciousness, that is what passes the scrutiny of modern thought, always comes out a different thing from what it is.

Nevertheless, it is necessary to make a distinction between modernity and modern. All that is modern is not modernity. As mentioned already, not everything modern is hostile to Christian truth. This is true of technologies, forms of government, social habits, etc. But in so far as these elements of modern civilization are subsumed by the culture of modernity they become dangerous, if not actively corrupting. Though they are not things which the Christian must forswear, in the cultural environment in which they flourish, they are somewhat "wild" because modernity places no serious moral boundaries round them. So, the Christian must be wary of their influence and is obliged to condemn their perversion or abuse.

It is then imperative that the Church be, especially in conjunction with her message of hope, extremely critical of the culture of modernity and its distortions of the temporal and natural orders ordained by God for the good of man. Even at her most critical, the Church always bears in mind the distinction between what is merely modern and secular in the innocent sense of those words and what belongs to the culture of modernity which secularizes – turns to its own material ends -- everything it touches.

While the culture of any advanced civilization must allow for the secular, the secular does not have its own rights *against* the sacred, as though man's natural and spiritual proclivities are irrelevant to or exclusive of each other. They cannot be inherently at odds because they are both ordained by God, Who has ordered man to both. While an advanced culture cannot, like a primitive one, render all of its actions sacred, it can allow for man's spiritual proclivities to show themselves symbolically in sign and in public acts which signify the transcendent realities to which man's spiritual proclivities are ordered. It is, of course, an unhappy fact that regnant democratic liberalism with its pluralist public orthodoxy is scarcely tolerant – despite "tolerance" being liberal orthodoxy's chief tenet – of any public displays of especially Catholic religiosity and is absolutely opposed to the confessional state. It is, nevertheless, imperative that the Church and her theologians insist, if only quietly, on her proper role as the supreme moral and spiritual authority in society and, in principle at least, on the confessional state as the most advantageous to her mission and, concomitantly, to the good of the members of a given society. Prudence may bid the Church speak *sotto voce* on the subject of the confessional state given a hostile democratic milieu ready to misconstrue the slightest word suggesting political authoritarianism, which to its mind is virtually totalitarianism. The nineteenth-century popes were not shy to condemn liberal principles, which, as they manifested themselves in European society and politics, denied the supreme moral authority of the Church. Catholics must heed, aside from that found in *Gaudium et Spes* and *Dignitatis Humanae*, the clearer and more emphatic teaching of earlier exhortations: the *Syllabus of Errors* (Pius IX), *Immortale Dei* and *Longinqua* (Leo XIII), as well as *Quas Primas* (Pius XI) in the 20th century, in which these popes condemned in principle the purely secular state. If those popes were bolder, it is in part at least because totalitarianism had not yet arisen in Europe and liberal democracy thus had not yet become by a fiat of liberal dogmatism an amendment to the natural law and something like a fundamental principle of human existence.

Vatican II's Declaration on the Church on the Modern World, *Gaudium et Spes*, underestimates the danger of modernity to Catholic thought and Catholicity in general; for the Council fathers seemed to be unaware of the considerable influence of modern thought on Catholic scholars and intellectuals and especially on themselves. Certainly, there were those in Rome and on the Council who were very much aware of the dangers of modern thought and warned of its influence on the Council, but it was not their political influence that prevailed in the end.

The influence of modernity upon the Catholic mind in the 19th century was subtle and insidious and has its roots as far back as the nominalism of William of Ockham in the 14th century. Among those most susceptible to its siren call were, curiously, apologists for the faith who wanted, as did the apologists of the early Church (like St. Augustine) to challenge the prevailing grounds for unbelief of the modern world. But these later apologists made the serious mistake of defending the Faith on modern philosophy's (viz., Kant and Hegel) own ground, arguing their conclusions to be wrong, while assuming uncritically their presuppositions to be correct. Still later apologists, like Maurice Blondel, wanted not merely to defend the Faith but to bring Catholic thought up to date by conforming to philosophical principles, which they were convinced would make Catholic belief relevant and thus appealing to modern man. The odd and ironic thing is that Blondel *et al.* were reacting in part to what they considered the desiccated rationalism of their scholastic predecessors. Leo XIII's call to arms against modernity and modernism (as its manifestations in Catholic thought were called) under the banner of St. Thomas Aquinas was the Church's response to the challenge of modern thought to Catholic truth. But even the Pope's effort, by promulgating his encyclical, *Aeterni Patris*, to clarify the true foundations of Catholic thought, was in some degree compromised by the way in which St. Thomas was understood by Catholic theologians who had received their Thomism from certain dominant Thomists, like Josef Kleutgen. These Thomists had been misdirected by modern thought to extract from St. Thomas a theory of knowledge with which to answer the questions posed by modern epistemology. The unintended result was a distortion of Thomism into a form of thought that was uniquely modern and alien to the scholastic tradition, rendering Thomism one more contending player in the dysfunctional, open-ended game that is modern thought. This may suggest how difficult and intricate the influence of modern thought had become. By the time of the Council a number of contending Thomisms had developed, which had complicated and impeded the good intentions of *Aeterni Patris.*

After Vatican II, the theological modernism which the Church had fought steadfastly for the first sixty years of the 20th century had, it seemed, finally prevailed. The "spirit of Vatican II", the wind of change that would at last bring the Church fully into the modern world, had in a very short time succeeded in leveling every tradition in its path, making every accommodation to modernity it could bureaucratically manage. *Gaudium et Spes* did not explicitly call for this accommodation or, better, capitulation, to modernity; but neither did it provide any unambiguous and declarative principle that could silence those who would use it to that end.

The Church's fight against theological modernism as well as its critique of modernity was, as it turned out, only superficially successful. The disciplines she imposed on the study of theology and philosophy in the seminaries and Catholic centers of study to give precedence to the study of St. Thomas were only effective in driving the most radically disaffected with traditional Thomism underground. And many of those who were not yet disaffected found the rote and mechanical way St. Thomas was all too often taught, unengaging and awkwardly unintelligible or unpalatable to the intellectual milieu they knew outside the seminary or Catholic university. This problem was not necessarily the fault of either those who failed to make the Thomism they taught viable or of their students who rejected it. It was rather a misappropriation of St Thomas on both sides of the widening divide in the intellectual community of the Church. What seemed more useful to the students and scholars who rejected Thomism were the works of those Catholic intellectuals and theologians who recklessly, it seems now, accommodated modern thought and thereby rendered a fresh and "relevant" interpretation of St. Thomas and of Catholicism itself. Few of those so taken in by the new theologians and persuaded to give over the ancient traditions of Catholic thought for modern forms had ever considered how it was they came to be presented with such a choice nor what was the pedigree of errors that produced their new Catholicism.

This pedigree, well know among the critics of modernity, is long and distinguished, extending from as early as the 14th century's William of Ockham to Descartes in the 17th century and then to Immanuel Kant and Friedrich Hegel in the 18th and 19th centuries. The brightest light in all of philosophy of those four hundred and more years of growing skepticism and confusion was -- before it all began -- St. Thomas Aquinas, whose work marks the apogee and, perhaps too, the perfection of the scholastic tradition in theology and philosophy. In that period of the decline of philosophy and the growth of skepticism, whose culmination was the nihilism of Nietzsche, Thomism was obscured under the ashes of a scholasticism which in the larger intellectual community of Europe had been burned in effigy. The Thomistic school of the great Jesuit and Dominican commentators, like Suarez and Cajetan, kept Thomism alive in Catholic thought while Europe was rapidly ceasing to be Catholic. But these Jesuit and Dominican commentators also compromised Thomism in subtle ways that have only recently come to clearest light in the work of Alasdair MacIntyre and Ralph McInerny, though observed earlier by Etienne Gilson and Henri de Lubac. Although admittedly controversial, their critique of the Thomistic tradition was not intended to eradicate it but to correct and strengthen it. If the Church is to speak convincingly to the modern world, she must disabuse herself of the effects of modernity in her own house. But the solution is less like housecleaning than like physical rehabilitation. It is my contention in this book that she must begin to exercise again the great scholastic tradition and (especially) the Thomism that belongs to it which have been largely in desuetude for over half a century. The scholastic tradition and Thomism have not been discredited only impugned by its enemies and confounded by its friends. I argue that without the scholastic tradition, Thomism cannot remain itself, nor can the tangle of truth and falsehood in modern Catholic theology ever be sorted out.

I insist throughout this book that at the heart of the modern mistake has been a rejection of realist metaphysics. Until modern man is "converted" at the ground floor of his thinking, he will never see straight, but, like the dipsomaniac, will stumble and stammer his way to perdition. Man's profoundly cock-eyed vision of reality is not primarily a matter of morality which is in the order of the will, but is primarily a matter of thought, of deepest habits of understanding, to which morality is intrinsically bound. That is a matter of the intellectual order of things. There is no love without truth.

The Church and the Culture of Modernity

I

Gaudium et spes and Modernity

Since the French Revolution until the Second Vatican Council, the Church has exhibited what might be described as an intransigent opposition to the modern world, or rather to those principles and movements which, either vociferously or tacitly, are opposed to Catholic tradition as the reservoir of wisdom human and divine. But with *Gaudium et Spes*, that council's *Pastoral Constitution on the Church in the Modern World*, we were enjoined to drop the "fortress mentality" and engage the modern world with a fresh, new appreciation. The catchword to indicate the "spirit of Vatican II" was "*aggiornamento*", which means "an opening up to". The Church was then allegedly called (presumably by the Holy Spirit) to an open-mindedness about the world as we find it. With *Gaudium et Spes*, the Church was supposed to have commissioned a new, confident, and expansive dialogue with the contemporary world.[1]   There's an old adage, *tempora mutantur, et nos mutamur in illis,* "times change, and we are changed along with them". Now, after forty-some years of unprecedented disorder in the Church, it is reasonable to doubt that what *Gaudium et Spes* enjoined upon the Church -- to renew her relationship with the world in a broader theological framework[2] and to declare "the origin, the subject and the purpose of all social institutions to be the human person" -- has been a prudent modus operandi.[3]   The Church admittedly in her wisdom changes with the times, but it is another state of affairs to be changed *by them.*

No one need quarrel with the broad intention of the Council to render the Church more effective in her evangelical mission. If she is to fulfil that mission, the Church must speak intelligibly and meaningfully to the modern world. But such an intention begs some very important questions about the relationship of the Church to the modern world that *Gaudium et Spes* does not address, or, at least, not well. The primary question is: How should this thing we call the "modern world" be *understood?* Once we understand the fundamental character of the modern world, what we may refer to as "modernity" or the "culture of modernity", because it is both an intellectual and cultural

---

[1] Tony Kelly, CSsR, *"Gaudium et Spes: Too much Joy and Too Much Hope?* In *The Australian EJournal of Theology,* August 2003.

[2] John Paul II, *Motu Proprio, History and Aim of the Pontifical Academy of Social Sciences.*

[3] *Gaudium et Spes,* 25.

milieu with which we have to do, we can begin then to understand what the Church's relation to it must be. Whatever that relation should be, it has much to do at bottom with the Catholic theological tradition, for, while we may agree that a "broader theological framework" is required to engage the modern world effectively in her evangelical mission, that framework must not be so broad that it incorporates principles of thought and action that are alien to the perennial mind of the Church.

Although *Gaudium et Spes* has much to say to us about the modern world (and not all of it is commendatory), for present purposes it is more important to consider what it does *not* say, particularly about the nature of the culture of modernity. *Gaudium et Spes* fails to theologically define what it wants the Church to understand and conditionally appropriate. The document gives what appears to be a positive treatment of modern culture, but it does not give any clear idea of what such difficult and polyvalent concepts as "culture" and "modern" mean.[4] It supposed uncritically that modern culture and Christianity were somehow fundamentally compatible; this notwithstanding the tremendous weight of published argument to the contrary by highly reputed Catholic and non-Catholic scholars who had long been known as critics of modernity.[5]

---

[4] See Tracey Rowland, *Culture and the Thomist Tradition*, Chap. 1, pp.17-34.
[5] *Ibid.* "According to Cardinal Garrone, Jacques Maritain's 1937 work *Humanisme intégral*, which was a development of an earlier work, *Religion et Culture* was an important influence on the formulation of *Gaudium et spes*. It

No doubt, it was the Council's good intention in *Gaudium et Spes* to "freshen" the air in the Church, if by that we mean an intention to reconsider how best to address the modern world in order to evangelize it. It is reasonable to suppose that in the last hundred years before the Council a need arose for the Church to conduct her evangelical mission to the modern world, especially Western Europe and America, in a way that involved more than (but by no means excluded) the emphatic condemnation of its errors. Definition and condemnation of moral and philosophical error were certainly necessary, but that is ever only preliminary to her mission in the world, which is to teach the Truth of Christ to the world and thus to beckon men to Him. To find error is certainly a pedagogical necessity, but it is far from the teacher's complete purpose, which is not only to correct but to *form* his students by what he teaches. The Council fathers (or many at least) understood that Europe could no longer be regarded simply as a wayward son of the Church now that it had become thoroughly secularized. America, though never a Catholic society, it could be said, was, in a very circumscribed way, a Christian one; at least it was the founders' as well as the framers of the Constitution's tacit intention that the ends of the Christian religion (as they understood it) be freely pursued but that the state be indifferent to any particular religious claim. Europe's formal apostasy and America's abandonment of the founders' intentions to preserve and protect the practice of the

---

was this work in particular which provided a philosophical framework for the project of synthesizing the Liberal and Thomist traditions. " p.22

Christian religion in American public life and its consequent secularization have since created conditions for the Church quite different from those which obtained in the time before the advent of modernity. From their initial anti-clericalism and anti-Catholicism the societies of the west progressed to a profound and prevalent ignorance of Catholic doctrine. More than a century of progressive secularization had rendered a once Christian civilization almost pagan. I say "almost", because the fact of its apostasy and the continual presence of the Church and her influence make any genuine paganism impossible. So, what began as an intellectual tergiversation became eventually a *cultural* transformation.

Where *Gaudium et Spes* is weak is precisely in its explicit understanding of the total secularization of modern western culture and the consequent loss of not only faith but an understanding of the faith and its corresponding truths in the intellectual and social orders, and how all this affects the conditions of the Church's relationship to the modern world. While it is by no means heretical, as some very misguided Catholics claim, *Gaudium et Spes* is seriously deficient in its comprehension of what is problematic in the culture of modernity. This is so much the case that the document is difficult, though by no means impossible, to interpret in accord with Tradition.

If we suppose that a *rapprochement* with the modern world is required, there is the vital question of how to *safely* accomplish it. It is hardly an exaggeration that the cultural influence of the modern world is a contagion. For a culture is not defined by ideas per se but by their myriad and subtle consequences, that shape the unexamined subtleties of linguistic and social habits, customs, and sensibilities of a people. But to put the entire matter in terms of *rapprochement*, a harmonizing of two things, is to misunderstand the fundamental nature of the Church and of the world in *any* age, especially as the idea presumes it is the *Church's* responsibility to make peace with the modern world it is supposed to have misjudged. The Church is not a worldly organization whose aim is to help make the world a harmonious place; she is the Mystical Body of Christ, a spiritual society, whose finality is not in this world at all. And even while she continues her pilgrimage here and acts as leaven in the world, penetrating civilization and investing it with religious significance that all things may point to God and man's need of Him, she inevitably finds, even in formally Christian societies, conflict and antagonism. As Christ Himself perpetually reminds His Church: "If the world hate you, know that it has hated me before you. If you had been of the world, the world would love its own: but because you are not of the world, but I have chosen you out of the world, therefore the world hates you" (John 15: 18-19). Hence, it is not a question of the Church -- whose doors are never shut and who never ceases her appeal to man -- harmonizing with the world (in St. John's use of the word) but the other way round.

With modernity it is not simply a matter of the world's hostility to the truth of Christ which our Lord indicated is at some level inevitable even when there is no formal rejection.

The culture of modernity is not merely hostile to Christian truth, but *uncomprehending* in a profound way that only an intellectual as well as spiritual apostasy can make possible. How that is the case, I will explain in a later chapter. At this point, let us look at how *Gaudium et spes* treats of modern culture and how it has helped to sow so much confusion about the Church's relation to the modern world.

I have already mentioned the fundamental weakness of *Gaudium et Spes*, which has, with what seems a kind of heedless humanitarianism, called the Church to a new assessment and appreciation of the modern world, but which surprisingly leaves the cultural and intellectual character of the modern world largely unexamined.

At the time of the Council, the Church's Magisterium was curiously well disposed toward modernity as it understood it. Catholics breathe the same air as the rest of the world; and in the air in 1960 was a palpable euphoria about the future boosted by the tremendous -- and tremendously naïve -- confidence of the liberal societies of the west in the wisdom of its technological science and political and economic institutions to solve the obvious problems that beset them. The presidency of John Kennedy rode that wave to an unprecedented popularity. Within the Church, the preponderance of the material achievements of the modern world that were beneficial to mankind all but overwhelmed the Church's formal criticism of modernity from nearly every pope since Pius IX. The modern world's apparent moral achievements were perhaps even more imposing: the defeat of fascism, the establishment of the United Nations with its *Declaration on Human Rights* (1948), the civil rights movement, the fight against poverty, and the many other projects of a putatively benevolent liberalism that was the distinct creation of the modern world: liberalism, we might say, was modern thought *reified* -- its political, economical, and moral embodiment. It was in those days the climate of opinion that in the most highly developed civilization in history, man had matured and what he had left behind in all the areas of human culture and social organization were the beliefs, habits, and playthings of man's childhood. The idea of and, still more, the tenacious belief in Progress, was still looming and powerful in spite of the ravages of the twentieth century.

Widely held in the Magisterium was the belief that the social trends of the 1950s and early 60s indicated a working out of God's providential design. They enjoyed the somewhat vague conviction that what was developing under foot was a new age in which the Church, united with all other Christian churches, and the world would no longer be enemies but, embracing the universal values of "truth, justice, charity, and freedom", would join hands in making a thoroughly just, though thoroughly secular, society in which the conditions for "human flourishing" will reach an unprecedented degree of perfection. We find this optimism expressed by Pope John XXIII (who called the Council) in his *Pacem in Terris* (1963), in which he regards the highly developed sense of rights and duties in the liberal societies of the west as a "kind of *preparatio evangelii*" that will bring man to a "better knowledge of the true God".

> When the relations of human society are expressed in terms of rights and duties, men become conscious of spiritual values, understand the meaning and significance of truth, justice, charity and freedom, and become deeply aware that they belong to this world of values. Moreover, when moved by such concerns, they are brought to a better knowledge of the true God Who is personal and transcendent, and thus they make the ties that bind them to God the solid foundation and supreme criterion of their lives, both of that life which they live interiorly in the depths of their own souls and of that in which they are united to other men in society.[6]

The optimism expressed here is interesting if only for the apparent association of secular liberal values and religious ones. Pope John seems to place the supreme liberal value of freedom on the same plane with the theological virtue of charity and the cardinal virtue of justice, and all bringing one to a greater knowledge of God. I say "seemed" because John XXIII was no doubt expressing a rhetorically poised sentiment rather than Catholic doctrine.

---

[6] *Pacem in Terris*, 45

In his opening address to the Council (1962), John XXIII expresses his expectations for the modern world still more strongly:

> In the present order of things, Divine Providence is leading us to a new order of human relations which, by men's own efforts and even beyond their very expectations, are directed toward the fulfilment of God's superior and inscrutable designs. And everything, even human differences, leads to the good of the Church.[7]

It is this optimism, which now seems insupportable, and the apparent confusion of spiritual and secular values that pervades *Gaudium et Spes* and underlies the entire corpus of the Council's documents. It was on the basis of this optimism that the Council fathers in *Gaudium et Spes* expressed a wish for a *rapprochement* with and a new respect for the modern world. Still more was this optimism the basis for the operative interpretation of the document according to the principle of *aggiornamento*. That understanding of *Gaudium et Spes* and the acceptance of modernity it helped to engender in the Church is still prevalent if somewhat shopworn after forty years. It is that new and uncritical respect for modernity that has written the program by which the Church's traditional critical stance toward modernity has over those forty years have been largely replaced by an alarming degree of ambivalence and even fondness.

---

[7] W. Abbott, *Documents of the Second Vatican Council*, London: Geoffrey Chapmen, 1967, pp. 712-13.

But the conciliar fathers themselves were less certain about the meaning of the document and especially its theological foundations, for, as Dr. Tracey Rowland has observed,

> . . . all commentators agree that *Gaudium et Spes* was a compromise document --- that it was the outcome of quite intense debates about the relationship between nature and grace and in particular the tension between the incarnational and eschatological dimensions of Catholic theology.[8]

Thus was there inevitably a certain lack of clarity in the document, for this "tension" was not resolved in the final writing. The fathers had struggled long to strike a balance between conflicting points of view. Passing through many revisions, the drafting of *Gaudium et Spes* began in the second session of the Council and was not adopted till the fourth, only one day before the end of the Council. The fathers' lack of agreement on fundamental issues of Catholic theology meant that they had to find a point of counterpoise with the result that the document born of this tension had, as one historian of the Council put it, a "dialectical character with multiple contrasts".[9] The document lacked "an overarching theological framework in which the contrasts

---

[8] T. Rowland, *Culture and the Thomist Tradition*, London: Routledge, 2003, p. 17. I refer the reader to the entire chapter of Dr. Rowland's book in which she treats of *Gaudium et Spes* and upon which I have depended in the following pages.
[9] Charles Moeller, "History of the Constitution" in *Commentary on the Documents of Vatican II*, Vol. 5, H. Vorgrimler, ed, New York: Herder & Herder, 1969, pp. 60-1. (Cited by T. Rowland, *op. cit*, n. 25, p. 173.)

can be reconciled."[10] As a theological compromise of opposing ideas woven together into a loose patchwork, *Gaudium et Spes* was certain to be the subject of a "riot of interpretations."[11]

The lack of a theological framework certainly made *Gaudium et Spes* peculiar among Church documents, but that was not all. In spite of its title, the document lacked the juridical form of a constitution which requires the precise definition of key terms, and thus it fails to examine the exact meaning of concepts such as modern, modernity, culture, etc., that are central to its message.[12] A word like "modern", for instance, is what C. S. Lewis called a "dangerous" term[13] because it has multiple senses, which will, if the sense being used is not precisely defined and distinguished from other possible senses, leave the text vulnerable to any amount of misunderstanding. But *Gaudium et Spes* treats "modern" as a synonym for contemporary.[14] "Culture" its authors understood to be a concept with many sides, but nowhere do they tell us exactly what they mean by it.

A further result of *Gaudium et Spes*'s looseness of form is its peculiarly indecisive character, moving as it does between sociological observations and theological propositions (we observed a similar tendency in Pope John's *Pacem in Terris*) and between dogmatic formulations and pastoral

---

[10] *Ibid.*
[11] T. Rowland, *op. cit.*, p. 18.
[12] See T. Rowland, *ibid.*
[13] C. S. Lewis, *Studies in Words*, Cambridge: Cambridge University Press, 1964.
[14] See Rowland, *op. cit.*, pp 18-19.

instructions and appeals without any apparent determining principle.[15] The resulting indecisiveness – one might almost say ineptitude -- is the all but inevitable effect of theological inclarity.

It is no wonder then that *Gaudium et Spes* became after the Council the ready and potent weapon of the modernists in the Church, against which few could stand, for it seemed to say the things they claimed it said. It was the interpretation of *Gaudium et Spes*, as denoted by the well-known metaphor, "opening of the windows", used by Pope John XXIII in an unofficial speech to an ambassador, that was the most widely known and accepted. It is remarkable that this, almost offhanded utterance, would become the key to understanding *Gaudium et Spes*, for it became commonly accepted with little criticism as the meaning of that airy slogan of the Council, "*aggiornamento!*".[16]

Aggiornamento or, as it is often rendered, "accommodation" is the notion that the Church, faced with the modern world, has to accommodate herself to it if she is to "live effectively" in it. To do so she must adapt herself to the contemporary culture.[17] It was a leading notion in the Church at the time of the Council (with varying degrees of assent) that the Church was incomprehensible to modern culture and that it was, therefore, incumbent upon her to adopt the prevailing cultural forms and sensibilities in her liturgy, religious life,

---

[15] See Rowland, *ibid*, p.19.
[16] See Rowland, *ibid*, p. 19
[17] Cf. E.E.Y. Hayles, *Pope John and His Revolution*, London: Eyre & Spottiswood, 1985). See also Rowland, *op. cit.*, p.19 where Hayles is quoted in full.

moral discipline, and not least of all her theology. This understanding of the relation of the Church to modernity is more plainly expressed in the Council's *Decree on the Appropriate Renewal of Religious Life* in which it is recommended for the education of religious that the religious life "should be adapted to the requirements of a given culture" according to the "prevailing manner of contemporary social life, and its characteristic ways of thinking and feeling." But even here there are other possible interpretations which would be less compromising toward modern culture. For instance, as Dr. Rowland has pointed out, "adapted to the requirements of a given culture" need not mean to accommodate the culture in the sense of following it or mimicking it:

> The idea that *aggiornamento* might mean an updating of theological resources to provide a coherent critique of the culture of modernity, rather than a simple accommodation to it – that is, an interpretation which coupled the concept of *aggiornamento* to the pre-Conciliar *Ressourcement* project which sought to effect a richer synthesis of the Patristic and Scholastic heritage – never succeeded in influencing the *Zeitgeist* of the Council as the accomodationist interpretation did. [18]

The problem with *aggiornamento,* and especially its accomodationist interpretation, as the key to understanding *Gaudium et Spes* is that it admonishes us to accommodate uncritically the modern world, itself

---

[18] Cf. Rowland, *op. cit.,* p.19.

offering no framework by which to understand modernity critically. There is no critical -- philosophical or theological -- examination of the culture of modernity in *Gaudium et Spes*. This may be because the fathers did not have any clear notion of modernity as a culture whose peculiar formation and identity in history renders it necessarily hostile to the Church. If, on the other hand, they rejected this understanding of modernity, it is not because the resources for the critical examination of modern culture were not known or available to them. The criticism of modernity had been a matter of serious intellectual endeavour for many decades prior to the Council. The work of Venerable John Henry Newman, Christopher Dawson, Romano Guardini, Erich Przywara, to name only some, were well known and their writings still in print in 1964. And too, of course, an unaccomodating view of modernity was writ large over every encyclical having to do with the modern world since Pius IX. Yet curiously these critics of modernity and especially of the liberal tradition were ignored by the authors of *Gaudium et Spes*. No one was invited to the Council who would have made explicit the connection between liturgy and social criticism and moral and cultural responsibility. Instead, it was the influence of theologians and *periti* (experts) like Karl Rahner, who emphasized assimilation to the secular culture and deemphasized transcendence and immortality, that went almost unopposed. Rahner has been understood to imply that the culture of modernity, the Enlightenment and "progress" were as necessary as the

Cross[19]. The theology of Karl Rahner and others like him (e.g., Edward Schillebeeckx) have been in some ways more like that of the German romantic theologian, Ludwig Feuerbach, who rejected transcendence and immortality and provided the philosophical foundation to Marx's atheism.[20] Alasdair MacIntyre has said of this secularizing theology that, "nothing has been more startling than to note how much contemporary Christian theology is concerned with trying to perform Feuerbach's work all over again".[21] *Gaudium et Spes*'s lack of a definite theological nor philosophical framework in which to define the relation of the Church to the culture of modernity, is not the result of an *absence* of philosophical influence. Its treatment of culture bears the marked philosophical influence of Jacques Maritain, whose political philosophy attempted to define a *rapprochement* between Catholicism and the Liberal tradition.[22] The general thesis of his very influential work, *Integral Humanism* (1937), is that liberal democracy, albeit a "revitalized" democracy reoriented to the fundamental truths of religion and the tenets of the *philosophia perennis* (especially metaphysics), was the best political order for the fulfillment of the human

---

[19] Cf. *Mission and Grace*, 1963

[20] Cf. Mark and Louise Zwick, "What Happened to the Tremendous Renewal Possibilities after the Second Vatican Council?" in the *Houston Catholic Worker*, Vol. XXIV, No. 2, March-April 2004.

[21] *Marxism and Christianity*
[22] Cf. Rowland, *ibid*, p. 22

person. Maritain was a notable Thomist who believed that the philosophical tradition of Thomism in Catholic thought was fundamentally compatible with liberalism, especially as it had developed on American soil. He rejected every kind of secular humanism and its materialist foundations, but argued that fundamental to a theocentric humanism is the philosophical recognition of the human person as a spiritual and material being whose principal and fundamental relation is to God and that this truth must, therefore, be reflected in ethical deliberation as well as social and political institutions.[23] Hence, he also rejected the secularism of the European society that formally rejected man's religious nature and its supernatural ends. But there is that in Liberalism, he argued, that has its source in the Christian and specifically Thomistic conception of justice.

For Maritain it was the Catholic tradition of natural law, founded largely on St Thomas's exposition of it, that provided the link between Liberalism and Catholic tradition. Natural law provides the criteria by which the best of Liberal tradition could be sorted out from the worst. As a Catholic and a Thomist, Maritain held that the natural law is "universal and invariable" and is not founded on human nature, but is rooted in divine

---

[23] Cf. Sweet, William, "Jacques Maritain", *The Stanford Encyclopedia of Philosophy (Spring 2004 Edition)*, Edward N. Zalta (ed.), URL = <http://plato.stanford.edu/archives/spr2004/entries/maritain/.

reason and in a transcendent order (i.e., in the eternal law), and 'written into' human nature by God. The first principle of law, founded upon the natural law, is that good is to be done and evil avoided, and from which follow necessarily those rights and duties fundamental to a just order of society.[24] These rights are antecedent in nature and superior to the state; and because God has ordained man's end to be moral and spiritual perfection, it is in the order of natural justice that each person have the right to the means of achieving that end. It is because these rights serve man's fundamental nature that they are called "natural rights". This accords with the Thomistic principle of justice, that we should distribute to each "what is truly his or hers".[25] And in Maritain's view what belongs most fundamentally to every human being and thus to be preserved by the natural justice of the political order is his inherent dignity. Man's dignity is then, according to Maritain, directly related to his natural rights and their fulfillment.

It was largely upon his theory of natural law and natural rights that Maritain proposed his democratic and Liberal view of the state, arguing that a just order of society requires that it be pluralist – because Liberal democracy is otherwise impossible -- and inspired by moral values inherited directly from Christianity. He considered democracy to be "the

---

[24] *Ibid.* See also Maritain, *Man and the State*, pp.90, 97-98
[25] *Ibid.*

profane name of the Christian ideal"[26] and that sovereign authority, the state's authority to rule, derives from the people, who have a natural right to govern themselves, though the ultimate source of their authority is God.[27] Thus, Maritain's conception of the just state is the Liberal democratic state baptized by a Thomistic understanding of natural law, which he then transmutes into natural rights, which in turn, he claims, determines the common good and secures and defines the freedom of the individual within the community.[28] I am not here interested in answering the question of whether Maritain's idea of the Christian/secular state is sound, but only in pointing out that its optimistic view of a possible relation of the Church to liberalism which lay at the heart of modernity that provided the Council fathers and their advisors with a philosophical foundation for their own optimism.

At the time of Council, before the institutions of democratic liberalism began to visibly and rapidly deteriorate as happened in the later 1960s, this was (and still is for many) a very persuasive position, especially as it dovetailed the thinking of Father John Courtney Murray, who was, as a *peritus* or theological advisor to the Council, also a large influence on the Council fathers' deliberations, in his case with respect to a similar document, the

---

[26] R. Kraynak, *Christian Faith and Modern Democracy*, (Notre Dame, IN: University of Notre Dame Press), 2001, p. 150.

[27] Maritain, *Man and the State*, p, 127

[28] Cf. Maritain, *ibid.*, pp. 106-107 and *Integral Humanism*, p.184

"Declaration on Religious Freedom" (*Dignitate Humanae*).[29] But whatever its influence, the idea of a Christian liberalism had no part in Catholic thought, indeed the Church had little good to say for nineteenth-century bourgeois Liberalism or for its inherent secularism. And this, despite Liberalism's appropriation to its own materialist ends portions of Christian morality -- but without the Christian metaphysical baggage. Even since Vatican II officially recognized democratic liberalism, the Church remains among its severest critics.

In so far as the principles of democratic Liberalism dominate *Gaudium et Spes*'s view of modernity, it compromised its theological integrity, not because the Church cannot appreciate liberalism's nobler aims (after all those aims originate with the humanism she did so much to foster in European culture) but because the liberal tradition was formed by modern concepts of the nature and purpose of man that were themselves effected by a philosophical rejection of the objective truth of Christianity as taught in the Catholic theological tradition. Liberals, like the contemporary thinker Richard Rorty, who wrote extensively in clarifying the principles of liberalism, abhor an objective moral order and are little more than what Rorty himself called "freeloading atheists". Christians who espouse democratic liberalism may accept Rorty's political principles while rejecting his philosophical ones, but the one cannot be

---

[29] See John Courtney Murray, *We Hold These Truths: Catholic Reflections on the American Proposition* for the full development of his thought.

so easily divorced from the other as we shall see. I will later discuss at more length how liberalism is antithetical to Catholic principles; for now I want to show how misleading is the undeveloped conception of culture in *Gaudium et Spes*.[30]

In one passage, *Gaudium et Spes* warns of the "increased exchanges between cultures" as having the undesirable effect of "endangering the character proper to each people" and "overthrowing" their "traditional wisdom".[31] As stated, this warning, in the context of the relation of the Church, whose divine message is supra-cultural, to the modern world, bears no obvious relation to Catholic teaching and could be understood to express ideas which have little or nothing to do with Catholic principles. For instance, "the character of each people" that is "endangered", could be understood to mean the Herderian idea that each national culture, whatever its character, Christian, pagan, anti-Christian, has its own unique, intrinsic, and objective value and may be judged only by its own standards. According to Johann Gottfried Herder, the eighteenth-century German romantic philosopher,

> . . . every nation bears in itself the standard of its perfection, totally independent of all comparison with that of others; [for] do not nationalities differ

---

[30] I am following loosely and on points elaborating upon Dr. Tracey Rowland's fuller exposition of the treatment of culture in *Gaudium et Spes* in *Culture and the Thomist Tradition After Vatican II*, p. 22 ff.
[31] Cf. *Gaudium et Spes*, II, Chapter 2.

in everything, in poetry, in appearance, in tastes, in usages, customs and languages? Must not religion which partakes of these also differ among the nationalities?

On this view, there can be no standard of judgment from theological, moral or any other set of criteria in so far as those criteria are brought adventitiously to it from another culture or *any other source*, including the Church, and which cannot be said to be superior to it in any way. If the missionary were directed by a Herderian conception of culture, it would mean those very elements of the given culture that frustrate his work of evangelization would be inviolable and therefore off limits to any inculcation of Christian principles that do not agree with the prevailing cultural norms. Evangelization would be at bottom indistinguishable from social work and any way of clearly distinguishing the cultural from the spiritual would be lost.

Herder's principle would doubtless be disastrous to the Church's evangelical mission. And yet it would seem the principle of enculturalization, which has dominated the post-conciliar Church's disastrous effort to render Catholicism agreeable to the indigenous society, derives ultimately from Herder. If this be so, it results not from any positive teaching found in that document but simply from a failure to define the meaning of culture. If *Gaudium et Spe* had carefully considered the meaning of culture vis-à-vis the Church, it might have forestalled any likelihood of this

German romantic sense of culture (*kultur*[32]) ever becoming entrenched as it has in Catholic thought. Instead, *Gaudium et spes* leaves so ambiguous a word unqualified.

In another section, entitled "Some Principles for Proper Cultural Development", *Gaudium et Spes* again easily opens itself to heterodox interpretation. Here it is said that by work in the fields of philosophy, history, mathematics, and the sciences and by cultivating the arts, a man can "greatly contribute towards bringing the human race a higher understanding of truth, goodness, and beauty, to points of view of universal value; thus man will be more clearly enlightened by that wondrous Wisdom, which was with God from all eternity, working beside Him like a master craftsman, rejoicing in his inhabited world and delighting in the sons of men."[33] There is nothing in this statement that could not be squared with the perennial teaching of the Church, who has always embraced the truth wherever she has found it. One is reminded of Origen's metaphor of "Egyptian gold"[34]. But it can only be so squared by

---

[32] Cf. Rowland, *ibid.*, p. 21

[33] *Gaudium et Spes*, paragraph 57., *op. cit.*, p. 961

[34] Cf. "A Letter from Origen to Gregory", *Ante-Nicene Fathers*, Vol. IV. "I am anxious that you should devote all the strength of your natural good parts to Christianity for your end; and in order to this, I wish to ask you to extract from the philosophy of the Greeks what may serve as a course of study or a preparation for Christianity, and from geometry and astronomy what will serve to explain the sacred Scriptures, in order that all that the sons of the philosophers are wont to say about geometry and music, grammar, rhetoric, and astronomy, as fellow-helpers to philosophy, we may say about philosophy itself, in relation to Christianity. Perhaps something of this kind is shadowed forth in what is written in Exodus from the mouth of God, that the children of Israel were commanded to ask from their neighbors, and those who dwelt

supplying from those sources what is not present in the text. What is absent – and what must be assumed -- is the notion of spiritual formation and that distinct from intellectual and cultural formation. In the modern world especially it is clear to all that the study of philosophy, history, etc. has not brought man closer to truth, goodness, and beauty, nor enlightened him to "that wondrous Wisdom", which is Christ. As we shall see, the very opposite has been the case. So much is a plain fact of history. That the study of philosophy, history, mathematics, etc. *can* enlighten us, there is little doubt. But if they are to enlighten, these various forms of inquiry into the nature of the world and man must be ordered to truth. That is a condition which modern civilization has not met because it has formally abandoned the intellectual tradition on which *any* study of philosophy, history, and mathematics can serve their proper aim, which is truth.

Consider Origen's metaphor: out of the gold the Hebrews took from the Egyptians they made the holy things of the temple with which they would serve God. So too did the Fathers with their understanding of Greek Philosophy, Roman law, and other useful elements of classical pagan

---

with them, vessels of silver and gold, and raiment, in order that, by spoiling the Egyptians, they might have material for the preparation of the things which pertained to the service of God. For from the things which the children of Israel took from the Egyptians the vessels in the holy of holies were made, the ark with its lid, and the Cherubim, and the mercy-seat, and the golden coffer, where was the manna, the angels' bread. These things were probably made from the best of the Egyptian gold."

culture, out of which they formulated the Faith as received from the Apostles. The Church's essential humanism – we might here with Maritain even call it her "integral humanism," is what formed the civilization of the west. But she was only able to do so because she understood that all truth is God's in Whom all things have their being, and that – in agreement with the tradition of classical thought -- the truth must be the mind's apprehension of what *is*. Truth, beauty, and goodness in the Christian theological framework, which is squarely within the western intellectual tradition of classical realism, are not merely abstract concepts cooked up by philosophical minds; they are transcendental properties of being which have their ultimate source in God, Who is. That theological framework, founded as it is in part upon the philosophical premises of the western intellectual tradition of natural reason, is ultimately founded upon divinely revealed truth, and thereby confers upon us the fuller apprehension through faith of the highest order of realty, namely God, Whom to know (and to love and to enjoy forever) is the finality or purpose of our existence as human beings.

The idea, as suggested by what *Gaudium et spes* does *not* say and by what it fails to clarify, that the study of philosophy, history, the sciences, and the arts – the highest activities of culture – in and of themselves foster the formation of the whole person, that they do *necessarily* bring one closer to the truth and thus to the Divine Wisdom, is contrary not only to fact but to the perennial teaching of the

Church. The Christian humanism of the Church has never regarded education, intellectual ability, or intellectual accomplishments as ends in themselves even when they are properly ordered to their natural ends. They are her concern only as indirect – because they belong to the natural order -- means to ultimate spiritual ends which fundamentally define us. Of the immediate ends of those activities the Church is not unconcerned, but they are not her first priority because their importance is secondary to her essential mission. The Church, of course, does not contest that those activities and endeavors cultivate us in the sense of self development (the German word for culture, *bildung* -- as distinct from *kultur* -- is more precise), but the natural ends of any culture must not conflict with the supernatural ends of man, which God has ordained, if that development is to be *virtuous* and if that culture is to expect the full cooperation of the Church. The naturalistic conceptions of truth, beauty, and goodness of eighteenth-century neo-classicism or the later German and English Romanticism, for instance, have helped to form some of the highest secular Liberal ideals of nineteenth-century Europe. Fundamental to these was the principle of the greatest degree of individual freedom within the boundaries of the, then, still putatively Christian civilized order. But according to the Christian concept, freedom, moral and political, is oriented ultimately to a spiritual order in which the ends of man and human society are established by God and not by the state or any other human institution.

While the Christian conception recognizes the natural ends of culture and the ways in which those ends involve the formation of the person physically, socially, and intellectually, it is rooted more deeply in a theological understanding of the relation in which stand truth and moral goodness to being and its Source. In other words, it is not what a culture makes of us that is the final determination of what we are but what God has already made of us in creation. Our supreme finality is to know and love God and enjoy Him forever; culture is the only the set of natural conditions or 'soil' in which we learn to fulfill both our spiritual as well as our natural ends. What must not be ignored is that these ends are ordered in a hierarchy of values in which the natural are subordinate to the supernatural, the lower to the higher, and *only by that proper relation* serve the same end.

The Church understands the role of Grace in human development, or the spiritual development of man through all of his natural faculties, as a created unity of spirit and body toward the supernatural end ordained for man in creation. *Gratia naturam non tollit, sed perfecit*, as St Thomas famously phrased it. And this principle is fundamental to the Church's essential humanism. But any conception of human development, as what can be construed from the above passage from *Gaudium et Spes*, that excludes Grace and the spiritual ordination of man is essentially Pelagian. For in that case, man's development is then necessarily ordered to himself or at least strictly to natural ends as was nineteenth-century Liberal humanitarianism.

This implied Pelagianism in *Gaudium et Spes* did not escape the notice of then Cardinal Ratzinger, who in his 1969 commentary on *Gaudium et Spes* described its terminology in various sections as "downright Pelagian"[35]. The Cardinal directed his complaint especially to the document's use of the idea of freedom as that especially which gives it its Pelagian flavor.[36] *Gaudium et Spes* does this because it fails to observe the distinction between the Christian and the Liberal conceptions of freedom. The supreme principle of Liberalism is freedom from restraint, that no one should be prevented from satisfying his desires if in satisfying them he does not trespass upon the freedom another to do the same. It is a fundamentally negative concept, for it pertains only to restraints -- our freedom *from*. It does not acknowledge what it is *for which* we are free, that is our freedom to *do* that which is incumbent on us according to our specifically human nature as creatures of God who exist for a definite purpose. It follows from this very modern conception that freedom is its own end; there is then nothing beyond freedom – it is the one absolute of modern thought, man alone enjoying the supposed blessings of his autonomy. Hence is liberalism's preoccupation with the individual as the essential unit of the social order. On the other hand, the Christian concept of freedom presupposes that prior to our

---

[35] "eine geradezu pelagianische Terminologie", *Commentary on the Documents of Vatican II, op. cit.*, p. 332
[36] Cf. paragraph 17

freedom – to our very existence -- is the created order as the foundation of all morality. For in the order of nature as in the order of grace everything that exists has a nature or essence and according to which is its finality or purpose for existing. We are free *in order that* we may love God. But the morality of Liberalism leaves God out of the equation, because it is beholding to modern philosophical principles that reject the western intellectual tradition of philosophical realism to which Catholic thought has always subscribed. So, for Liberalism there is only the individual, autonomous man and the order *he* makes collectively by social contract and the exercise of his rights within that order to live as he pleases.

Any notion of self development expressed in the terms of the Liberal conception of freedom, even without any intention of propounding that conception, is at least implicitly Pelagian. While the Church, contrary to the Calvinistic doctrine of Irresistible Grace, recognizes man's essential freedom to choose good and evil, she does not allow that man can perfectly conform to the will of God without grace. If this is so for the individual, it must also be so for society as well. The Liberal idea that reason and knowledge can alone direct the will toward the good is thus fundamentally at odds with Christian doctrine.

In paragraph 41 of the document we find what can only be said to carry its Pelagian spirit to a still higher level. The first sentence of the section begins: "Modern man is on the road to a more thorough development of his own personality, and to a growing discovery and vindication of his own rights."[37] Modern man, the statement seems to say, is superior to pre-modern man; that modern civilization is advancing toward a level of unprecedented moral achievement. This has the strong odor of the Liberal idea of Progress with its fundamental confidence in the moral and social evolution of man. Whatever interpretation one gives those words, they do not clearly express (even if they don't not plainly contradict) the mind of the Church. The idea of progress lost the devotion of most intellectuals after the First World War. But ideas as powerful as this die hard. I have already suggested that the conciliar fathers were somewhat under the spell of the conspicuous material and social achievements of the post-war world. It was a time when despite the worries presented by the cold war, urban decay, pollution, and the decline of traditional morality in western societies, an underlying confidence persisted that even if mankind wasn't marching to utopia there were ready modern solutions to these very modern problems. If the Council fathers shared that confidence it is certainly not to their credit. All that *Gaudium et spes* might have said in the way of qualification, definition, historical analysis, and theological reflection based on Christian doctrine it did not say. Paragraph 41 fails to mention explicitly grace at all; it only somewhat incongruously states that

> it has been entrusted to the Church to reveal the
> mystery of God, Who is the ultimate goal of man,

---

[37] *Gaudium et Spes, op. cit.,* p. 940-1

she opens up to man at the same time the meaning of his own existence, that is, the innermost truth about himself. The Church truly knows that only God, Whom she serves, meets the deepest longings of the human heart, which is never fully satisfied by what this world has to offer.

Although this seems to make the necessary qualification to the previous sentence's Pelagianism, it explains nothing of what God has to do with the worldly progress just extolled. It goes only so far as to say rather feebly that God is somehow in the process. God is man's "ultimate goal" and the Church "reveals the mystery of God"; yes, but what do these things mean with respect to the culture and more specifically the problem of cultural formation in the modern world? What must be the Church's relation to a culture which excludes Christian principles? We see again in this passage another instance of that particular distemper in *Gaudium et Spes* of confusing the sociological and the theological. It is a babble of voices in which one may as readily hear the voice of liberal progressivism as he might the voice of Catholic belief.

We may be sure *a priori* that the Council fathers were not teaching Liberal progressivism; but we know that liberalism still largely constituted the climate of thought in their day and that their deliberations over the writing of *Gaudium et Spes* were carried on under the powerful influence of Maritain, who thought as many still do today that a reconciliation between Catholicism and Liberalism was both possible and desirable. And although Maritain distinguished clearly between an anthropocentric humanism and a theocentric humanism,[38] that distinction never found its way into *Gaudium et Spes*. Those who are familiar with the Catholic philosopher's work may readily see it implied in the Council's document, but few outside of a very small class of professional scholars would be able to do so and assume that crucial distinction. The average educated reader is likely to be misled, especially under the influence of the document's popular accomodationist interpretation. By the time one gets to paragraph 54, where he will read, "we are witnesses to the birth of a *new humanism*, one in which man is defined *first of all* by this major responsibility to his brother and to history"[39] (my emphasis), what is he or she to think but that it "sounds more Hegelian than creedal Christian"?[40]

Even admitting the material benefits of the last half-century's technological achievements, it is difficult for most of us who have lived through it to unqualifiedly admire the mass or democratized culture it produced; a culture that by a former higher cultural ideal was considered to be decadent. But in early 1960s, urbanization and industrialization and consumerism were, though not without their critics, hailed as the unmistakable marks of progress and accompanied by an equally -- almost millenarian -- look to the future, mitigated only by the ever-

---

[38] Cf. Rowland, *op. cit.*, p. 25
[39] *Gaudium et Spes, op. cit.*, p. 959.
[40] Rowland, *op. cit.*

present threat of nuclear war. Even in the theological establishment of that era one can find a sanguine acceptance of mass culture. In the grip of this intellectual optimism that characterized the climate of opinion at the time of the Council, the fathers seemed to embrace the values or ethos of modernity as they narrowly viewed it. They saw the ethos of modernity in terms of scientific and technological advancement in the service of alleviating human suffering and poverty and raising the general standard of living, and the post-war international cooperation between the developed and developing nations and between members of the scientific community. In the same section (56), *Gaudium et Spes* specifically identifies these admirable and auspicious values of modern culture:

> Study of the sciences and exact fidelity to truth as scientific investigation, the necessity of teamwork in technology, the sense of international solidarity, a growing awareness of the experts' responsibility to help and defend his fellow man, and an eagerness to improve the standard of living of all men, especially those who are deprived of responsibility or suffer from cultural destitution.[41]

These "values" of modern civilization have lost most of their brilliance in the forty years since *Gaudium et Spes*. We have seen the corruption and inefficacy of the United Nations, the moral dereliction of technological development, the

---

[41] *Op. cit.*, p.962

corruption and mendacity of experts in the scientific community, the depredations of urban planning and absurd theories in social science made public policy, and the worsening conditions in the Third World through war and state corruption and poverty, which has been made all but ineradicable by war and irresponsible leaders. Yet all of these actual effects of the structures of a new world order (as it is now ominously called) were in some degree evident in 1964, if one had eyes to see them. But the critics of modernity, except in their own circles, were unpopular in the climate of opinion of that time. The climate was indeed already changing in the 1960s and had indeed already changed in the intelligentsia and the generation it so profoundly influenced that was in twenty years about to take the helm of social and political responsibility.

We can reasonably infer from the sheer magnitude and comprehensiveness of the failure of the culture of modernity to meet the expectations of even the most modest optimism, that what drives the culture of modernity is something other than what many of the Conciliar fathers supposed. In their apparent naïveté, they failed to ask the critical question of whether the culture of modernity is suitable for the formation of the Christian virtues or whether a Christian culture, of which those virtues are the moral foundation, is what is even to be aimed at, or if that moral foundation is rather to be, as Liberalism would have it, personal freedom.

It was more than naïveté or even the ostentation of modernity's achievements that rendered the bishops and their *periti* obtuse to what should have been so obvious a question. Nor was it at bottom the influence in their thinking of certain premises of secular Liberalism, although that was a consequence. Dr. Rowland has pointed out that a principle "motivating force" behind the writing of *Gaudium et Spes* was the rejection of "integralism" with respect to the Church and secular society.[42] Integralism, often mistaken for a form of theological fascism, is the belief that society is an organic unity and naturally hierarchical and co-operative between the social classes with a view to the common good. This is essentially, but not exclusively, a Catholic conception of society and is in many fundamental ways at odds with the Liberal one. In this conception the Church is integral to society and its governance by virtue of its spiritual, or, at very least, moral authority which the state recognizes and obeys. It obeys, not because its own authority is subordinate to the Church, but because it acknowledges the authority of God from Whom its own ultimately derives. Thus the Church is not a political body but a kind of adjunct to the state *in her role as* a moral authority. This role for the Church is of course completely incongruous with the Liberal notion of the secular state that recognizes no higher authority that itself (whatever public sentiments to which it may pay lip service). Rejecting integralism as a species of theocracy was then a rejection of any role for the Church's authority in the secular order. Consequently, the spheres of politics and economics, for example, are the exclusive province of the state or the marketplace or professional experts and

---

[42] Rowland, *op. cit.*, p. 27

bureaucrats. The operative principle behind this rejection is the complete dichotomy of Church and state, secular and sacred, of the supernatural and the natural, of nature and grace.

While the Church does not teach integralism per se, she does insist upon three things that amount to much the same thing: her moral and spiritual authority in and *for* the world with respect to her evangelical mission (for she is not just one religion among equals), the spiritual or supernatural ends of man, and the divine ordination of the state as opposed to the modern view of the state, based as it is on Hobbes' and Locke's convenient theories of its purely natural origin. The Enlightenment and its offspring, Liberalism, rejected the first two of these doctrines because it rejected the Church's supernatural claims, acknowledging her only as a hostile or, at best, uncooperative institution to be rendered innocuous. Hence, Aloysius Cardinal Ambrozic, Archbishop of Toronto, can say of *Gaudium et Spes* and of the thought of the Council in general that he was convinced that it was either mainly or at least significantly, an attempt to reconcile the Gospel and the Enlightenment".[43]

Walter Cardinal Kasper has likewise, perhaps approvingly, spoken of the Council's rejection of integralism, as the Church's recognition of the "autonomy of secular fields of

---

[43] Aloysius Cardinal Ambrozic, "Dialogue with Secularism" in *Culture and Faith* VIII-I, Civitas Vaticanum: Pontificium Consilium de Cultura, Plenaria 2000, 41 – 46, at 44.

activity".[44] In accepting modernity at face value, the Council seems to have embraced secularism, not, of course, for the Church, but as the proprietary right of everything that is not the Church. Society as an organization of human activity and ends exists exclusively in its own realm with its own values and laws, to which those of the Church and of religion in general are irrelevant. To the authority of the secular, absolute in its autonomy, the Church must defer as to an equal. In this way and for this reason did the Council fathers do homage to the "superior" products, achievements, and competencies of modern civilization. This explains their uncritical optimism about the modern world and their deference to the culture of modernity. By its willing deference to the secular it has also accepted with the same sense of propriety the demotion and sequestration of the Church in society.

We have only to take note of the remarks of Giacomo Cardinal Lercaro made in his interventions in the first debate on the schema of *Gaudium et Spes*, which were "decisive" in their influence,[45] to see the Council's own thinking in action. Cardinal Lercaro expresses his conviction with what perhaps now seems a facile -- even a trifle oily – persuasiveness, appealing as he does to the counsel of evangelical poverty, that the Church should confess herself "culturally poor" and make herself "more and more poor" by courageously divesting herself entirely of her cultural

---

[44] Walter Cardinal Kasper, *Faith and the Future*, London: Burns & Oates, 1985, p. 4.
[45] Rowland, *op. cit.*, p. 27

patrimony, and only thus be fit for the modern world. He says,

> . . . the Church preserves certain riches of a glorious but perhaps anachronistic past (scholastic system in philosophy and theology, educational and academic institutions, methods of university teaching and research). They must have the courage, if need be, to renounce these riches, not to pride itself on them and to be more and more cautious of trusting them . . . [for] they may prevent the Church from opening itself to the true values of modern culture or of the ancient non-Christian culture. . . . Such a renunciation of the cultural patrimony is not an end in itself but a way to acquire new riches, and, humanly speaking, greater intellectual acumen and a more rigorous critical sense.[46]

The argument is rhetorically persuasive but rationally weak, which is what makes it dangerous. What is most alarming about -- or should have been at the time – about it is not the premise that there could be weaknesses in the Church's cultural patrimony or, more precisely, in her appropriation of that patrimony, but that the *entire* patrimony is to be renounced, not just the "vagaries" of Scholasticism or ineffectual methods of research or modes of communication,

---

[46] The quotation was taken from Dr. Rowland's *Culture and the Thomist Tradition*, p. 27-8. See also her note 69 on Cardinal Lercaro's liturgical views.

but the whole of the Church's inherited past, including her liturgical tradition. And all this must be renounced because it has stood in the way of her assimilating the "true values" of modernity and pagan antiquity. It is before those two monolithic non-Christian civilizations, between which lay the entire expanse of Church tradition and Christian civilization, that the Church is to do her humble obeisance.

What Cardinal Lercaro's argument overlooks (or tacitly assumes, if we were to give him the benefit of the doubt and give his words a favorable interpretation) is that the culture of the west is historically founded under the direct influence and participation of the Church and that its development since the division of Christendom into separate and alien religious traditions (Catholic and Protestant) and its consequent secularization have estranged western societies to the mind and purposes of the Church which are not the playthings of time and cultural change. The very humanist tradition, to which modern culture still, if only weakly, pays respect, but which Lercaro and the Conciliar bishops profoundly admired, was in fact a creation of the Church, in so far as she was at the heart of the Christian culture that developed out of the culture of classical antiquity into which she was born, and not the creation of a lot of fifteenth- and sixteenth-century scholars disaffected with an arid scholasticism and who had a wealth of new-found classical texts at their disposal. For Lercaro as for any modernist it is fatally easy to overlook this fact and suppose that humanist values are fundamentally and even necessarily secular or non-Christian in their origin and, therefore, that the specifically Christian civilization of the Middle Ages is forever irrelevant to the civilization that supposedly recovered those forgotten values from the antiquity in which they flowered. According to this progressive mentality, modern secularization has outdone and surpassed in an evolutionary way the old Christian civilization to which it bears as much relation as a human does to the chimpanzee, sharing a remote ancestor, but the one never advancing beyond its primitive origin and the other evolving far beyond it into a wholly other and superior species. And for some secularists in their hostility to and fear of Christianity it is easiest to deny any descent whatsoever.

What lay at the bottom of this is something antecedent to the Enlightenment and to Liberalism; it is a fundamental misunderstanding of the relationship between the order of nature and the order of grace. This is a profound subject in theology and I do not intend to even begin to plumb its depths. It is enough to say here that what was operating in Lercaro's mind and in the minds of many of the bishops of the Council and their *periti* was not a Catholic understanding of the relationship between these two orders of reality. The idea that was evidently operating was something more protestant. The Church has always distinguished between sanctifying and actual grace. Actual grace we may define generally as that which moves the will toward an acceptance of God's sanctifying grace, which is alone necessary for salvation. Any person, place, or thing which moves the intellect and will as well as the emotions and pre-dispositions to accept that saving grace is actual grace by any traditional definition.[47] It is equally traditional in Protestant theology to reject this conception of grace. But then, without actual grace, as so defined, there can be no participation of the natural in the supernatural or *vice versa*. Neither then can anything in a culture, which is in the natural order, be a medium of grace. On this reckoning, all theological considerations can be left out of account when judging the value and effects of cultural life and anything true or good or beautiful can have no transpositional value. It follows then from traditional Reformed Protestant thought, for instance, that there is Divine Revelation but no natural order of the intellect by which man is ordained to know and love God. Nor is there (traditionally) in this theology a natural order of moral goodness – a natural law – ordained by and derived from the Eternal Law, only the moral actions of individuals which can never make one righteous in the eyes of God.[48] And here even beauty is

---

[47] Cf. Frederick Wilhelmsen, "Faith, Sign, and Society" in *Faith & Reason*, Summer, 1994

[48] Luther's idea of sanctification excludes any moral effort. The following is from his Lectures on Romans (1515-16). "Since the saints are always conscious of their sin, and seek righteousness from God in accordance with his mercy, they are always reckoned as righteous by God (semper quoque iusti a deo reputantur). Thus in their own eyes, and as a matter of fact, they are unrighteous. But God reckons them as righteous on account of their confession of their sin. In fact, they are sinners; however, they are righteous by the reckoning of a merciful God (Re vera peccatores, sed reputatione miserentis Dei iusti). Without knowing it, they are righteous; knowing it, they are unrighteous. They are sinners in fact, but righteous in hope (peccatores in re, iusti autem in spe)...

made subordinate to morality, placed exclusively in the service of moral practice. The Protestant tradition of theology thus has no conception, apart from extrinsic theocratic notions, of an intrinsically Christian culture, on the mistaken principle that what is "merely" natural is *necessarily* secular.

Of course, the view of nature and grace operating in *Gaudium et spes* is not so thoroughly protestant as the Calvinist or Reformed view I have delineated, but neither does it quite square with the Catholic doctrine. As we have seen, this view regards the secular order as in a purely natural way leading man to God – certainly a natural theology not found in the Reformers. But this happens not by the operation of actual grace as Catholic theology has traditionally defined it. In this, what I will call the Accomodationist view, grace and nature merge, as we shall see later in the theology of Rahner and others, and are not in their subordinate relationship as traditionally defined. It posits the secular order as *independent* of the order of grace or so infused with grace *naturally and inevitably* that the two orders are indistinguishable in (at least) their cultural effects. The traditional Catholic (Thomistic) view is based on different metaphysical principles in accordance with the realist tradition than the either the Protestant or Accomodationist views, which derive from modern philosophical presuppositions that reject that tradition. And it is the weakening and eventual (de facto) abandonment of the realist tradition in Catholic thought that is at the root of the ambivalence toward modernity in *Gaudium et spes* and especially the Church's apparent capitulation to it since the Council.

The Church and the Culture of Modernity

II

The Sacred and the Secular

By regarding a secularized culture as wholly autonomous and thus on a par with and, in its own realm, superior to the Church, *Gaudium et spes* seemed to fling open the doors as well as the windows of the Church with an almost reckless insouciance. If culture can be wholly autonomous of the transcendent order, governing itself *by its own self-determined rules or ethos*, it follows that the culture of modernity is simply a natural development of it own autonomous existence and the Church has little prudent choice but to make its peace with modernity. To do what the Church has always done, even when she has been an outlaw, which is to preach the whole truth of Christ to a spiritually, morally, and (as follows) politically disordered world, would be, on this view, like one sovereign nation telling another how to run its internal affairs. She is then left to preach the Gospel circumspectly, careful to attend only to the "spiritual" welfare of men and to counsel her own, all questions of justice and the common good, being strictly the province of the secular order in which she has no authority and can have nothing to say, are left out of account. If this was not the mind of the Council fathers, certainly it is what follows from the unacknowledged principles operating in *Gaudium et spes*.

Doubtless, there is a separate realm of the secular with its own institutions, legal, political, and social, which the Church is neither called nor necessarily competent to govern. The alternative is theocracy, for which the Church has no interest or calling. It is also true that while the Church has a greater moral authority than the state, her moral and spiritual authority do not *formally* extend to, say, economics per se, or, still less, medical research, or urban planning. That is to say, the Church does not formally govern economic life nor medical practice, etc. But because no part of human social existence is lived outside of the moral order; because all our actions and choices – economic, intellectual, artistic, and so on, are directly or indirectly morally ordered, the Church's moral authority obtains in every aspect of our cultural experience. So too, her spiritual authority, from which her moral authority cannot be separated, everywhere obtains. The deep and uncritical assumption of modern secularism is that culture need not be and modern culture should not be religious, that is directed to religious ends. After all, the secularists remind us endlessly, the Christian civilization of medieval Europe was a total failure ending in schism and devastating religious wars. While religion may be one of the engines of culture, it is neither integral to it nor salutary. Therefore, the Church and Christianity, the secularists insist, apart from an adventitious moral influence, have little to do with modern cultural life which is sustained by its own values. In fact, the secularists would say, the truth is quite the reverse. If religion is anything it is a product of culture not the other way round.

The modern secularist view of culture requires from us a critical distinction between that which is secular and that which is secularized. The secularist would hardly be likely to observe that distinction to have much importance apart from an historical one, because he assumes that religion is the by-product of culture which he insists is the primary thing. But any honest historical consideration of the foundation of culture will find that religion is always and everywhere primary and formative.

I should point out here that if medieval civilization did end in failure it was not because of its own principles but because new and alien ones were introduced into it. No one, whether sympathetic or not to the fortunes of the Church, seriously disputes that the Reformation and the philosophical nominalism, which infected scholastic thought in the 14th century and eventually led to the Protestant rebellion, had destroyed the unity of medieval civilization. Nor was that civilization theocratic. It was not the ecclesiastical authority of the Church per se that created the remarkable degree of social and intellectual unity that was the great and unique cultural achievement of the Middle Ages, but the Faith itself that through the patronage of the Church made for a spiritual unity that was not only theological and political but necessarily cultural as well. It was only after that unity was broken, that scientific inquiry and economic activity, now "liberated" from the spiritual and moral authority of Church, became problematic for Christian society. For, in the centuries that followed, which witnessed the steady diminution of the Church's authority and influence in society, it was the movements and developments in science (under the influence of a materialist worldview) and economics (under the influence of bourgeois liberalism) that proved to be the two most powerful forces of secularization in western culture.

Now let's consider what secularization means as distinct from the merely secular. Our English word is from the Latin, *seculum*, and can mean simply that which is not *religio*, what has to do with religion, and, therefore, temporal, earthly, worldly, transitory, or pagan. In this sense, the secular is merely that which is concerned with things outside the temple. In primitive societies unaffected by modern civilization, as Christopher Dawson has observed, there is no secular. Society was entirely organized by religious values and custom and belief. "The simpler a culture is the closer is its relation with religion, not of course because a lower culture is more spiritual than the higher one, but because the narrow limits of its control over nature increases man's sense of dependence, so that it seems impossible for society to exist without the help of the mysterious powers that surround him."[49] The religion of primitive man was not private or an experience of individual conscience but exclusively communal; it had to do with everything within his experience, pertaining especially to life, food, rain, the seasons, procreation, and in which he sees the hand of God or the gods and the working of sacred magical forces that with him make up the world.[50] The ways in which primitive peoples live and the crises of their lives are "inextricably interwoven with religious beliefs and practices to form the pattern of culture."[51]

In such societies men live by every action the way of the gods; their lives in its very minutiae are bound up as much (or more) with Them as with one another. This reality was not for primitive man an abstraction of metaphysical or theological speculation but a *lived* reality. Their consciousness as social and cultural beings (the *idea* of the "individual" was yet to be born) and their religious experience was a *single* experience. Thus, as everything for primitive man signified or, rather, was a living manifestation of spiritual realities, there was no possibility of the secular. Everything was religious. Everything was experienced as a manifestation of spiritual reality.

---

[49] Christopher Dawson, "The Secularization of Western Culture" in *Christianity and European Culture, Selections from the Work of Christopher Dawson*, ed. Gerald J. Russello (Washington, DC: Catholic University of America Press, 1998), p. 171.
[50] Cf. Christopher Dawson, *op. cit.*, p.172
[51] *Ibid.*, p.172

Peter L. Berger has argued, that the roots of secularity can be discovered in the religion of ancient Israel,[52] which defined the Hebrews as the covenanted chosen people of the one true God and therefore set apart – consecrated, a sacral state – from every other culture and people, who with their false gods were forever and unconditionally outside the divine favor. Thus began in the Old Testament what Berger calls the "disenchantment of the world". But with the coming of Christianity, secularity takes on a subtler and more complex character. Under the New Covenant, the people of God are no longer the Jews by a racial inheritance but anyone who is baptized into the Mystical Body of Christ, His Church. As was the tribal nation of Israel, the Church is a visible institution with its sacred rites and orders, but unlike ancient Israel, whose mission was to remain faithful to God's Law and keep itself exclusively from its pagan neighbors and the rest of the world, the mission of the Church is to "go out to all the nations" and to "restore all things in Christ".

While, as the Bark of Peter, the Church is sacral and set apart from the world as a spiritual society, the world, now that God Himself has entered it and eternally joined Himself to Man by the mystery of His Incarnation, is now not understood simply as everything that is not the Church but only that which *rejects* her and thereby the Gospel (or *vice versa*). The

---

[52] Cf. Peter L. Berger, *The Sacred Canopy, Elements of a Sociological Theory of Religion* (New York: Doubleday Anchor Books, 1969)., p. 113.

secular, that which simply has to do with the world, is no longer a thing to be rejected in itself. For world which lay outside the Church (the new Israel) it is now her Apostolic mission -- her *raison d'etre*, -- to engage and bring herself into some relation to it -- even when compelled to be an outlaw -- while keeping herself from being tainted or absorbed by it. The primary end of that engagement is the salvation of the world, not its cultural enrichment. To that end the Church has always in view the moral good of man. She has always recognized that outside her strict confines there exists a (by definition) *secular* order which is ordained by God and contiguous with His created order, which has determined not only the laws of physical nature but those too of the moral order and the nature of Man whom He made in His own image. And in this secular order, as divinely ordained, the Church understands -- what the secular order may itself not understand -- that it too is the object of divine grace and can itself, in its language, institutions, and customs, be a secondary or tertiary means of conveying the same grace that flows primarily from the Church. The Church administers to her faithful those sacraments which God has entrusted to her alone; and the faithful, in turn, by virtue of the sanctifying grace received thereby, communicate -- inevitably if nothing hinders them -- *outside* the temple by word and action, by sign and symbol the spiritual realities and irreducible truths they have experienced and learned *inside* the temple. By doing so, they communicate collectively and individually an *actual* grace to every other person and thereby (in a certain sense) "sacralize" the world, encouraging it to greater virtue and making it aware of the spiritual realities that continually impinge upon it (but which do not *inhere* in it) and which govern the nature and destiny of man. The two orders, the secular or temporal and the sacred or the spiritual, do not thereby merge and lose their respective identities, as certain tendencies in modern theology have supposed, but cooperate. The Church's Apostolic mission is to evangelize the world; she cannot make for herself the isolation demanded of Israel under the old covenant.

The process of sacrilization that I have described in the broadest terms is the Christianization that occurred after the legalization of Christianity in the classical world in the East and throughout the so-called Dark Ages of the 9th and 10th centuries in the West. What obtained as a result of that process, though a Christian society, was not a theocratic one. But it was sacral in the sense I have explained; and while the Church in the west remained separate from the state and in a necessary and proper tension with it, Europe was by virtue of Christianity's (largely) unencumbered influence upon it, a society shot through with every significance of the Faith it had embraced and through which every man received a measure of actual grace and the sanctifying grace it often leads to.

The distinction between sanctifying and actual grace has always been part of the Church's theological tradition. Actual grace is that which, acting through any person place or thing upon the whole man, in his intellect, will, emotions, and pre-dispositions, moves him to accept that sanctifying grace necessary for salvation.[53] It is this actual grace which makes sacral that which is naturally and properly secular. If we understand the secular to be merely that which is not specifically religious but upon which religion will cast its influence, then the sacral and the secular are not mutually exclusive. Far from it; they are, rather, as integrally related as flour is to dough. If you want bread, as opposed to mere water, you must add flour. Water is a natural element and necessary, but it is not food; to make bread requires that other thing which is other and elementally different from it. Thus, the secular order in itself, though natural, is sustaining but not nourishing; it requires to be infused with something fundamentally different from but not alien to it. (My analogy hobbles somewhat given that water is equally necessary to life, but it is saved by the fact that while religion does not exist apart from culture, neither is culture its efficient or its formal cause.) Religion is the foundation of culture (the very word is from the Latin *cultus*, i.e., religion), and is that foundation which alone makes it nourishing to our nature as it is a genuine effect of the life of creatures made in their Creator's image.

The sacral acts upon the secular only through the members of a society; they in their cultural life infuse it with the sacred and are in return fed by it. That man should be

---

[53] Cf. Frederick D. Wilhelmsen, "Sign, Faith, and Society" in *Faith & Reason*, Summer, 1994. In the following paragraphs, in which I discuss sign and symbol, I rely throughout upon his elucidation of the subject in this article.

spiritually nourished by his secular social and cultural environment is a natural and, unless powerfully thwarted, an inevitable manifestation of his fundamentally spiritual and social nature. It was a fiction of Enlightenment thought that man in his original "state of nature" existed naturally in isolation from his fellows and lived, as Hobbes famously expressed it, a life "solitary, nasty, brutal, and short". Human society was on this theory a contractual invention by individuals for their mutual benefit and protection from one another, each man being the natural enemy of the other. But man is by his very nature a social being, born not in isolation but within the most intimate of societies, the family, which itself exists within a social fabric that surrounds its individual members. This broader society which can either nourish each, buoy him up in the many and inevitable crises he confronts in his human condition, or it can oppress him.[54] Every man is "saved by God or is damned by himself within some society in which he is born, nurtured, raised".[55]

What modern philosophy has forgotten or denied the ancients knew well. Aristotle reminds us that only the gods and beasts can live alone, but man is by nature a political animal and therefore a social one. As such "his very political life demands . . . an at least implicit code of manners and a tacit agreement on the meaning of the good life and,

---

[54] Cf. Frederick D. Wilhelmsen, *op. cit.*
[55] *Ibid.*

therefore, on the meaning of man within the total economy of existence."[56]

Because man cannot live alone but must live in society, his consciousness is ineluctably preoccupied with "the other", especially the other person, the human world that surrounds him. In such a condition, it is natural and all but an epistemological necessity that what man knows he communicates. Both St. Augustine and St. Thomas Aquinas affirm the principle that intellection is communication – *intellegere est communicare*, that we can only be sure we understand anything when we can first tell ourselves what we know, then, through the instrumentality of signs and symbols, "gesture" it to the world. The two acts, knowing or self-communication and communicating to someone else, are substantially the same.[57] So as a man conditions the world around him by what he knows and, therefore, communicates in a multitude of gestures – sign and symbols of which verbal language is only one kind, though the most elaborate and complex -- so is he also conditioned by it, for we can only know what is presented to us to be known, the content of the world, both nature which God made and culture, which is the world we make by virtue of being that which God made us.

It is thus a mark of man's spirituality to "sign" the world with meaning. The world of man is therefore full of signs

---

[56] F. Wilhelmsen, *Christianity and Political Philosophy* (Athens: Univ. of Georgia Pr., 1978), p.36.
[57] *Ibid.*

and thus full of meaning. Now, it is true that the thing signified is present in the sign, for every sign makes known what it signifies. The neutral or arbitrary sign (street signs for instance) can be changed at will. But when the sign is also a symbol, it is a different matter. A symbol is a sign that has become more than itself. For a symbol not only points to something beyond itself; it participates in the reality it signifies, making the signified, as John of St. Thomas put it, *present* in the sign and constituting thereby a new being or essence, another mode of existence.[58] Crosses, images of Our Lord, of the Blessed Mother and the saints, blessed palms, etc., therefore, we treat with a particular care and give them special regard. As symbols they, as Frederick Wilhelmsen expressed it, "live the life of the symbolized".

The symbol acts upon man in a way that, say, a street sign cannot; it stirs the will by engaging his emotions, triggering into consciousness the lived history that established its meaning, and thus activating his intelligence to reflection. Very few symbols are completely neutral so that they are wholly powerless to attract or incite to some degree, for such is the nature of the sign. If they so act upon us and are inescapable in a world of signs which we have put there by our own inevitable human cultural activity, then it becomes a very important question whether or not the signs with which we sign the world are good or bad, whether those signs signify a truth or a falsehood, move us to virtue or vice, distract us from or are an ever present reminder of

---

[58] *Ibid.*

those unseen spiritual realities that really surround us and of our ultimate end as human creatures.

Take the words of the Jesuit poet Gerard Manley Hopkins:

> THE WORLD is charged with the grandeur of God.
>
> It will flame out, like shining from shook foil;
>
> It gathers to a greatness, like the ooze of oil
>
> Crushed. Why do men then now not reck his rod?
>
> Generations have trod, have trod, have trod;
>
> And all is seared with trade; bleared, smeared with toil;
>
> And wears man's smudge and shares man's smell: the soil
>
> Is bare now, nor can foot feel, being shod.

Hopkins bemoans the destructive effects of bourgeois industrial capitalism; the world "charged with the grandeur of God" has been befouled by modern man's heedless and frenetic activity. The grandeur of God which man saw in nature and in the revealed Faith of the Church and, seeing it, signed his world with it by everything he built, painted, wrote, sculpted, by every law and custom, with every word, every gesture, this grandeur he has effaced from his world, desacralized it. Nature remains objectively what God made it, but modern man is blind to that grandeur which is God's own signature and so has stripped his world of any sign of it. No one needs to be persuaded that the culture of modernity allows little or no place for religion, especially Christianity. Western culture *was* Christian, not only by virtue of the predominance of Christian doctrine but by virtue of that doctrine having informed not only the minds of every person but also everything created or impressed by those minds. That culture has been desacralized, denuded (with the exception of the architectural remains of Christendom) of the signage of a thoroughly imbued Christian consciousness that had been impressed upon the life of Europe before the French Revolution and the advent of political and economic liberalism. To speak of the "secularization" of secular society seems tautological. But the impress of Christian faith and imagination and sensibilities on the fabric of social life did not destroy the secular, but transposed it into a new and higher set of values and experience, even though they were not, strictly speaking, religious. We might better use the word desacralize than secularize, but I will use both throughout to mean the cultural effect of the cultural and intellectual de-Christianization of society.

The secular, then, while it is by definition non-religious, is not opposed to religion but rather can be profoundly and inevitably *impressed* (in the literal sense) by it through man's natural cultural activity but only when man's religious instincts enjoy a full berth in his cultural life. When those religious instincts are suppressed or granted a niggardly political tolerance by the state that limits its expression to what is strictly personal or private, *public* life is effaced of any religious expression beyond the neutered and banal like congressional prayers. Admittedly, this formal limitation would be less effective if there were *already* a vital religious culture in the west. However, what obtains in western societies beyond the formal restrictions of law, what lay beneath and behind those laws, is the deeply rooted public orthodoxy of democratic Liberalism that defines our conceptions of freedom and the common good according to exclusively *secular* principles.

Peter L. Berger's definition of secularization admirably makes the same point clear in somewhat different terms:

> By secularization we mean the process by which sectors of society and culture are removed from the domination of religious institutions and symbols. When we speak of society and institutions in modern Western history, of course, secularization manifests itself in the evacuation by the Christian churches of areas previously under their control or influence – as in the separation of church and state, or in the expropriation of church lands, or in the emancipation of education from ecclesiastical authority. When we speak of culture and symbols, however, we imply that secularization is more than a social-structural process. It affects the totality of cultural life and of ideation, and may be observed in the decline of religious contents in the arts, in philosophy, in literature and, most important of all in the rise of science as an autonomous, thoroughly

secular perspective on the world. Moreover, it is implied here that the process of secularization has a subjective side as well. As there is a secularization of society and culture, so is there a secularization of consciousness. Put simply, this means that the modern West has produced an increasing number of individuals who look upon the world and their own lives without the benefit of religious interpretations.[59]

What Berger has defined is a society which is no longer inclined to and thus is no longer conducive to the reception of grace, but is in various ways hostile to it. What he calls the "secularization of consciousness" is precisely the result of the desacralization of culture. The question, already answered by the secularist, of whether man is better off in a sacral order or out of it, is seemingly undecided among Catholic theologians, at least those who think very much along the lines of the popular interpretation of *Gaudium et Spes*. The question is crucial to the Church's mission to evangelize the world and to re-evangelize the West and even her ecumenical efforts since the Council, for it is generally agreed that Protestantism is one of the historical causes of secularization and of its consequent desacralization.

Protestantism has been described by Berger (a Lutheran) as an "immense shrinkage of the scope of the sacred in reality" and, therefore, a "radical truncation" of the Catholic

---

[59] Peter L. Berger, *op. cit.*, pp. 107-8

universe.[60] For the Protestant Christian, nature and grace are mutually exclusive; nature is impermeable to grace. The two orders of reality are radically polarized and there is no commerce possible between them; like heaven and hell, between them lay a "great gulf fixed". It follows then that human nature and, by extension, all human culture, is fundamentally unfit as a *vehicle* of grace; it can never be more than an *object* of grace, to which grace is strictly alien and adventitious.[61] The world of nature and the world of man, that is, the secular order, are, in the Protestant conception, absolutely closed to the sacred.

Peter Berger, again, explains this with a trenchant clarity:

> The Catholic lives in a world in which the sacred is mediated to him through a variety of channels—the sacraments of the church, the intercession of the saints, the recurring eruption of the "supernatural" in miracles—a vast continuity of being between the

---

[60] *Ibid.*, p.111

[61] "Lutherans come to their view because it best satisfies the biblical data and it finds a firm basis in the great Reformation principles which recognizes the total depravity of man and more especially the magnificence of God's grace in the salvation of man, the *sola gratia*. The doctrines of the total depravity and the *sola gratia* stand in such a delicate juxtaposition that the slightest imbalance can introduce fatalism or synergism. While Lutherans in the *Formula of Concord*, the last of the historic Lutheran Confessions, set forth the biblical support for their doctrine of election, they had indeed set their position forth in the *Augsburg Confession* in the articles on original sin and justification. (3) Man is so perverse that left to his own desires he despises the things of God. Only a divine act of grace can rescue man from continued and final exclusion from salvation." David P. Scaer, *The Doctrine of Election: A Lutheran Note:* An excerpt from *Perspectives on Evangelical Theology*, Kantzer and Gundry, eds., Grand Rapids: Baker Book House 1979, Chapter 9.

seen and the unseen. Protestantism abolished most of these mediations. It broke the continuity, cut the umbilical cord between heaven and earth, and thereby threw man back upon himself in a historically unprecedented manner. . . . It only denuded the world of divinity in order to emphasize the terrible majesty of the transcendent God and it only threw man into total "fallenness" in order to make him open to the intervention of God's sovereign grace, the only true miracle in the Protestant universe. . . . [I]t narrowed man's relationship to the sacred to the one exceedingly narrow channel that it called God's word.[62]

All the necessary ingredients for secularization or desacralization were already present in Protestantism, but which the Protestant world could forestall so long as it could still maintain this "one exceedingly narrow channel" -- its 'biblical faith' -- against the torrent of rationalism that increasingly battered it and to which it finally gave way. Once this narrow channel of the mediation of grace was cut, the floodgates of secularization were thrown open upon the whole of Protestant Europe and, through its own newly-formed channels in modern culture, eventually the whole world.

[W]ith nothing remaining "in between" a radically transcendent God and a radically immanent human world *except* this one channel, the sinking of the

---

[62] Berger, *op. cit.*, p.112.

latter into implausibility left an empirical reality in which, indeed, "God is dead". This reality then became amenable to the systematic, rational penetration, both in thought and in activity, which we associate with modern science and technology. A sky empty of angels becomes open to the intervention of the astronomer and, eventually, of the astronaut.[63]

Secularization has by now run its course. But for a few remnants of ancient and medieval architecture and a few shrines the sacral has been erased from western culture and from the conscious daily experience of western man.

Certainly then, it does not seem that the task of the Church is to embrace secularism in the way that thinkers such as Jacques Maritain and John Courtney Murray have urged and which *Gaudium et Spes* has been interpreted to prescribe. Their idea was that the Church should collaborate with all men of good will to build a secular order that is "Christian" only by virtue of a common acceptance of certain principles whose foundations are not specifically Christian but which agree with or do not contradict Christian principles and which Christianity has always fostered whether directly or indirectly. These principles are to be found in the natural law, from which can be built a consensus among Christian and non-Christian to form a just and virtuous a society.

---

[63] *Ibid.*, pp. 112-13

Besides the rather doubtful expectation that a liberal democratic society would be willing to thus cooperate with the Church, there is, on the face of it, nothing to object to in that kind of cooperation in so far as the society is already secularized. But such cooperation *leaves* the society secularized and the culture consequently empty of religious content. It is not, after all, abstractions such as the concept of natural law that move men toward the good, but what they see and feel and imagine -- what only a culture can provide, even a beleaguered and suppressed one, though with poorer results. The natural law as an abstraction (and theories of natural law vary even among Catholic theologians) cannot make a society cohere and its members to pursue collectively the common good. But the natural law, as lived and living in the customs and institutions--the entire cultural life--of a people, can. This is so because the natural law is not merely an abstract set of moral principles nor has it ever been embraced as such by a people. It is rather the existential experience of the natural law, as it is embodied in every tradition, in law and custom, in every social relation and activity, and as it is grasped in the moral imagination of a people, which informs their moral sense. In other words, the natural law is not something imposed adventitiously as a means of social control by positive legislation; it is rather what *informs* the making and administration of law by first informing the minds and hearts of everyone under the law, which in any possible just society means *every*one.

By saying that the natural law obtains as an "existential experience" I do not mean to imply that the natural law is the subjective creation of "values" we rationally conceive and which grow out of our response to moral situations. No, the natural law bespeaks an objective moral order that is necessarily antecedent to any moral situation let alone any moral "values". "Values" is a dangerous word in ethics, because it implies that the force of the moral law depends upon our *valuing* it, when the truth is we can "value" it only *because* the moral law exists independently of whether we "value" it or not, that is apart from our subjective response to it. What matters is not our subjective response but our objective compliance with it, for obedience to the natural law accords with the purpose of our existence and thus with an objective reality we had no part in making. Our moral responses, rather than producing the natural law, themselves grow out of it, for the natural law is natural to man whose nature was made to accord with the moral order. The natural law is that which naturally follows from the rational participation of man's being with the rest of reality as he encounters it. Man does not rationally scrutinize a moral situation to know the dictates of the natural law, he can know what is right or wrong in a given situation because the law is "written" into his nature which is a rational nature. Thus, the first principles of moral reasoning are not themselves the product of his reasoning but that which makes any moral reasoning possible. The first principle of the whole moral order is: "Good is to be done and evil avoided"[64]; but to the question, "Why seek the good?", there is no answer, for there is no getting behind

---

[64] Cf. St. Thomas Aquinas, *Summa Theologica*, I, 94,2

first principles, as C. S. Lewis once put it, we might as well pluck out our eyes in order to look a them.

The natural law then is known intuitively and understood rationally as a set of abstract principles or precepts which overarch and inform our understanding of all our experience. All moral inquiry then reasons from those known precepts to the moral good aimed at. But we know the precepts of the natural law because it is our nature, that is, it is the natural end or purpose of our intellect and will to know the good (what is good for us as human beings) and to pursue it. The purpose of intellect is to understand the truth about reality (and conversely to avoid error) and the purpose of the will is to act according to our understanding. The will is naturally oriented to pursue the good as the intellect understands it. Now, the intellect is not of course indefectible and while it always seeks what is good, it can choose a good that is not good *for* the subject (the acting person). A disordered intellect will persuade the will *against reason* that the thing desired is good to do or have. It is against reason because reason when in accord with reality reveals what is truly good for us.

The name notwithstanding, the natural law is not, like physical laws, a product of natural forces, but is derived from and participates in the Divine Law. Physical laws of course derive from God's creative act, but not in the same way that natural law derives form the Divine Law: gravity and inertia are not part of the Divine Nature, but Justice is. The natural law, when conceived as having no transcendent source, can have its ground in nothing more than human behavior itself, and determining the good becomes an empirical exercise like Adam Smith's *Theory of Moral Sentiments*. There is no *purely* natural moral authority. The ultimate moral authority must be Origin of the Good, and nothing in nature can fill the bill. Because the natural law only has authority or moral force by its participation in the Divine law, no political order can long endure that dedicates itself to the natural in isolation from or in exclusion of revealed truth. While it is granted that it works in the abstract, historically it has never been known to work and none but modern secularized societies have ever tried. The natural law's relation to Divine Law necessitates a spiritual authority competent to interpret the natural law's often difficult applications.[65] No other authority than the Church has both a divine commission and almost two thousand hundred years of accumulated moral wisdom.

Some modern Catholic theories of the natural law claim that knowledge of God is not necessary to fully understand and obey the natural law. After all, if the natural law is "written on our hearts", not by a supervening grace, but by nature, then we only need to perceive the good to which the law points and choose it. But St. Thomas Aquinas teaches that the moral precepts of the Mosaic Law, even those which command us specifically regarding our relationship to God, belong to the natural law and thus our knowledge of God

---

[65] Cf. Frederick D. Wilhelmsen, *op. cit.*

plays a crucial role in our moral progress.[66] Reduced to a mere abstraction or isolated from the Divine Law and the authority of the Church the natural law becomes a paper lion that few would wish to so narrowly restrict their freedom. Allow me to quote here Christopher Dawson:

> . . . the principles of natural law, essential as they are, are only the minimal basis of common action . . . . . No secular remedy can meet the world's need; no merely moral effort can restore true peace and spiritual order to society. The only final end to which Christian action can be directed is the restoration of all things in Christ. All Catholic teaching on social action during the present century [up to 1942] has been based on the doctrine of the Universal Kingship of Christ.[67]

Dawson uses "secular" here to mean that which excludes the Church, not only as an ecclesiastical institution, but what she teaches regarding the spiritual ends of man and of human society and her supreme authority to teach it. The Christian society of medieval Europe, though secular in that other sense I have tried to define (of being a separate sphere outside of the Church's immediate jurisdiction with its own laws, courts, governance, etc.), recognized those spiritual ends and in its own sphere cooperated, however imperfectly, with the Church to realize them. Even at the

---

[66] Cf. MacIntyre, op.cit., p. 141
[67] Christopher Dawson, The Judgment of Nations, New York: Sheed & Ward 1942, pp 166-68.

height of her own political powers, when she was in direct conflict with the secular powers, the Church has always recognized their legitimacy and sought their cooperation. What she could not and should not tolerate, let alone approve, is the triumph in society of the secular (in my and Dawson's sense) or secularization and which I have described as desacralization.

The intimate relation between natural and divine law invites the question of the relation between natural order and grace or the supernatural order. As I have said before, this theological matter is profound and difficult and very important to almost all the thorny problems faced by the modern Church. Though it is not a subject I can treat in depth, I will, however, aver that whatever the precise relation is between nature and grace, it is a mystery, the dogmatic definition of which will not of course come by the (by no means fruitless) disputations of speculative theologians but by the infallible declaration of a future pope probably after a dogmatic ecumenical council. The question of nature and grace bears a special relevance to the question of the relation of the Church to modernity and will continue to crop up throughout this work. But in the immediate context, I will only say that the natural law has no force unless related to divine authority. The natural law is operative without the action of supernatural grace, but only the operation of the supernatural order and not (independently) the natural moral sense in man can guarantee that the law will be faithfully (I do not say perfectly) observed. Of course, such observance alone will not guarantee his eternal salvation, which only sanctifying grace can do. The ancient civilizations certainly had conceptions of a binding natural law and in the Stoics we find a comparatively close approximation to the Christian conception among the Romans (at least the patrician class), but no one without blinders would claim any of these societies just by *Christian* standards. The admiration the Christian Middle Ages had for classical civilization was for a civilized *order* that approximated and in certain ways foreshadowed the new Christian order, but they had it from St. Augustine himself that it could be *only* an approximation and shadow of a thoroughly Christian social order; that, however imperfect, only Christian truth could realize.

In *Gaudium et Spes* the Church again rightly acknowledges the secular "fields of activity" (to borrow a phrase from Cardinal Kasper) that are not directly under the authority and governance of the Church. But *Gaudium et Spes* fails to distinguish between the secular and the secularized. It does not take into account, let alone explore, the phenomenon of secularization. It does this, in part, because it supposes that those secular "fields of activity", politics, economics, etc., are not only outside the Church's jurisdiction, but intrinsically unrelated to all theological considerations.[68] Culture, on this view, is autonomous of the sacred, of religion, and, therefore, secularization is the *proper* state of culture, or at least of modern western culture, given the historical and philosophical developments (assumed to be normal and

---

[68] Rowland, *op. cit.*, p.29.

constructive) that have produced it. Bernard Lambert, a *peritus* at the Council and intimately involved with the drafting of the final version of *Gaudium et spes*, went so far as to say that secularization is the necessary process of the "logical development of creation".[69] Secularization he defines as "the process by which a society frees itself from religious notions, beliefs, or institutions which used to order its existence."[70] We meet again in this definition the idea of the evolution of culture, of man growing up and thus *out*growing old, outworn beliefs and ideas, a process of maturation by which the secular becomes autonomous from and even superior to the sacred. The religious nature of man becomes, so to speak, "privatized", cut off from his cultural life. He need no longer sign his faith in what he does, for what he does, culturally at least, is unrelated to the transcendent realities he believes in. In fact, as Lambert, so clearly implies, the autonomy of the secular, the complete divorce of religion from culture, is grounded in man's being.[71] For in his view, secularization is a necessary part of man's natural development and the maturation of his relationship to the order of creation. Man himself is the

---

[69] B. Lambert, "*Gaudium et spes* and the Travail of Today's Ecclesial Conception" in *The Church and Culture Since Vatican II*, J. Gremillion, ed., Notre Dame, Indiana: University of Notre Dame Press, 1985, p.36. Citation and quotation found in Rowland, *op. cit.*, p.29.

[70] B. Lambert, "*Gaudium et spes* hier et aujourd'hui" in *Novelle Revue Theoloque* 107, 1985, pp. 321-46, at 327. Cited and quoted by Rowland, *op. cit.*, p.29.

[71] Cf. Lambert, "*Gaudium et spes* and the Travail of Today's Ecclesial Conception" in *The Church and Culture Since Vatican I*, p.38. See also Rowland, *op. cit.*, p.29.

foundation of culture and not his relation to God living in a world ordered by God.

It is not surprising then that Lambert understands *Gaudium et spes* and indeed the Council as a whole to declare that secularization is not necessarily evil and to approve "a frank acceptance of secularity".[72] Lambert's extrinsicism respecting the Church and culture belies the authentic teaching of the Church on the mystical relationship of nature and grace. It is also belies the Christocentric character of other parts of this document and of others of the Council (viz., *Lumen Gentium,* paragraph 54). Paragraph 22 of *Gaudium et spes* states:

> The truth is that only in the mystery of the incarnate Word does the mystery of man take on light. For Adam, the first man, was a figure of Him Who was to come, namely Christ the Lord. Christ, the final Adam, by the revelation of the mystery of the Father and His love, fully reveals man to man himself and makes his supreme calling clear. It is not surprising, then, that in Him all the aforementioned truths find their root and attain their crown. . . . All this holds true not only for Christians, but for all men of good will in whose hearts grace works in an unseen way. For, since Christ died for all men, and since the ultimate vocation of man is in fact one, and divine, we ought to believe that the Holy Spirit in a manner known

---

[72] Lambert, *ibid.,*p.51

only to God offers to every man the possibility of being associated with this paschal mystery.

Behind Lambert's interpretation of *Gaudium et spes* are the broader theological and philosophical understandings that we have already met with in Kasper's and Lercaro's notions of secularity, namely Karl Rahner's theology and especially Maritain's "integral humanism". Rahner argues that the secularization of modern culture was an historical necessity. While he admits that the culture of modernity is inimical to Christianity, he regards to be, like the Cross itself, a part of salvation history.[73] It follows that secularism is necessary and that a Christian society is no longer possible in salvation history – perhaps not even desirable. There should be, then, no opposition to secularism, for Christian civilization is by God's own design dead and the Church must in the humility of Christ submit to that reality.

This way of thinking about secularism has its foundation in a deeper line of Rahner's thought that Walter Kasper, a thorough-going Rahnerian, clearly articulates and in doing so exposes its weakness:

> Evangelization and inculturation necessarily belong together. This does not only apply to the Third World; the unity of the two is also a program for the churches in the Western world. They must not be satisfied with the existing dualism of the Church and secular culture, nor must they adapt to

---

[73] Rowland, *op. cit.*, p. 31.

the secularized world: they must seek to penetrate it anew from within.

Together with its efforts to overcome dualism, the Council also turned its back on integralism. It emphasized the distinction between God and the world, creation and redemption, Church and culture, Church and politics. It taught that *there is room within the order of salvation for a rightly understood integrity of earthly realities as these possess their own laws, their own truth and goodness, all of which can be recognized step by step by human reason.* According to the council, it is only the recognition of God's transcendence that assures the transcendence, that is, the freedom of man. Because *the gospel binds only in the moral sphere, conscience,* it liberates in purely worldly spheres and in the questions of concrete cultural and political formation. [italics are mine][74]

Kasper's reasoning here is rather confused even while he states his point of view very clearly. The "secular" referred to here is not the secular in the ecclesiastical sense but in Dawson's cultural sense, that is, what has been *made* secular or estranged to religious belief, by being desacralized. The culture of modernity has been de-Christianized and

---

[74] Walter Kasper, "Nature, Grace, and Culture: On the Meaning of Secularization" in *Catholicism and Secularization in America*, David L. Schindler, ed. Huntington, Indiana: Our Sunday Visitor Books 1990, p.45.

consequently a "dualism", to use Kasper's word, necessarily exists between it and the Church. But, Kasper argues, the Church must "overcome" this dualism and at the same time retain her integrity from the secularized culture; she must rather "penetrate" the secularized culture "from within". Now, a thing cannot be penetrated from within unless it is already inside, in which case penetration is unnecessary unless its intention is to get *out*. But the Church by virtue of the dualism Kasper supposes is already outside modern culture; yet this dualism is not a satisfactory *modus operandi*. So, the Church must be at once part of, in, and excluded from the culture of modernity. One can only wonder if Kasper meant to be so utterly paradoxical or if he could be so confused. It may be he had in mind St. Paul's distinction of being in the world but not of it. But then he would be saying what the Church has always believed and understood about herself. And what can he have meant by "overcoming" the dualism? Is the Church to remove it or, perhaps, somehow step around it or, again, turn it to her own purposes? None of these make any sense in the context of Kasper's argument. He says that the Council had "emphasized the distinction between God and the world, creation and redemption, Church and culture, Church and politics" in renouncing integralism, but how does emphasizing such distinctions help her overcome this supposedly besetting dualism? It seems rather to encourage it.

There seems to be operating here two "dualisms" which Kasper fails to distinguish. The one he assumes is bad, a consequence of the integralism he abhors, because it is an *inimical* dualism setting the Church in opposition to the culture of modernity. The other is good, a consequence of the inculturation of which he approves, because it is an *irenic* dualism by which the Church can relate peacefully with the culture of modernity, leaving the culture of modernity *as such* untouched, adopting to modernity the policy of live and let live, and exerting her influence on individual souls which is her proper province. If, as Kasper insists, the elements of culture "possesses their own laws, their own truth and goodness", and if that autonomy must be respected because "there is room within the order of salvation for a rightly understood integrity of earthly realities", and thus eschewing integralism the Church may not Christianize the secular order, then she has only two options. The first is to ignore the culture of modernity, which she cannot rightly do; the second is to make it her own, that is convert it from within respecting its own integrity, but without becoming herself secularized and thus wholly lose her identity. It is a sort of marriage of convenience, like that between a virtuous woman who marries a vicious and unrepentant criminal for the sole purpose of reforming him. Far from convenient to the purpose, such a *mesalliance* is doomed to failure and worse, the corruption or destruction of the virtuous woman.

Most significant in Kasper's argument is the statement: "the gospel binds only in the moral sphere, conscience, it liberates in purely worldly spheres and in the questions of concrete cultural and political formation." The Gospel, on this view, cannot inform the Church's relation to culture; culture is not within the purview of Church's mission; her object is strictly the individual conscience, to which alone, it is supposed, the truth of the Gospel pertains. Kasper assumes that no relation exists between culture and religion except in and through the individual conscience. It seems that he believes them to be wholly extrinsic and belies everything we know about the fundamentally religious nature of culture. The two are, as Dawson observed, "impossible to separate,"[75] and the social nature of man, whose conscience is not formed in isolation -- in fact, his entire self-development -- necessarily takes place within his cultural experience. And, to quote Dawson again: "it is never possible to get beyond culture"[76], that is, there is no human experience that is not mediated by culture, any more than breathing can occur without atmosphere.

Until the Council this concept of the relation of the Church to secularity and the nature of the secular was understood to be contrary to the entire social doctrine of the Church. From

---

[75] Christopher Dawson, "The Secularization of Western Culture" in *Christianity and European Culture Selections from the Work of Christopher Dawson*, Gerald J. Russello, ed., Washington D.C.: Catholic University of America Press 1998, p.171
[76] *Ibid.*

the 19th century through the first half of the 20th, what informed the papal encyclicals against liberalism and modernity is a very different understanding of that relation. It was understood to be a relation of mutual antagonism: the Church saw in European liberalism and in particular the liberal anticlerical state a tremendous threat to her authority and her efficacy in what were still predominantly Catholic societies. The welfare of those societies was seriously threatened by a secularism foisted upon them by the liberal state. It was genuinely a clash of authorities: the new secular states wanted to secularize society, to liberate it from the Church's authority -- or rather to usurp that authority for itself; and the Church wanted to retain her authority and influence – especially in education – in order that society would *not* be secularized. The consequence of secularism she knew would be disastrous for society *as* a secular (in the benign sense) order and deleterious to the spiritual welfare of its people, who are necessarily affected by that order in which the development of the whole of their lives obtains. The Church understood that culture was the preserve of religion and that religion could not flourish outside of it – for there is no "outside". She understood this in her divinely inspired wisdom, but not as an article of intellectual or cognitive knowledge, for the study of culture was unknown yet to historical studies which was still a new field of inquiry. Hence, it could be only implicit in her teaching on the consequences of secularization. But it has since been made abundantly clear by a number of Catholic intellectuals, such as Guardini, Przywara, and MacIntyre, who have considered culture as fundamental to the growth and practice of religion in a society.

Maritain's "integral humanism" proposed a new conception of a Christian order whose cultural forms are secular but whose beliefs are Christian or, at least, informed by Christian principles. He too held the idea that modern western culture, is and should be autonomous of religion, that man's cultural life and his most profound beliefs about reality should not, or need not, meet. "The secular order has in the course of the modern age built up for itself an autonomous relation with regard to the spiritual or consecrational order."[77] Maritain regards this state of secularization not as a catastrophe or even an impediment but an "historical gain".[78] A sacral order is, for Maritain, the mark of an immature culture and religion. And this in one sense is true. Primitive cultures, as we have already observed, do not distinguish, or not clearly, the difference between nature and grace. But what "historical gain" (or any other kind) is there when nature and grace are estranged in our cultural experience? And what can that "autonomous relation" to the sacred that modernity enjoys be but an estrangement? How can a culture be independent of sacred meaning and at the same time embrace it? Maritain would say that man's essential freedom makes that independence necessary. But Maritain is here in the grip of an idea; he overlooks the

---

[77] J. Maritain, *Integral Humanism*, Notre Dame, Indiana: Univ. of Notre Dame Press, 1973, p.170
[78] *Ibid.*

fact that culture is *essentially* religious, and remained so till modernity in the interests of the liberty Maritain so values slowly uprooted the culture of western Europe. Culture then is not "necessarily independent" of religious meaning; it in the modern world did not naturally and inevitably matriculate into that autonomy but rather chose it by *rejecting* religious meaning as it had already rejected religious truth. We are assured that modern man has grown up and no longer needs sign and symbol, the external reassurances of primitive societies, to confirm what he believes. Hence, a modern social order to be "Christian" no longer needs to externalize or signify its faith. Modern man does not have to "sign" his culture with his faith to make it spiritually intelligible or meaningful to him; he is presumably intellectually and imaginatively capable of *being* Christian without leaving any external mark of that most profound internal mark on his being. Again Maritain would have us believe that such "freedom" is the inevitable result of the development of modern consciousness, evolved into a thing superior to that of medieval man to the extent that he no longer requires the symbolic to realize his faith. Though critical of Maritain, I do not wish to suggest that he wanted, any more than did the Council fathers, to subordinate the spiritual order to the secular. Rather, he seems to have thought that the secular could be at once subordinate to and autonomous from the spiritual order. But if so, Maritain seems to have forgotten a basic principle of hierarchical order, that the higher is always greater and therefore subsumes the lower. Maritain, I believe, is not (unlike, perhaps, Rahner) being paradoxical; it is the same confusion of thought (unaccountable in so masterly a Thomist) that we saw in Rahner *via* Kasper.

What, again, does it mean for an autonomous social order, all of whose forms of cultural life are secular, that is, desacralized, to be subordinate to the spiritual order? A secular democracy that is itself not secularistic is not only defective theoretically but it is, as Frederick Wilhelmsen has called it, a "psychological impossibility".[79] It is precisely this psychological necessity for man to sign his world with his faith or his deepest beliefs that Maritain overlooks. Maritain argued that the Christianity can preside in the heart without ever taking any shape in the physical, external world of the office, classroom, boardroom, ballpark, etc. But to quote Wilhelmsen again: "Our Faith is incarnational and if the Cross weaves its grace into my heart, then I will gesture it into physical existence."

Thus, a desacralized order that is also a Christian one is an ontological impossibility. Wilhelmsen explains:

> A sacral society appeals not only to the intellect and to the will but to man's sensibility and emotions. We might recall here with benefit St. Thomas Aquinas' insistence that the human person is the *totem*, the totality of any man in existence. Not even my soul is my person

---

[79] F. Wilhelmsen, *op. cit.*

argued the Common Doctor: my soul is *personale*, personal, and although the resurrection of the body cannot be demonstrated by natural reason, that resurrection is suggested by the very unity of the human person, body and soul, emotions and will, intellect and senses. It is the whole man standing on the soil of this earth who is the person. To dissect one part of him—the religious—from the whole—the political from the religious, man as worker from man as player: *homo fabor* from *homo ludens*: the economic from the familial; the aesthetic from the social, is to sunder into smithereens he who is a unity in existence.[80]

It is no more possible for the social and political order to be at once Christian and sunder all man's religious affirmations from his cultural life than it is possible for a cadaver to be a person.

It would seem that *Gaudium et Spes*, following Rahner and Maritain, assumes that culture is a strictly neutral medium for the moral and spiritual activity of a society and, therefore, the evils that obtain in it are extrinsic to it. The evils of modernity are supposed to be like so many poisonous plants, it is the plants not the soil that is poisonous; a non-poisonous plant grown in the same soil would be perfectly edible and even wholesome. The social

---

[80] *Ibid.*

evils of corporate capitalism and abortion, for instance, are not supposed to be intrinsic to the culture of modernity, but are only the collective effects of the moral transgressions of individuals who would have acted otherwise, given different stimuli. (What stimuli, one would ask, might that be for one outside the Church in a desacralized culture?) The problem, on this view, lies not at the structural or cultural level where obtains the public orthodoxy of a society, but at the level of the individual's moral derelictions which alone the Church can address without ever having to reject the cultural milieu in which he lives. It is supposed that a good society is made by making the individuals that make it up good. But how, it must be asked, can man, who is a social creature by nature, be made to be good when society is disordered without rejecting that society? Nowhere in *Gaudium et Spes* does the notion occur that the culture *itself*, as the soil in which natural man develops, with its mediating structures of language, custom, imagination, rational discourse, and sentiment, *on which the Church herself depends to fulfil her mission*, can be unsuited to the growth of moral and intellectual virtue. This failure to come to terms with the true nature of modernity is what makes *Gaudium et Spes* so unreliable a guide for addressing the problem of the Church in the modern world.

The last (at least) 40 years have demonstrated the mortal folly of taking modernity as you find it and making your peace with it, coaxing it, adopting its ways and means, speaking its language, alternately chiding and flattering it all in the hope that it will embrace the one thing to which it is diametrically spiritually and morally opposed. Suppose a nation is at war with its mortal, vicious, and far more powerful enemy, who has no interest in terms of peace, and suppose too that this nation decided that it could prevail on its enemy to accept its terms by withdrawing its troops and sending a delegation of peace to persuade its enemy not only to disarm but to give up its sovereignty too, all in the interests of the brotherhood of man. There is no doubt of the outcome. As long as the Church remains in this world she is the Church *Militant*, embattled but never the aggressor. No defending army will send a delegation of peace to an entrenched and numerically superior enemy that does not intend to surrender.

III

The Church and Classical Culture

Although few would deny that the modern world has seen tremendous evils, some may ask how is it that in being "modern" modern evils are more alarming to the Church than were the evils of previous ages? Also, in what way are the evils of modernity peculiarly "modern", except in so far as they occur in this age and not in some previous one? There are, of course, the obvious differences between the ancient, medieval, and modern worlds, but what makes modernity's relation to Christianity *essentially* different from that of the ancient and medieval worlds; and especially, what makes modernity any more deleterious to Christianity than pagan antiquity which persecuted the Church and medieval Christendom which is supposed to have compromised her? Is not human nature the same in every age and doesn't it make, then, every age equally dangerous to the Church? These inevitable questions lead to the question I wish to answer in this chapter: Why should the Church have to eschew the culture of modern civilization like the plague, when she has always by her essential humanism appropriated the prevailing culture? After all, the Christian civilization of medieval Europe was in part the result of the Church's appropriation of certain aspects of classical pagan civilization.

On that consideration, one might be inclined rather to agree with the modernists and secularists in the Church that modernity is not the *enemy* only a thorny problem to come to terms with. Culture, we may be sure, is not a neutral medium and that the Church is necessarily conditioned by (but not a product of) culture because she has to do her work in a cultural medium and in doing so affects culture and is affected by it. But modernists and secularists cannot agree that modern culture is *inherently* antithetical to Christianity. If the Church is at odds with modernity, it is, some say, because she has needlessly alienated it by her hostility; that modernity would welcome her if she only properly understood it and made her peace with it. Note that the modernist supposes that it is not Christianity but the *Church* that is at odds with modernity. It is, they say, the hidebound and reactionary Church with her "fortress mentality" (the modernist thinks the Church has not sufficiently lost this mentality since Vatican II) that refuses to accept modern thought (though its acceptance has been (at least) insinuated in a thousand statements of the Magisterium for almost 50 years). Supposedly, then, the impediment to the modern world's acceptance of Christian truth is the Church not modernity. Modernity, it is supposed by this view, would, but for the Church hidebound resistance, receive her message and, like classical civilization, be seamlessly woven into the fabric of Catholic thought and practice. The modernist will remind us that the culture of classical paganism was also hostile to Christianity and yet the Church very wisely appropriated its language, philosophy, legal tradition and structures, etc. and made the civilization of the Christian Middle Ages.

Setting aside the question of The Church's use of classical pagan civilization, I want briefly to consider the separate but preliminary question of the Church's traditional regard for modernity, her "fortress mentality". The modernists and secularists insist that this defensiveness is unnecessary and that it is long since time that the Church recognize that the modern world, far from being evil, has brought tremendous good to mankind. Liberalism, for instance, that great *bête noire* of the pre-conciliar Church, has spread political freedom and unprecedented wealth throughout the world, which before had known so much physical misery and political oppression. Surely, they would say, in the face of so beneficent a civilization, whatever its faults may be, the Church should forgo her old contrariness that the Council of Trent had induced in reaction to the Protestant

Reformation. But what was, they concede, perhaps a reasonable reaction to a difficult and politically threatening situation in the 16th and 17th centuries after the breaking up Christendom when the Church was surrounded by political as well as theological enemies, became by the middle 19th a fixed and unreasonable frame of mind by which the Church saw the world dualistically: only what submitted to her will and authority was good and all else necessarily hostile and a threat to her. This dualism reduces simplistically to an historical view by which the world before, say, the Reformation was good and after it all the good was lost. This dualism greatly intensified during the 19th century by Liberalism's political and social transformation of Europe, and so reduced, it is argued, the Church's ability to understand and communicate with the modern world that it only served to antagonize its so-called "enemies" who only sought political justice even if it was at the expense of the Church's political power.

Certainly, it would be fatuous to suppose any such dualism. And certainly no one, even the most ardent traditionalist, would wish to partition history in such a way as though good and evil were chronologically selective. But it is equally fatuous to suppose that the Protestant Revolt was not a great divide in European history; even to deny that the fortunes of European civilization were necessarily linked to its submission to the Church's moral will and authority as distinct from her political will and authority, which are not easily distinguished.

It may help to further clarify the terms being used. By the "modern world" I mean the present state of western civilization and its sphere of influence. That state, which I am calling the culture of modernity, is the result of an historical development driven by certain philosophical premises that have rendered it fundamentally opposed in principle and practice to Christianity and to a Christian order of society. In one sense, of course, the present world in any age is "modern", even what we call the medieval world was, of course, not "medieval" to those contemporary with it. But I am speaking of a culture and ethos that defines our civilization in the west. The appellation of "modernity" is apt because the philosophical principles that gave it birth were, in the main, themselves the product of the post-medieval civilization. It is then not what is "modern" that is at fault, but modernity, which is, as will become clear, the modern turned, like Narcissus, in upon itself.

Modernity is to the modern world what rabies is to an animal. If I say the dog is rabid, I have said something true and very important about the dog, but I have not said all that may be true about the dog, that it is a mammal and a quadruped, for instance. We have observed first and more emphatically its rabid state because the dog while it is rabid presents an immediate danger and will continue to until it can be returned to a normal state or destroyed. Modernity is not a normal state for a civilization or culture because it has excluded religion, especially Christianity, and thus presents moral and spiritual dangers that are enormities in any human society.

To return now to the main question: if the Church could successfully appropriate the culture of classical paganism, why should she not do the same with the culture of modernity? The reason is because classical culture, while in many ways incompatible to Christianity, was not *inherently* hostile to it; and because modernity stands in a very different relation to Christianity than did classical culture. The difference between the two relationships is precisely that between the way a pagan relates to Christianity and the way an apostate relates to it, between being a stranger and being estranged. To the pagan (not the Jew, of course), and thus to someone outside of the pale of Christian truth, Christianity is still a foreign and unintelligible religion, which was sufficient reason for him initially to reject it. But the apostate (sufficiently) understands the faith and rejects it. The apostate has rejected Christianity from within; he rejects the truths he once embraced and which had formed his mind and life. And his apostasy is not just intellectual; he rejects not just a set of principles and beliefs, but the whole life of grace and ultimately the Person of Jesus Christ Himself. Thus, the apostate's is a spiritual choice, an act of will involving his entire person. To reject something we have been intimate with puts us in a different relation to it than if we had never known it. This is why divorce is more destructive to the human personality than is disappointed love or why treason is more terrible a crime than perjury. Pilate only dispensed (guiltily) with a problem; Judas betrayed a Person.

I will come back later to the apostate nature of modernity in the next chapter. But here it is necessary to consider the relation of the Church and Christianity to classical paganism.

It would be a mistake to suppose either that the Church thoroughly or that she decidedly embraced classical culture, as if it were the most straightforward and the most obvious thing for her to do. It was neither. Both the Greek and Latin churches were always uneasily aware of a "double tradition,"[81] the Church's native tradition and the tradition of the classical past. Despite her rejection of pagan religion, the Church did not wholly reject the philosophy and literature of pagan civilization. She instead wisely appropriated it, but it was neither easy, straightforward, nor without danger. The great work of the Fathers of the Church of making Christianity intelligible to classical culture and it acceptable to Christianity was the patient work of centuries. It was not until the second half of the fourth century that an acceptable synthesis was finally worked out in the East between Christianity and Hellenic philosophical

---

[81] Cf. Christopher Dawson, *The Formation of Christendom*, New York: Sheed & Ward, 1967, p. 114.

tradition, which we find in the writings of the Cappadocian bishops, St. Basil, St. Gregory of Nyssa, and St. Gregory Nazianzen.[82]

What is generally called classical culture was Hellenic culture or Hellenism as it was diffused first by Alexander the Great and then by Roman imperialism throughout the civilized world from Rome to Antioch and Alexandria and further east into the heart of Asia. While the classical Greek expression of the tradition and spiritual wisdom of Hellenism is to be found in the Platonic dialogues, by the early second century it had become a rational monotheistic religion and culture shared by the entire western civilized (i.e., Greek-speaking) world whose inspiration was the ideal of moral perfection.[83] Hellenism's importance to civilization had little to do with political power, though that was a means of its wide expansion, but rather with its cultural power by virtue of its intellectual character, a training of the mind and moral character, which gave it its enduring power and penetrating force in a variety of alien cultures, carrying with it wherever it went its great tradition in literature and education, its philosophy, science, art, and physical culture.[84]

But its diffusion made inevitable the influence and inclusion of non-Hellenic elements from the East. Classical Hellenism was typified by both an intellectual attention to and a religious reverence towards the natural world as "the

---

[82] Cf. Dawson, *ibid.*, pp. 120 – 121.
[83] Cf. *Ibid.*, p. 103.
[84] Cf. *ibid.*, p. 118.

visible manifestation of intelligence and order"; but the religious traditions from the east were darker and irrational and thus spiritually alien to the Hellenic tradition. The eastern religious influences were characterized by a deep pessimism towards life, the belief that the entire cosmic order was ruled by demonic forces, from which forces and the consequent evils of the body, which included birth and procreation, one looked for a way of salvation.[85] The common name given these ancient religious beliefs and attitudes is "gnosticism". If classical Hellenism was itself problematic for the Church to assimilate, this foreign gnostic element was destined to be a great trial to her. And, as Eric Voegelin, has made very clear, gnosticism in its myriad forms has been the poison of the intellectual life of the modern as well as the classical world.

Gnosticism became the scourge of the Church and, because it characterized the intellectual culture in which the Arian heresy grew, remained so long after the Church ceased to be persecuted. For as gnosticism was alien to the classical Hellenic ideal, which was intellectual and moral, not mystical, it was still more fundamentally alien to Christianity whose mysticism is of a different order. For what is common to the many gnostic traditions of the ancient world, such as Mithraism, is their dualism and an anti-materialism according to which creation is evil and God is, therefore, not the creator. Denying the goodness of the material world, gnosticism sought salvation in the world of

---

[85] Dawson, *ibid.*, p.104.

forms, that is to say, of the mind, and therefore in the secret *gnosis*, the theosophical knowledge of the supreme secrets of cosmology and metaphysics.[86]

Gnosticism, as the Church found it in Hellenic culture presented a problem for the Church, which she solved by using the classical elements of Hellenism against it. The Church was a living, organic, and spiritual society in possession of a divine revelation and gospel, a sacred tradition founded upon it, and a new way of life. And she was quite sure of herself, but had up to this time not yet formulated a reasoned defence of Christianity, a body of doctrine that could answer the various abstruse questions of metaphysics that gnosticism raised. This presented a serious impediment to her evangelical mission and her own integrity as gnosticism had already wormed its way into Christian thought.

While one cannot say the Church was predisposed towards classical Hellenism, she was, nevertheless attracted to its usefulness to her task of confronting gnosticism and converting the gnostics. She needed the language and structures of philosophic thought that the classical tradition made readily available and which were already intelligible to every educated person of the Hellenic world, and which only needed to be informed by Christian revelation. Hellenism was the culture into which the Church was born, and was as such the natural and necessary means by which she could accomplish her spiritual ends.

---

[86] Cf. Dawson, *ibid.*, p. 106.

By the end of the second century and during the first half of the third, the Church began to lay the foundations for the development of a scientific theology. Begun by St. Irenaeus and Tertullian in the West and Clement of Alexandria and Origen in the East, the work was not finished till the age of the great councils.[87] It was at this stage the eastern rather than the western Fathers who sought in the classical tradition the "Egyptian spoils" they needed. Though also imbued with the literary culture of Hellenism, the western Fathers were at first less receptive. St. Irenaeus used almost exclusively Christian and biblical sources and little or nothing of philosophy in his apologetics; and Tertullian, with his famous *"Quid Athenae Hierosolymis?"* (What has Athens to do with Jerusalem?), set himself against the whole of pagan culture and to the greatest possible extent withdrew from it, declaring "there can be no reconciliation between the oath of allegiance taken to God and that taken to man, between the standard of Christ and that of the devil, between the camp of light and that of darkness. *Non potest una anima duobus deberi*: it is impossible to serve two masters, God and Caesar."[88]

The Greek Fathers, on the other hand, led by the catechetical school of Alexandria, followed a different course. They recognized that there existed a basic knowledge of truth common to both Christianity and the

---

[87] Cf. Dawson, *ibid.*, p. 107.
[88] Tertullian, *De Idolatria*, 18 & 19, quoted by Charles Norris Cochrane in *Christianity and Classical Culture*, (New York: Oxford Galaxy Books), 1957, p. 213.

classical tradition in philosophy, that the wisest of the Greeks had to some degree anticipated the true, historical Logos, the Incarnate Christ, the Word of God, and as such they were a *praeparatio evangelii*, a preparation for the coming of Christianity. The School of Alexandria, Origen being its greatest representative, accepted the challenge of Hellenistic thought, as the more traditional theology of St. Irenaeus did not, to demonstrate that the answers to their profoundest intellectual and moral inquiries are to be found in Christian revelation.

Accepting the terms of Hellenistic thought was a bold move. Earlier Greek apologists, like Justin Martyr and Athanagoras, had made a tentative approach, but Clement and Origen and the Alexandrians gave to philosophy a higher status in the Christian approach to the knowledge of God than anyone had yet given it.[89] It was dangerous, too. Greek orthodoxy was eventually to reject much of Origen's theology and condemn his works, but not before his tremendous influence had made its mark on Christian theology and culture. Origen had crossed a line, beyond which, in certain important aspects of his theology, he was thinking less like a Christian than a classical Hellenist. Although he regarded the Logos as the Eternal Image of the Invisible God, he clearly thought, like a neo-Platonist, that God, the Son, was on an order of being inferior to that of God, the Father. But this was before Nicaea, and was a relatively easy mistake to make given the powerful force and

---

[89] Cf. Dawson, *ibid.*, pp. 108 -109

influence of Hellenistic thought upon the educated eastern Christian mind especially in the absence of a fully-developed Christian philosophical tradition that was still in the cradle. All that said, it must be borne in mind that a strong monastic tradition had already grown up in the East in which men forsook the "modern" world as they found it by a complete withdrawal.

The Hellenization of Christian culture began in the East and extended throughout the Mediterranean world. Greek was the language of even the Western Church and remained so till late in the third century. But, though the Christian culture of the Hellenistic East dominated – it practically created the younger culture of the Latin West -- the Church in the West had its own disconcertingly original response to the "modern" world. This was Tertullian's response, who was, as first of the Latin Fathers and a writer of considerable genius and power, the founder of Latin Christian literature and one of the most powerful formative influences on the Christian culture of the West.[90] Tertullian was, at least to a modern historian, somewhat of an ironic figure, if not even a paradoxical one, because, while he rejected as demonically inspired the whole of pagan culture, he was thoroughly Roman in his thought and ideals. "He is the last representative of the great Roman moralists, like Lucretius and Juvenal and Tacitus, and the moral indignation which made Lucretius an atheist and Juvenal a pessimist makes Tertullian the champion of the Christian faith against the

---

[90] Cf. *Ibid.*, p111

corruption of the pagan world."[91]   But the same qualities made him a puritan and a heretic. The Montanism he left the Church to follow was excessively ascetic and anti-intellectual, and, against the admonition of the Church, *sought* persecution and denied that once fallen, one could be restored to a state of grace.

Contrary to Tertullian's fears, it was not the baptizing of Hellenistic thought that presented the greatest danger to the Church's integrity, but the conversion of the Roman Empire. So long as the Church was an outlaw and persecuted, she was acutely aware that between her and the immense material order that was the Empire of the Romans, her persecutors, was an apparently unbridgeable gulf, that as she was the beginning of a new, spiritual order and life, she could have no part in justifying or enjoying the fruits of the old order that was sustained by so much injustice. The principle of her life was utterly subversive of that which made that civilization what it was.[92]   She accepted the Roman state as ordained by God, Who in His sovereignty appoints all the rulers of the earth, but she did not and could not participate in its common life. The early Christians then removed themselves from society, living their own common life concealed from the heathen world around them, to which any connection they had was external and accidental. For by their membership in the Church, the City of God, as a new society with new spiritual relations between its

---

[91] Dawson, *ibid.*, p.112
[92] *Ibid.*, p. 116

members – male, female, slave, freeman, Gentile, and Jew -- they had forsaken their membership of the City of Man.[93]

In such conditions did Tertullian write. But when the Roman Empire became Christian, Christians were no longer the persecuted minority they had been. Christianity was now the established religion of the *orbis terrarum*, the entire civilized world, and of the largest and most powerful and well organized empire the world had ever known. The partnership between Church and Empire that would eventually develop and that would last more than a thousand years marked a revolutionary turning point in the history of Christian culture and of the world and would forever change the meaning of secularity. For as long as Christendom would last, the aims of the Church would conditionally and by an ideal never realized become the interest if not always the direct purpose of the civilized order. But, of course, at first, the edicts of toleration by Galerius and Constantine (311 and 313) only made Christianity *legal*; it did not become the established religion of the Empire and the *only* legal religion until 380 under Theodosius and Gratian. But the immediate consequence, broadly speaking, was that the Church no longer could maintain the isolation from the life of the Empire in which she once held herself.

The alliance between the world Empire and the Catholic Church meant that her relation to classical Hellenism would now be more intimate still, a closer, more complex and

---

[93] Cf. *ibid.*, p. 117

reticulated association that would demand of her a greater ability to manage its powerful influence upon her. For the Empire was already (nominally) Christian by the time a synthesis between Christianity and the Hellenic philosophical tradition had been worked out in the third quarter of the fourth century with the aim of Christianizing that tradition and through it an entire civilization, to which Christian thought was still not wholly intelligible. And of that union between the Roman Empire, Hellenism, and Christianity was born the basis of the Byzantine culture and Empire which lasted till the Fall of Constantinople in 1453. But the Church in the East found herself a thrall to a powerful Oriental despotic state. For while the Empire remained Roman, the oriental element in classical culture had, in the East, become predominant. Lost were *romanitas*, the old Roman moral ideal of piety (i.e., adherence to the old republican Roman customs and traditions), as well as the Roman imperialist ideal of a constitutional monarchy based on a privileged citizen class and a society of self-governing cities, and with them much of the public virtue that characterized old Rome. The revolutionary crises of the third century transformed the Empire into what more resembled Tsarist Russia at its most autocratic than the old Augustan principate.[94]

We can find three kinds of responses in the ancient Church to classical culture represented by three very different Christian apologists: Tertullian, Lactantius, and St.

---

[94] Cf. Dawson, *ibid.*, pp. 122-123.

Augustine. We have already mentioned Tertullian's wholesale and uncompromising rejection of pagan culture even before the western Church began critically to make use of it. I suspect that Tertullian would not have rejoiced over the edicts of toleration, nor, perhaps, over Constantine's conversion or, at least, what followed from it. But Lactantius most certainly did rejoice.

Lactantius (ca. 240–320) was the bishop of Caesarea, and (under Diocletian) a former professor of rhetoric and, therefore, a thoroughgoing classicist. Like so many of the early Christian authors, he was dependent on classical models and perfunctorily true to the requirements of his profession. Called the "Christian Cicero", Lactantius exhibits many of the literary graces of the master of Roman oratory. But the beauty of Lactantius's oratorical style far exceeded his grasp of Christian principles and his knowledge of Scripture.[95] St. Jerome laments Lactantius's ignorance of his religion, wishing that he had "stated our position as effectively as he demolished that of our opponents,"[96] and Gibbon observes that he "was almost entirely ignorant of Christian teaching and much better versed in rhetoric than theology."[97] The Christian Cicero was so called for more reasons than for his rhetorical skill; more significantly, it was that he *thought* like Cicero, the statesman and philosopher. With Cicero, Lactantius as a Christian could believe that the

---

[95] Cf. The Catholic Encyclopedia, 1917 ed. under "Lactantius".
[96] Quoted by Charles Norris Cochrane, *op. cit.*, p.218.
[97] Gibbon, *History of the Decline and Fall of the Roman Empire*, ed. J. B. Bury, (London: Methuen, 1896-1900), chap. V.

moral had an objective existence in nature and that the state's principal purpose was the rule of justice. And as a Christian, he could, with Cicero, look to the civilizing effects of the Roman civilization to ameliorate the barbarians, to teach them the virtue of Roman citizenry, which he regarded, with Cicero, as both an end and foundation of civil society, but which he believed were also consistent with Christian principles.[98]

But Lactantius was far from being uncritical of classical thought. He considered it to be vitiated at its roots because it was unilluminated by faith, and its hostility to the new religion only alienated it further from the truth of Christ.[99] In this he anticipated St. Augustine, limning the beginnings of a specifically Christian moral philosophy. He understood that only a philosophy inspired by faith could demonstrate the inefficacy of the classical notion of justice, which proposed that each man be given his due. Pagan justice, Lactantius argued, was divorced from the sources of justice deeper than reason alone, namely, human affection and love. The higher justice can only be achieved if all men are known to be brothers under the Fatherhood of God, bound thus to the same Creator and the final Dispenser of Justice. Lactantius saw clearly that *Romanitas*, however venerable, had not worked to save the Empire from decay and disintegration. Though he honored Cicero for his noble conception of natural law, it was a conception Lactantius

---

[98] Cf. Wilhelmsen, *Christianity and Political Philosophy*, Athens: University of Georgia Press, 1978, p.89.
[99] Cf. *ibid.*, p.90

insisted was doomed practically to fail of justice because it was not understood to be an expression of the divine law. And the classical notion of virtue he regarded as defective because it was not founded on a love for God. The citizen's love of God as his Creator, he argued, was the only effective motive to pursue the common good and so achieve social justice. Roman *pietas* did not misconceive the good of the commonweal, only the foundation by which that good could be achieved. The profoundest needs of a commonweal and of a civilization are ultimately spiritual not physical, and *Romanitas* could not satisfy them.

So far Lactantius's understanding and somewhat complex appreciation of classicism were sound. But what was critical for Lactantius and for the Church was the confidence he placed in the forms of the old classical politics and their corresponding virtues, which he believed the new Christian Emperor would reestablish. Lactantius expected the problem of classical politics to automatically resolve itself with the establishment of a Christian emperor. Charity would triumph in the polis by means of the power of the state. For the natural virtues, *Romanitas*, which on their own could not sustain the fortunes of the Empire which were waning, would through charity be supernaturalized and Rome could then look to a millennial future, an Empire of love. Thus, In Lactantius' mind (and, much later, in Dante's), the spiritual ends of Christianity merge with the political ends of the Empire. But, of course, he was wrong; for Christianity does not promise victory in this world. Those today who would baptize liberalism in the belief that it can achieve the ends of the Church make the same mistake about a political ideology that is even less conformable to those ends.

Lactantius' mistake is better understood if we consider that the Cross had no continuous *historical* meaning for him. The paradox of the Cross and even the finality of the Apocalypse do not seem to dim his enthusiasm for the progress of Roman classical civilization, against which the Antichrist himself is hardly a match. It is evidence of his deep attachment to the entire classical tradition that he had only superficially Christianized it. The failure of the Roman ideal was a scandal to him and Christianity was the technical solution to its preservation and efflorescence. There should be, in Lactantius's mind, a permanent and peaceful existence for a Christian polity assured by the triumph of human virtue. Against this, "unintelligibility, chance, the absurdity of sin, tragedy, the scandal of evil crowned and goodness scorned, the constant pressure of disorder and the ever tumescent indecency of failure"[100] -- in short, the perpetual working of Original Sin in the world -- seem to him but paper monsters. Lactantius understood the importance of love to justice and to the political order and thus understood better than his pagan predecessors the meaning and limits of virtue. But the Christian Cicero, enamored of the classical ideal and its embodiment in *Romanitas*, who dedicated his *Institutes*[101] to the Emperor Constantine, could scarcely help

---

[100] Wilhelmsen, *op. cit.*, p.94.
[101] *The Divine Institutions* (*Divinarum Institutionum Libri VII*). This was the most important of his writings, an apologetic treatise intended to point out the futility of pagan beliefs and to establish the reasonableness and truth of

but confuse the finality of "Eternal Rome" with the finality of the Kingdom God. It seems in the spirit of his age that Lactantius confused politics with theology. Though with much less excuse, he was thinking with his Emperor. Both Constantine and even Theodosius after him (who, unlike his predecessor, went so far as to institute the forms and order of the Catholic state) required of Christianity that it should subserve a definitely social and economic function.[102] What none of them realized or would not entertain is that Classicism and Christianity were fundamentally irreconcilable. This is not because they had nothing in common but because they served ultimately different ends.

The poignant irony (to the modern person) of the Church's position in the historical situation of the fourth century should not be missed. Catholics in this period, even those of Lactantius's ilk, were necessarily in the role of the "modernist" relative to the "traditionalist" pagan who would preserve the classical tradition at all costs. The Church found herself at the vanguard – indeed the chief agent -- of a movement of human history into a new age. The ancient world was at the crossroads, in a process of transformation. To a Julian (the Apostate) or a Symmachus[103] the rise of a

---

Christianity as a response to pagan critics. It was the first attempt at a systematic exposition of Christian theology in Latin.

[102] Cf. Cochrane, op. cit., p. 356.

[103] Quintus Aurelius Symmachus (c. 340–c. 402), A pagan representative of the traditional cursus honorum, Symmachus was an opponent of Ambrose, archbishop of Milan. He implored the new emperor, Valentinian II, to restore the famous Altar of Victory, symbolic of traditional Roman civil religion, to its accustomed place in the Senate. He pleaded for tolerance for traditional cult

Christian state and the corresponding decline in the fourth century of the classical Roman state and the fortunes of the Empire "meant the end of civilization and with it everything that gave value and significance to human life". But these momentous developments, it was becoming apparent to the Church, were a preparation for a new and radically different age. A new civilization and culture were forming around her and the Church understood it to be in the interests of the Kingdom of God to help form it. But it then fell to her to "civilize" the barbarians (which now meant also converting them), who coveted the stability and prosperity of the civilized world. The Church accomplished this dual program of at once civilizing and converting the barbarian in part by assuming custody of the very literature that, throughout classical times, held the spiritual nourishment of the old civilization and, in part, by giving them something of the spirit of order and discipline which she had acquired from her long association with the fallen Empire.[104] Lactantius could see this much, but he still held onto the ideal of *Romanitas* as something essential and eternal, which others, who better expressed the mind of the Church, thought should perish from the earth.[105]

One of these others who better expressed the mind of the Church was Saint Augustine. He was, like Lactantius, also a teacher of rhetoric and steeped in the classical tradition.

---

practices and beliefs which Christianity was about to suppress in the Theodosian edicts of 391.
[104] Cochrane, *op. cit.*, p.357
[105] *Ibid.*, p.356

Born thirty years after Lactantius's death, by the time Augustine came into the world, the moral and intellectual foundations of classical Hellenism were in all but total ruin. For more than a millennium men had labored to realize the classical ideal of the commonwealth; the genius of Rome was supposed to have finally achieved it as Vergil had declared at the dawn of the Empire. By the end of the third century *Romanitas* was already lame, unable to stand up to the pressures of the political and cultural changes taking place in the ancient world and to most nothing seemed capable of restoring its original vigor. Lactantius, as we saw, was convinced that Christianity would restore it and the Emperor Julian, believing Christianity to be the chief enemy of *Romanitas*, tried to restore it by suppressing the new religion and reviving paganism. But both were whistling in the wind and the Emperor came to defeat and death in Mesopotamia. By the time Augustine was twenty-one, Rome had been defeated at Adrianople and her military fortunes forever reversed. One can only wonder what Lactantius would have thought of this rapid decline.

Like Lactantius, Augustine too urged recognition of Christian principles as the one true foundation for a new science of politics. It was from the famous passage in Book 5 of his *The City of God* (chapters 21-26) that Charlemagne learned how to be a Christian emperor of a restored Rome.[106] But unlike Lactantius, Augustine did not advance Christianity as a solution to any concrete political problem.

---

[106] Cf. Wilhelmsen, *op. cit.*, p.95

He made it perfectly clear that the problem of realizing the classical ideal of the commonwealth can only be addressed by a transposition of the pagan concept of virtue with the Christian conception. St. Augustine understood that the pagan concept of virtue, whose operating principle, Excellence (*arché*), had no transcendent goal, based as it was on a thinly veiled materialism, and that the Christian concept grounds *effective* virtue in a personal relationship between man and God, his creator, whose grace is necessary and fundamentally gratuitous. Outside of that relationship, he declaimed, "Prudence leads nowhere, Justice distributes nothing, Temperance moderates nothing, except to the end that men may be pleased and vainglory served."[107] The call to virtue can only be fully historically realized when it becomes something personal – to desire my own perfection because I love God Who desires it of me and Who made me for Himself -- rather than the merely civic pursuit of public honors. The motivation in classical virtue was insufficient to realize the moral excellence necessary to sustain the classical commonwealth. Beyond man's fundamental freedom to accept or reject his own perfection, Classicism's call to fulfill one's own nature ethically through virtue lacked anything that could sufficiently motivate him to struggle for moral perfection -- to be prudent, generous, chaste, honorable, and just. Though the classical literary tradition extolled those virtues and some men possessed them in a high degree, the moral debility of the ancient world is certain evidence that they were in very short supply among the mass of men.

---

[107] Augustine quoted by Wilhelmsen, *ibid.*

Indeed, the classical call to the life of virtue was, as Wilhelmsen expressed it, "like asking a man to die on the battlefield for the third law of thermodynamics."[108]

If there was any hope for political happiness, it was through Christian virtue in a Christian polity; in the purely classical struggle of virtue against barbarism, virtue was losing. Nevertheless, Augustine was equally emphatic that virtue, even Christian virtue, guarantees neither success nor failure. "We do not attribute the power of giving kingdoms and empires to any save to the true God, who gives happiness in the kingdom of heaven to the pious alone, but gives kingly power on earth to the pious and to the impious, as it may please Him, whose good pleasure is always just."[109] Success or failure in political life, as in personal life, ultimately falls within the power of God and the Divine Will, for the ultimate meaning of political events rests solely in the will of God.

Augustine was not then a partisan of the Empire in the way that Lactantius was. The Christian ruler should, while he may, make political power "the handmaid of His majesty by using for the greatest possible extension of His worship", but what God has given in His sovereignty He may just as readily take away. The Christian ruler's reward for wise and just governance is not necessarily enjoyed in this world, though it is certainly in the next. The irrational in history, the dark forces of mischance, classical philosophy could

---

[108] Wilhelmsen, *op. cit.*, p.100
[109] Augustine, *The City of God*, 5,20.

never adequately account for; it was an unaccountable and embarrassing paradox. But Christian metaphysics, as Augustine understood it, rejected the absolute status classical thought had given nature and thus rejected too the absolute status of nature's enemy, chance, fortune, or the unintelligible in history and our personal experience.[110] In Christian and specifically Augustinian thought the unintelligible ceased to be the *bête noir* it was in classical thought. Though unintelligible, it was no longer necessarily irrational. The chance event — our good or bad luck — which is admitted to be existentially absurd because its meaning is inscrutable in the order of finite or efficient causality, is understood in the order of *final causality* to have a rational transcendent cause, viz., God, Whose intelligence and will are not bound by the finite order and Who is the Cause by which that order exists. Thus, Augustine argued (and Boethius after him), only a Christian can be reconciled to our experience of the "absurd," because ultimately the absurd is impossible.

We may now be prepared to see in the modern post-conciliar Church's relation to modernity the fundamental difference as well as the similarity between it and the ancient Church's relation to classicism. The Hellenic or Graeco-Roman classical tradition exerted a powerful influence on the Church whose leadership was largely drawn from the upper classes and hence educated in that tradition. We may

---

[110] Wilhelmsen, *op. cit.*, p.100 -101

recall that St. Jerome berated himself for being more a Ciceronian than a Christian. The Church in her new role as the religion of the Empire faced the twin problems of civilizing the barbarians as well as converting them and maintaining her own integrity as a spiritual society sojourning in this world where she was given no lasting city – not even Rome. It was, thence, the task of the Fathers of the Church in this period to take account of that tradition. She recognized that it was at once an approximation of Christian truth (a *preambula fidei*), for it acknowledged a transcendent reality (e.g., in Plato and Aristotle, in whom the tradition reached its apogee), and profoundly flawed since it apprehended no operative relation between the transcendent and man and thus primarily oriented to man and not to God his Creator and Redeemer. Even Cicero, who believed in a fixed and overarching natural law, did not acknowledge the Divine Law from which it necessarily derives. The Church's theology needed to take account of the profound questions raised by classical philosophy, not because she felt threatened by them, but because they were being asked by those whom she sought to convert to whom they were of deep importance. The classical pagan world began to despair of any rational solution to a profound alienation from belief in a rational existence, as evidenced by the popularity in the third and fourth centuries of the philosophy of the Cynics and the attraction of oriental irrationalism (the religion of Mithraism, for example). Once asked, these critical questions could not be left unanswered, despite the dangers of engaging pagan thought. And, as we've seen, there were dangers: the danger of demystifying Christianity, of reducing it to a mere rational or ethical religion, or of making it a mere tool of Empire for the spread of the Roman ideal; or, what was more threatening, the danger of making Christianity a purely mystical and esoteric religion by the subtle influence of the Church's old enemy, Gnosticism, which lay in the deeper recesses of neo-Platonism

But the Church's appropriation of classical thought and forms could be of mutual benefit to her and to civilization, because Christianity was not an irrational religion. All truth concerned her because Christ is the Truth and all truth expresses what is real, the reality which is God's. St. Paul's warning to the Colossians against "philosophy and vain deceit" was not to decry philosophy, but the *substitution* of reason for faith. At the very heart of Hellenistic thought is the rational principle of the *logos*, which means both reason and word, and that not to act in accordance with that principle is to act against nature. It was St. John, under the inspiration of the Holy Spirit who first made the connection between Christ, the Second Person of the Blessed Trinity, and the Greek concept, declaring that the divine, transcendent God had revealed Himself as *logos*, and as the Logos, became man and as such eternally and supremely manifested His love for His creatures. Christianity was united with classical Greek thought in its understanding that the world was intelligible and that a fundamental relationship existed between the mind of man and intelligible reality. It also agreed that all of a man's moral and intellectual virtue depended upon his conforming to the demands of that relationship and that upon virtue depended in turn the achievement of every human good. But for Christianity the ultimate source of the moral order was God, the I AM, Who is Being Himself, and His Divine law, it was not only nature that one acted against in failing to accord with the principle of the *logos*, but God, Who is the Logos, Reason Himself.

These profound affinities made it possible then for the Church to critically purify classical thought and thus make use of it not only in her civilizing mission, but also in the continual development of the Christian mind, the mind of the Church. That development St. Anselm precisely formulated as *fides quarens intellectum*, faith seeking understanding. Classical tradition in philosophy, at its best, was in search of truth, and in grasping certain primary truths it developed forms for intellectual inquiry that proved tremendously useful tools to the Church in the development of her understanding of the truth revealed to her.

The Church and the Culture of Modernity

IV

The Origins of Unbelief

C lassical culture could offer Christianity what it did not inherently possess, a structure of thought within which it could formulate its theology. It could provide this because certain important affinities existed between the highest expressions of the culture of classical antiquity and Christianity. But there are no such affinities with the culture of modernity. I have already mentioned that the relation that the culture of modernity bears to Christianity is that of an apostate. Hence, modernity's profound rejection of Christianity puts the Church in a necessarily different relation to it than was classical antiquity. But one would not think so to read *Gaudium et Spes* or from the way most Catholics embrace modernity. So, it requires some explanation.

The Church and the Culture of Modernity

Modernity has always viewed itself in relation to the past declaring itself superior. Since the 18th century what is "modern" has been given, so to say, preferential treatment. The Renaissance studied antiquity as the quaint province of historical preoccupation to the exclusion of the Middle Ages, which, though it knew less of antiquity than the Renaissance, in some ways took it much more seriously as a *predicate evangelii.* Far from being just another age in the history of civilizations, the modern age has regarded itself, as the culmination of human endeavor and achievement arising from, as though out of the primordial slime, the long benighted age of the Church. Measuring itself against its predecessors, the modern age knows more and has achieved more for the benefit of humanity than any other age and has raised man to a height he has never before attained. We are obliged at least to admit as historical fact the *material* progress of modern civilization in science, technology, the distribution of wealth (depending on the country you live in), and medicine. But we are also obliged to admit as historical fact that these achievements of modern civilization had their provenance in a Christian civilization, medieval Europe. Modern man, of course, has not felt himself so obliged; in fact he has consistently denied as a matter of public orthodoxy the Christian origins of western culture, despite what honest historians find to the contrary. The European Union's refusal to acknowledge in its constitution its Christian past is perhaps the most blatant example. But why is this?

Let's first consider the word "modern", which is one of those semantically complex words. The simplest (and earliest) sense of the word is nothing more than "of the present or recent times".[111] But the word, which would never have been but for a consciousness of the past, gathered to itself a sense of the comparative worth of "the present or recent times", thence the superiority of things *modern* against things ancient. Far from a simple term to differentiate the ancient and medieval from the present age, *modern* has acquired the sense of a *preference* for the present age to anything before it. We see this to be the case with the rather drab epithet "post-modern", used to denote our present age and to indicate a change in preference, like a change in regime, a preference for anything that is *not* modern. Of course, depending on the speaker's or writer's tastes, sensibilities, and intellectual affinities, the word *modern* could also be used to denote the *superiority* of the new over the old, or of innovation against tradition.

The rivalry between new and old and a growing sentiment against the later we begin to see as early as the sixteenth century. It reaches a high pitch in France in the mid-seventeenth century under the influence of rationalism, under the auspices of British philosophy, especially Locke's sensualism and Bacon's "new science", to which Diderot's and d'Alembert's *Encylopédie* (1751-1765) pronounced a "principal

---

[111] Its first recorded use was in 1585. It comes from the Late Latin word *modernus* derived from the Latin *modo*, "just now".

debt"[112]. The *Encylopédie* itself helped enormously by its wit and "scientific" rigor to promote the modern disposition in eighteenth-century Europe. Not the least of those things which helped advance the prejudice for things modern was the "Debate of the Ancients and the Moderns" (*Querelle des Anciens et des Modernes*), a learned debate that arose over whether contemporary learning had surpassed the classical learning of the ancient Greeks and Romans. It was the "moderns", as they were called, epitomized by Bernard de Fontenelle, who, represented the new age of science and reason and the spirit of Progress, against the "ancients", whose proponents, for their part, argued rather weakly that all that is necessary to be known was still to be found in Virgil, Cicero, Homer, and, especially, Aristotle. To Fontenelle's "modern man", the so-called wisdom of the ancients was little more than the product of superstition unenlightened by science and reason; hence, modern man could see further having removed the blinkers of tradition and religious superstition. The controversy crossed the channel to England where it was taken up by Sir William Temple, who answered Fontenelle's contention in a work entitled *Of Ancient and Modern Learning* (1696). Jonathan Swift, who worked for Temple at the time, satirized the

---

[112] "In the prospectus Diderot had already said: "If we succeed in this vast enterprise our principal debt will be to Chancellor Bacon who sketched the plan of a universal dictionary of sciences and arts at a time when there were, so to say, neither sciences nor arts." D'Alembert acknowledged the same indebtedness. Thus, British influence was considerable both in shaping the doctrine of the "Encyclopédie" and in bringing about its publication." *The Catholic Encyclopedia*,1909, vol. V., under "Encylopedists" by C.A. Dubray,

controversy, but especially the moderns, in his own work, "The Battle of the Books", part of his *A Tale of a Tub* (1703). It should not be overlooked that the wisdom of the Christian Middle Ages was never taken into account by either side of the controversy, owing to that "modern" prejudice that, we noted, began in the Renaissance.

We can thus see how *modern* became a "dangerous" word, whose strict meaning is chronological, but which became laden with the semantic burden of representing a complex and conflicting body of cultural and learned attitudes about European and specifically Christian civilization. It was a contention of values. The semantic burden gets heavier as the prejudice deepens and diversifies.

Although Swift, in his satire, being partial to classical learning, gave the victory to the ancients, it was the moderns who really prevailed. The prejudice in favor of things modern took root in the European mind. By the eighteenth century the prejudice was no longer a position assumed in academic debate among literati, but had become a fixed principle of thought in the minds of a powerfully influential intellectual class of Europeans, especially in France and England. The European and Scottish Enlightenments, being the formative movements in European thought in the eighteenth and nineteenth centuries, were enemies of Europe's Christian past and would remake the civilization they inherited from the Christian civilization of medieval Europe. The European Renaissance was itself a cultured man's rejection of medieval civilization in favor of classical antiquity. But the Enlightenment's philosophical defection from its inherited Christian past was chiefly the eventual effect of the theological defection of the Protestant Revolt, which had broken the unity of Christian thought in Europe and to a considerable degree the cultural force of that thought.

Protestantism rejected along with the authority of the Papacy, the entire medieval tradition of the Church, which it regarded with imperturbable ignorance as a medieval anomaly. And while the Reformers persuaded themselves that they were returning to the original and pristine principles of Christ's Church, they were establishing principles and ideas which would form the foundation for the eventual complete secularization of European society. In their rejection of the Church's medieval past and thus, ineluctably, her Sacred Tradition, the Reformers had established the first *modern* Christian Church. Eventually and, perhaps, inevitably, what began as a theological revolt and an intellectual prejudice became in France and eventually all of Europe a political and cultural *revolution*, which at its worst, was directed against not merely a political regime but the entire traditional order of society, transmogrifying it into what became the first thoroughly secular society, the thorough exclusion of religious belief and values from its organization and common life.

It is evident that the history of "modern" is only evidence of a more profound and determining factor. Behind the history of a word is the history of the thought which the word denotes. And so it is in the beginnings of modern philosophy where we will find the origin and heart of modernity. Modernity expresses itself essentially, as we have seen, as a revolt against the past, against received tradition, not merely in custom and convention, but at the highest levels of rational human understanding, namely philosophy and particularly that part of philosophy that has to do with the principles of being itself and from which all other inquiry into the true nature of reality proceeds. And from this rarified height, descend by degrees the elements that form the climate of thought and the air that we all breathe. As thought is the precursor of doing, it is thus the foundation of culture, for we conduct our lives individually and collectively according to what we think is real and true.

Leo Strauss and Pierre Manent, among others, have observed that modernity started with Niccolo Machiavelli, in so far at least as Machiavelli was the first to explicitly abjure the Aristotelian and Christian doctrines of the state, which acknowledged the state to be responsible to ends higher than its own existence, in favor of "modern experience", *lunga esperienza delle cose moderne*[113]. As Manent points out, in Machiavelli modernity found an interpretation of itself that "determined the orientation of the European

---

[113] Machiavelli speaks of his "long experience in contemporary affairs" in his Dedicatory Letter to *The Prince* (1513).

mind".[114] Machiavelli substitutes purely political ends for moral ones, accepting evil as politically primary and obligatory to achieve those ends. In the same way did his intellectual descendants subordinate ethical truth to lesser ends, such as Marx who subordinated ethics to history and economics, Nietzsche to the will, and Freud to psychological forces. Manent observes that doubt of the good is one of the most deeply rooted characteristics of the modern soul; it was Machiavelli who raised in political thought the status of evil above that of the good and thus did the western soul lose its political innocence.[115]

As fundamental as Machiavelli is to the formation of modernity, especially in morals and politics, the revolt against the Church and Catholic principle would have been less profound and ubiquitous but for the occurrence at a much deeper stratum of thought. It was Rene Descartes' (1596–1650), by his rejection of the entire Aristotelian-Thomist philosophical tradition in metaphysics, who, "more than any other figure, marks the transition from the Middle Ages to the modern world."[116] After the breakdown of medieval philosophy since the 14th century, there followed a period of about two hundred years in which constructive philosophy and especially metaphysics had all but died in the care of a corrupted and incompetent scholasticism that

---

[114] Cf. Pierre Manent, An Intellectual History of Liberalism, tr., Rebecca Belinski, (Princeton: Princeton University Press 1994), 12.
[115] Cf. ibid., 14.
[116] R.M. Eaton, quoted by Etienne Gilson in The Unity of Philosophic Experience (New York: Scribners, 1937), p.125.

had been infected by nominalism and had brought low the whole scholastic tradition and given, in many learned circles, St. Thomas and even Aristotle a bad name. It was in the ruins of medieval scholasticism that Descartes wanted, not to rebuild what had collapsed, but to build an entirely new philosophical tradition. There were many since the 14th century who had criticized Aristotle, but it was Descartes' ambition to be the new Aristotle, to remake philosophy from the ground up. But let's put Descartes to one side for the moment to take account of the intellectual conditions that helped form Descartes' philosophical project.

If we are to trace the origins of modern thought we have to go further back than Descartes to the crisis in medieval philosophy that precipitated Descartes' thought. His philosophy was a desperate struggle to free all of philosophy and himself from the skepticism in which it had been steeped for two hundred years. The *Discourse on Method* was Descartes' direct answer to that supreme skeptic in an age of universal skepticism, Michel de Montaigne (1533–1592), whose *Essays* (1580) presented to Descartes a challenge that he eagerly took up.

But what made Montaigne a skeptic? The 16th century was an age in which philosophical thought was barren, for "rational metaphysics was dead and positive science had not yet been born" and philosophy as a purely rational discipline had abdicated to an open philosophical skepticism.[117] What made Montaigne a skeptic was the same thing that made Descartes the father of modern philosophy. The difference between Montaigne and Descartes is that Montaigne embraced skepticism and Descartes tried to destroy it. The question then is: How did philosophy get itself into this state of disorder?

It is worth noting that most historians of philosophy would not call the state of philosophy in the 16th century "disordered", for while they recognize that philosophy at that time faced a challenge to reorganize itself along different principles, they do not admit of a transcendent "order of truth" to which reason must conform, and certitude, as with faith, modern philosophy has wholly abjured. But Descartes was no modern; far from embracing uncertainty, he abhorred it and endeavored to banish it from philosophy forever. He was as far from Bertrand Russell or Jean-Paul Sartre as a theologian is from an atheist.

The skepticism of the 16th century is the child of the 14th. In that earlier century, the union of theology, the science of those things that are received in faith from divine revelation, and philosophy, the knowledge of those things which flows from the principle of natural reason, was beginning to dissolve. That union, which was the great achievement of the 12th century (especially the work of St. Thomas Aquinas), recognized that, because God is the

---

[117] Cf. Gilson, *ibid.*, p.118.

common source of both reason and revelation, theology and philosophy, if pursued along correct principles, will necessarily agree. Their union is understood in the recognition that the two sciences are essentially different: "only distinct things can be united; if you attempt to blend them, you inevitably lose them in what is not union, but confusion."[118] The Scholastic philosophy of the late Middle Ages under the influence of the nominalism of William of Ockham, began to forget that essential difference.

The separation of theology (faith) and philosophy (reason) began with nominalism, which claims that there are no universals, that they do not exist apart from the names we give them. Thus, the nominalist (and his cousin, the conceptualist) would say that there is no such thing as Triangularity, a real thing inherent in all triangles, but only this triangle or that triangle. Of the universal, Triangularity, he would say that it is a concept that exists only in the mind, a name we give to a group of like things that we perceive. In the realistic conception of universals, Triangularity exists objectively of the human mind and distinctly from any of the particular material or physical things it defines. Indeed, Triangularity is that which makes every individual triangle intelligible. Universals are, in the Aristotelian tradition of realism that obtained in medieval scholasticism, forms of things that determine what a thing is, what makes a triangle (however imperfect) triangular. However, the Aristotelian conception of universals, unlike Plato's conception of their

---

[118] *Ibid.* p. 62

objects existing in a "third realm", they do not have ontologically an existence separate from the things they represent, but neither are they reducible to those material things any more than they can be reduced to mere mental abstractions pure and simple. The mental concept of Triangularity is the certain result of the natural operation of the mind in abstracting and defining what the senses apprehend in objective existence. Though a mental concept, the universal then actually participates in extra-mental reality.

Ockham was himself a Scholastic, which means he was trained in a dialectical method of inquiry and a system of philosophical and theological principles that made much of Aristotle's philosophy, and which culminated in St. Thomas' synthesis of Aristotelianism and Christian theology. But because Ockham rejected Thomas' synthesis, his own philosophy was at odds with Aristotle's, particularly on the question of universals. Among Ockham's predecessors a variety of opinion obtained on the nature and reality of universals, all of it, however tenuously, was realist. Some, like Duns Scotus (who also rejected St. Thomas' synthesis but rejected Ockham's conclusion too), taught that universals were real entities (like Platonic Forms) apart from their existence as individual or singular things. Others, like Henry of Harclay were drawn to something very like Ockham's conclusion that universals have no extramental reality. St. Thomas Aquinas, however, believed Aristotle to be right about universals, that they are virtually present in individual things, from which, through the senses, they are abstracted by the intellect to present to the mind the general ideas we call universals. The Church, we may say, has always embraced philosophical realism even before the descent of Scholastic Aristotelianism, for while realism was the tradition of western philosophy since Plato, it is also how the unphilosophical mind instinctively understands its experience of the external world. As Gilson has observed: we are all realists until persuaded otherwise. And it was realism which the Church finally officially (though not dogmatically as *de fide* – it is not after all a matter of faith but of knowledge) adopted when Leo XIII in *Aeterni Patris* made St. Thomas the Common Doctor of the Church and established his writings as the Church's standard for theology and philosophy.

Ockham was ready to go further than even Harclay and give up altogether the realist understanding that in some manner universals, our general and abstract ideas, were themselves in some manner real or even corresponded to real things. Ockham insisted that our general ideas are neither images, pictures, nor mental presentations of any real or conceivable thing.[119] His reluctance to accommodate even the basic premises of realism had far-reaching and disastrous effects for medieval and modern philosophy. Like Descartes, Ockham started a revolution in philosophy, for which (so far as its effects are concerned) the best analogy is, I think, the Sin of Adam.

---

[119] *Ibid.*, p. 68.

Etienne Gilson's observation about how philosophical revolutions begin deserves quotation, because it identifies the dominant characteristic and fundamental philosophical error of modern thought that lies as the heart of the culture of modernity:

> Every time philosophical speculation has succeeded in circumscribing what we might perhaps call "a pure position," its discovery has regularly been attended by a philosophical revolution. Begotten in us *by things themselves*, concepts are born reformers that never lose touch with reality. Pure ideas, on the other hand, are born within the mind and from the mind, not as intellectual expressions of *what is*, but as models, or patterns, of what ought to be; hence *they are born revolutionists*.[120] [italics are mine]

Ockham's was the first revolution in what was to be an endless series.

Ockham decided that there was no other solution to the "problem" of universals than to substitute a new classification of the various types of knowledge for the old one. He accordingly divided knowledge into two classes, abstractive and intuitive, old terms to which he gave new meanings. According to Ockham, our intuitive knowledge is cognition from the immediate perception of a really existing thing, and which is, therefore, self-evident. Whatever is not

---

[120] *The Unity of Philosophic Experience* (New York: Scribners, 1937), p. 68.

intuition in our knowledge is abstraction. This includes all our abstract ideas, man, chair, democracy, which represent whole classes of individual things, as well as our mental representations of individual things, that is, the mental image or memory of a certain thing even with all the individual characteristics. What is born only in mind as the image or memory of something cannot be real, otherwise we would not have to remember or imagine it. Only that which comes by our immediate perceptions can be known. Abstract knowledge then is a kind of cognition or knowing by which nothing can be known about the existence or non existence of its object.[121] We see here in Ockham's doctrine the foundation of modern empiricism for experimental knowledge, as he called it, alone can be *science* or true knowledge.

If only intuition or the immediate impression of some object by an internal or external perception can give us knowledge of that thing's existence, then where does that leave the objects of abstractive knowledge or universals? Ockham did not dispute that universals *as themselves singular things* exist. But what kind of existence? Unicorns can be said to exist, but only in the mind. So, according to Ockham, we can say that universals exist but are not real. Ockham regarded universals as psychological facts, mental phenomena, for he called the universal a "quality of the mind", and as such are empirically observable facts but

---

[121] In my account of Ockham's epistemology I am following closely Gilson's. See *op. cit.*, pp.62 ff.

without any intrinsic reality. They are mere signs.[122] In other words, the sign itself exists, but its meaning or signification does not or, at least, we cannot know it. The meaning of a sign has no existence of its own, what exists is the sign (the universal or abstract idea) and my perception of it (the psychological phenomenon). The kind of sign that best demonstrates Ockham's doctrine is that of the spoken word because it bears no natural relation to its meaning or the thing it signifies. Hence universals are mere signs or words to denote real things, but which themselves are not real, because they are not found to exist but are *invented* and only thereby come into existence. Here we find too the seeds of Existentialism.

There are, of course, signs or concepts that have an obvious natural correspondence to what they signify and so always and everywhere mean the same thing. For instance, certain physical phenomena are natural signs of their causes such as heat, which is cause of fire, is also the natural sign of its presence. Ockham had to admit that there are such signs, but his theory could not account for them, because these signs indicated that universals existed in their own right, that the same image can signify certain distinct individual things to all human beings. He found that all the possible solutions to his difficulties were all realist solutions. But instead of retreating from his conclusions and reexamining them, Ockham simply made an "end run" around his quandary.

---

[122] Cf. Gilson, *op. cit.,* p. 71

One of those realist solutions had already been given by Abelard and should have appealed to Ockham if he had been prepared to accept a solution: that the universals if they exist nowhere else at least exist in God's mind. But, as though spotting a trap, he decided that realism was not possible even in the divine mind, denying that even in God could ideas exist that represent particular individual things. Refusing to give up the premise that universals are nothing real, Ockham concluded that God Himself is no more capable of conceiving them than we are. So, it must be that in nature no such thing as man or dog exists only the individual things – this man, this dog -- and if every individual dog resembles in certain fundamental ways every other dog (explained by the form or universal, doggness, in realist thought), that is simply how God created them and must remain a mystery of the Divine Will, for there can be no other explanation for things as they are than that God willed them so. That, Ockham thought, was the wisest philosophical position to take. Hence, it was his solid conviction that it was futile for the philosopher to speculate on the hypothetical causes of things that actually exist. We should take the things that actually exist as they are. But Ockham also believed that what actually exists might always be different from what it is, for the reason why things are as they are rests ultimately upon God's freely willing it and the possibilities open to the free will of an omnipotent God are infinite. The operations of nature are hidden from us and we cannot know what God will do next. Hence, philosophical speculation on the nature of things is ultimately empty because it is impossible to know their nature. This is the essential meaning of the principle of "Ockham's Razor": what you cannot empirically verify you must not suppose.

Ockham was a Franciscan monk and thoroughly orthodox theologically. But philosophically, he was a pure empiricist and his empiricism led him straight to a kind of provisional materialism, provisional because, although God exists, He cannot be known to exist for we have no immediate experience of Him. God was necessarily an object of faith not of reason. In the same way was the immortality of the soul a victim of Ockham's theological empiricism or "theologism". Ockham's empiricism could not rationally account for the causal relation of a material thing to an immaterial thing and yet that the soul was immaterial and, therefore, an immortal substance immediately created by God was an indispensable tenet of Christian theology and in full agreement with the tradition of Christian philosophy. Theology and philosophy also agreed that the soul was not only immaterial but also a knowing power that through the particular body it animates can establish relations with material things and thereby know them. Ockham insisted that, while we experience knowing, the result of that relation, we can have no experience of the relation itself because we can have no experience of an immaterial substance in the first place. Ockham did not want to cast doubt upon the teachings of the Church or the existence of God or the immortality of the soul. Despite his philosophical problems, he was entirely disposed to believe these things.

Let us by all means, he maintained, hold to such beliefs as Christians, for not to accept them as true is to cease to be Christians, but they should be held exclusively as articles of faith not reason. If this sounds familiar, it is because it is the very subjectivism that has infested Christian theology for 200 years.

Ockham was tenacious and was willing to go wherever his theologism would lead him. He had thrown everything into doubt that cannot be known intuitively, or empirically (for Ockham they come to the same thing), by internal or external sensation. But he found (no doubt to his dismay) that the boundry he circumscribed within which was everything that could be known with philosophical certainty, continued under his inexorable logic to recede till even intuitive knowledge was itself in doubt.

Ockham had taken it for granted that the objects of our intuitive knowledge must exist, for if it did not exist we could have no intuition of it. So much seemed obvious. But on closer inspection, it revealed another insoluble problem for his philosophy. He could not account for our intuitions of *non*-existent things. It was easy enough for Ockham to explain how existent things cause in us a mental sign of their existence, that is, the intuition of that thing, its object. Thus do we know a thing is, but it does not explain how we know a thing is not. How can that which does not exist, what *is not*, make us to know that it does not exist? A curious question perhaps to someone not entangled in the web of his own philosophy, but to Ockham it was trouble and he knew it. He tried to answer it in different ways, all of which, as Gilson has observed, "have merely driven to despair" historians of philosophy in their attempts to understand them.

Ockham's final solution, which was not a solution at all but a way of maintaining his philosophical principles, was to resort as before, but now with even less reason, to his theologism, now a kind of *deus ex machina*, by supposing that God alone conserves in us our intuitions of non-existing things. The problem with Ockham's "solution" is that it removes the certainty we enjoyed about the reality of actually existing things. For the same reason we are left in ignorance about the operations of nature because their causes ultimately depend not on secondary causes or known intermediate laws of nature but on the free will God, are we no better assured by pure reason, that is on philosophical grounds, that what we perceive as real really exists. On this reckoning, it is possible for God to deceive us by giving us the intuition of an object that doesn't exist. It is, after all, God's right to do so if He chooses and we cannot know it nor prevent it. The world could be, as Bishop Berkeley, another Englishman, three centuries later argued, a vast illusion against which there is no proof to the contrary.

We can see how the principle of causation itself, at the foundation of any rational understanding of the phenomenal world, is seriously undermined in Ockham's philosophy, where it is posited as an exclusively theological principle, that is, something we can only assent to by faith. The principle of causation, according to Ockham, is a supposition that cannot be confirmed by sensible experience. What we experience is only the regularity of one thing following another. Causation, on the other hand, is an abstract concept, which, for that reason cannot be anything more than a quality of the mind, a psychological event, and, therefore, nothing at all. Ockham's theologism alone preserved his belief in causality, which his empiricism would not allow him to admit rationally. So, instead of an autonomous order of nature, which he would not accept empirically, in which physical bodies have an efficient causality of their own in the natural order, Ockham posited the arbitrary power of God. We know by faith that God exists and that He is all-powerful, but an autonomous natural order has no theological confirmation. In such a world as Ockham conceived, combustion follows fire but not necessarily *because* of it, for God's free will and arbitrary power *could* have decreed that fire would always make wood burn without any causal relation between them, the heat being nothing more that what God creates directly in the wood whenever fire is present in it. Hume would later refine Ockham's argument and dispense with the principle of causation altogether.

The combination of empiricism and theologism was destructive of the concept of a stable, intelligible nature governed by its own internal necessity or laws. Ockham left nothing at all between God's will and absolute power and the countless individual things, beings, and events, all radically distinct from one another with nothing to unite them, that pass into and go out of existence. Nature could not be intelligible because what we understand nature to be, "that concrete order of intelligibility and beauty" does not exist. Unintelligible, the world can have no meaning of its own. In no ordinary sense could the God of Ockham's theologism be considered the "Author of Nature" as this God has abolished nature.

Gilson has observed that, more than "a shrewd logician and clear-headed philosopher, whose mind could not entertain a philosophy at variance with his theology", Ockham was also "a great publicist whose political doctrines, deeply rooted in his theology, were dangerously shaking the lofty structure of mediaeval Christendom."[123] His established notoriety, of course, gave ambience to his passionate theologism, and so what would have remained a mere curiosity in the history of philosophy became what Gilson called "the first known case of an intellectual disease." Ockham's was the first fundamental mistake in western philosophy; it is the "Original Sin" of modern philosophy because the consequence of it has been the confusion of the whole of western thought. It has in it the seeds of modernity. He has been called the "medieval Hume" with good reason, for their philosophical doctrines bear an unmistakable resemblance to each other. While there is nothing in St. Thomas Aquinas' theology that could possibly have led directly to David Hume's agnosticism,

---

[123] *Ibid.*, p. 86.

Ockham's combination of a crude empiricism and refined theologism had gone already at least half the way. All that was left for Hume, who, unlike Ockham, was not encumbered by a concern for the power and glory of God, was to dispense with Him.

But the immediate result of Ockham's nominalism was the breakdown of medieval philosophy and culture, especially of Scholasticism. We need not here go fully into the particulars of that breakdown, but only so far as to establish how that breakdown, in its turn, advanced our progress toward modern thought, which dates from the end of Scholasticism. Medieval philosophy and theology had, by the middle 13th century, achieved an alliance that produced an understanding of reality that was "an organic whole in which what reason knows about God and His creation is inseparable from the teaching of the revealed text".[124] Its culmination was the work of St. Thomas Aquinas. But it was not until the 19th century, when the vast intellectual foundation on which St Thomas built his system was gravely threatened on every side, that the Church officially adopted his work as a standard for all her theologians. Until that time, the fortunes of Thomism were varied (a matter I will discuss in a later chapter). St. Thomas' work, that near perfect synthesis of philosophy (particularly Aristotle's) and theology, of faith and reason, certainly had no immediate popularity; rather, it was highly controversial. And as a result, that marriage of clearly distinguished modes of

---

[124] *Ibid.*, p.92

intellectual inquiry (Ockham notwithstanding), grew uneasy and quarrelsome and eventually broke down.

We have concentrated on William of Ockham because it was his school of thought that was most destructive of that alliance; for by rejecting Aristotle and thereby too the reality of universals and (in effect) of causation itself, what followed was a skepticism, at the philosophical level, of all rational knowledge. But it was by no means the only school of thought so at odds. Intellectual disputation is a good thing and was certainly not discouraged in the medieval Scholastic milieu. The opposite was, in fact, the case. In the early 14th century, there was too much disputation, or rather, too many varieties of opinion on the same questions. Everyone was refuting everyone else: Thomist versus Ockhamist versus Scotist and so on. And, of course, everyone can't be right. In hindsight, the Church embraced Thomism, because it best expressed the mind of the Church, but too late to make it an easy adoption. The devastating problem of these scholastic wars was that the disputants were getting no closer to agreeing upon who *was* right. They were regarded by many to present a serious danger to the future of religion, because philosophical speculation was undermining theological truth. The complexities of the cooperation between the principles of reason and the revealed tenets of the Faith and the intricate and seemingly insoluble problems that arose were tremendously discouraging to many and helped to cast doubt upon the propriety of using philosophy at all (especially Scholastic philosophy) as an aid to theology. The conviction became widespread that as theology was the science of the word of God and as such its object was to advance the soul toward its salvation, philosophy, which was serving only to mire theology in interminable and ultimately *irrelevant* disputes that were contrary to the spirit of religion and of the Gospel. It was the Gospel, the critics said, that should be the focus of theological study and thus concomitantly the reading of the Bible and certain Fathers of the Church, such as St. Jerome and St. Augustine, as well as a thorough training in classical Latin.[125] This new attitude (not so new, really, for it was a resurgence in part of the Patristic theological tradition, which had been supplanted by the 13th century by the systematic use of dialectic in theological discourse) spelled not only the end of medieval scholasticism but of medieval civilization itself. In it fermented the beginnings of the Renaissance and of a new Christian humanism, as represented by Erasmus, which was unsurprisingly anti-scholastic and thus preoccupied with classical studies, and, as far as theology was concerned, with a simple return to the Bible, and the study of ethical problems as the only thing left to be attempted after the decline of Scholasticism.[126] The new humanism meant then a rejection of Aristotelian philosophy (for there was no other philosophical tradition yet to replace it) which it disdainfully identified with Scholasticism.

---

[125] Cf. *Ibid.*, p. 94
[126] Cf. *Ibid.*, pp. 94-95

It would be remiss not to note that the threat to a Christian philosophy in the 13th century came too from Averroës, the Spanish Arab commentator on Aristotle. Averroës and his Latin proponents taught that the conclusions of philosophy and those of theology, if each is left to follow its own methods, are necessarily contradictory. Thirteenth-century scholasticism had risen up to meet this challenge, which largely preoccupied the attention of the likes of St. Thomas, St. Bonaventure, Duns Scotus, and William of Ockham. It was their Apple of Discord. For their answers to Averroes' doctrine were various and far from agreeing with one another. They could not agree on the usefulness of philosophy to certain basic questions, such as the immortality of the soul, that concerned both philosophy and theology. St. Thomas's teaching best understood (as the Church has since recognized) the right balance between faith and reason, but at the time it was only one of many disputants and was far from being unanimously received. The others either put too much stock in philosophical arguments or too little. (It is interesting that Scholasticism has, since the modern era, been accused of being insufficiently rational, depending too much on authority, when the fact is its tendency was always to be *too* rational, too dialectic; but the modernist criticism has not overlooked this.) At the end of the day, it was Ockham's doctrine that seemed to carry the most influence. Much easier than determining the complexities of the relation of faith and reason was to suppose they had nothing to do with each other. According to Ockham, what cannot be proved by philosophy cannot be proved by theology, where certitude is grounded in faith not in reason. Consequently, there was a general failure of confidence in philosophy, the exercise of abstract or pure reason. The general impression was that if philosophy could not be trusted, it was to be left alone as a thing contagious to theology. Still, an ancient and venerable philosophical tradition could not be ignored as though it did not exist, and so the tendency was to show that it was not only incapable of proving anything against religion but of proving anything at all.[127] It was not yet an age of skepticism, the only faith that was so far lost was faith in philosophy's usefulness to theology. But that was just the beginning.

The discrediting of philosophy, and thus any synthesis of it and theology, was the opposite of Ockham's theologistic philosophy. Ockham failed to keep theology and philosophy distinct by trying to put philosophy on a theological footing. The result of his confusion of faith and reason was, we see, the indefinite estrangement of the two. So now theology was content to be on its own not only cut off from philosophy but estranged from it. But this meant that philosophy too would be set adrift, no longer directed by revealed truth.

The metaphysical skepticism that afflicted the late Middle Ages remained unresolved, so that by the 17th century it become the reason for Montaigne's loss of faith

---

[127] Cf. *Ibid.*, p. 97.

(and for his influence as well) and the great burden of Descartes' career. A new ideal of rational knowledge was emerging in the 15th and 16th centuries from Ockham's teaching and its influence, a rudimentary empiricism that so "severely restricted the field of rational certitude that practically nothing of it was left".[128] For this to be accomplished, philosophy would have to be discredited, and to do that Aristotle would have to be discredited by showing that nothing the Greek philosopher had concluded in his physics or (especially) his metaphysics was really demonstrated.[129] The intention was simply to undermine philosophy (principally, scholastic philosophy) and turn reason to better purposes than metaphysical speculation, viz., to ethics and practical religious life. But the means proved to be extremely dangerous to faith, because it implied that, if philosophy was useless to theology, then Christian dogmas had little or nothing of reason to support them. Much of the philosophical genius of the Renaissance was devoted to constructing the most elaborate logical arguments to demonstrate that nothing had ever been proved by philosophical inquiry, especially Aristotle's. The unintended consequence of this dismissal was the discrediting of formal logic, for there was no stopping what was fast becoming a juggernaut: why should logic not be thrown out with philosophy when it is the very instrument with which it tormented theology?

---

[128] *Ibid.*, p. 99.
[129] Cf. *Ibid.*, p. 102.

Francesco Petrarca, or Petrarch, the great fourteenth-century Italian poet and humanist, is a prominent example of the many who were profoundly affected by the skeptical milieu. Petrarch was moved to write a little book, published in 1367, entitled *On My Own Ignorance and That of Many Others*, in which he throws off the yoke of Aristotle: "I am confident, beyond a doubt, that he [Aristotle] was in error all his life . . . in the most weighty questions." Of Aristotle's *Ethics*, he said, "I dare assert, let my critics exclaim as they may, that he was so completely ignorant of true happiness, that the opinions upon this matter of any pious old woman, or devout fisherman, shepherd or farmer, would, if not fine spun, be more to the point than his".[130]   It is for this intellectual outlook that Petrarch was rightly called "the first modern man"[131] Petrarch was utterly disgusted with what he called "the noisy herd of scholastics" and allowed his mistrust of philosophy to guide his understanding of the moral life.

Moralism, the use of Ethics against metaphysics as the foundation of our understanding of the world, was the chief remedy the humanists of the Renaissance for philosophical skepticism. The most important problems, they insisted, are moral problems and for their answers one need look no further than the Gospel, the Fathers of the Church, and the pagan moralists (like Cicero, their favorite)

---

[130] I am indebted to E. Gilson (*op. cit.*, pp. 104-5; see his own footnote to his quotations) for the quotations from Petrarch's *On My Own Ignorance and That of Many Others*.
[131] By French Historian, Henri de Nolhac.

on whom even the Church Fathers relied. But in the breakdown of scholastic philosophy another remedy presented itself, mysticism. The moralist would discredit and thence abandon philosophy, the mystic would transcend it.

Mysticism was on the other side of the milieu of the rational skepticism of the 14th and 15th centuries and those centuries were rife with it. Certainly, the mystical is inherent in Christian theology and hardly unknown in the middle ages. Medieval theology universally taught that God is rationally known only by what He is not, for we cannot know what He is, as He is infinitely above anything we can say or think about Him. In St. Thomas's doctrine it acted as a general qualification that applied to all theological statements but also as an invitation to transcend theology and enter by love into the mysteries of God that surpass human understanding. But while he made this principle the foundation of his own teaching, St. Thomas is ever aware that if reason alone cannot know God, it is not because He has completely hidden Himself from us, but because He is above reason. Thomas understood that what is hidden in the mystery of God remains supremely *intelligible*, that is, it is hidden only from reason (*ratio*), which is the dialectical process of discursive thought, but not from intellect (*intellectus*), which is intuitive and therefore apprehends directly without thought.[132] Reason and mystery are not

---

[132] The reader is directed to Josef Pieper's excellent discussion of this distinction in *Happiness and Contemplation*", tr. Richard and Clara Winston (Chicago: Henry Regnery Co., Logos Books, 1958), pp. 77-78.

contradictories; reason is ordained to give way to -- to open up – to mystery, to achieve its own finality and in doing so give way to love. For mystery is not occult ideas or principles but the very life of the Blessed Trinity in which participates (at least rudimentarily) everyone who remains in a state of sanctifying grace. Love then sees into the darkness which reason's light could not penetrate. Reason, according to St. Thomas, is the only means to the threshold of the mystical life. Without it, the "cloud of unknowing" becomes a cloud of confusion. Reason and mystery are not the same, but neither are they at odds, for to reason God remains forever an intelligible though blinding light.[133]

But in the dissolution of the medieval synthesis of faith and reason, it was not St. Thomas's use of mysticism that took hold but the mystic, Johannes "Meister" Eckhart's (c1260–1327). Eckhart, whose writings are replete with closely reasoned arguments, borrowed heavily from St. Thomas, but with a profoundly different use of reason. St. Thomas uses reason to a mystical end but without mysticism; Eckhart's use of reason, on the other hand, is itself mystical. He was thoroughly persuaded, not only that God was unknowable, but that it necessarily followed that He must also be unknowable in Himself. In other words, God is not a blinding light but shrouded in darkness. Eckhart's use of reason, therefore, was bound, not to lead to that Light, but to throw a darkness to reason all about Him. God, according to Eckhart, is not is simply beyond the reach

---

[133] Cf. Gilson, *op. cit.*, pp. 108-9

of human knowledge, but is beyond *all* knowledge, even His own, and is thus unfathomable to Himself. In the "silent wilderness" which is the Godhead, there is neither Father, nor Son, nor Holy Spirit.[134] In the manner of the neo-platonic flight of the soul to the Alone, the end of the mystical experience of the fullness of God in His divinity is a flight to a place beyond God, beyond any intelligible idea or image we have of Him and thus beyond all thingness and meaning into nothingness.

Nicolaus Cusanus applied Eckhart's theological principles to philosophy. Like so many others who introduced revolutionary doctrines into philosophy or theology in the disorder that followed upon the breakdown of Scholasticism, Cusanus wanted to put an end to the pervading theological and philosophical disputes that gave rise to heresies, doctrinal condemnations, and schisms, that were destroying the unity of the Church. Disaster could be avoided if men could be convinced that their philosophical and theological differences were insignificant.[135] Cusanus contended that philosophy is merely a "learned ignorance" (*docta ignorantia*), by which he meant that philosophy is only a highly elaborate and informed ignorance. He ceased to believe that an exact knowledge of any object was possible and that without exact knowledge truth was impossible. The proper task of the philosopher then is to become increasingly aware of the imperfection of human

---

[134] Cf. *Ibid.*, pp. 109-10.
[135] Cf. *Ibid.*, pp. 112-113.

knowledge. Like Zeno's paradox, the more knowledge the philosopher gains, the more clearly he understands his ignorance. Theologically, as applied to the Godhead, Cusanus' doctrine meant that God, as the Absolute, is unthinkable because He is outside and above all relations and thus no principle of rational thought applies to Him, even the principles of identity and contradiction. God is, in Cusanus' formulation, a "coincidence of opposites" (*coincidentia oppositorum*). All disputants must fall silent before a Being of Whom we can have no true rational conception.

It is but a short step from that proposition to the proposition that the universe is also unintelligible. Cusanus held (quite rightly) to the principle of causality that the cause is in its effect and all effects are in their causes and, therefore, must bear a likeness to them. But Cusanus made the mistake of applying this principle of causation to God, which cannot be true. As the *First* Cause and Prime Mover, God must be entirely outside of or distinct from the things He causes to be. This is the significance of creation *ex nihilo*. He does not create from himself, otherwise He would be diminished by the act and with God that is intrinsically impossible. But in Cusanus supposes that the universe as a whole then bears to God, its Cause, the same likeness that all effects bear to their causes.[136] God is in the universe and the universe is in God as well as in everyone one of its parts. Such a conception of the world comes dangerously close to

---

[136] Cf. *Ibid.*, p. 116-17.

making the world almost as unintelligible as God Himself is supposed to be. If the world is a coincidence of opposites, then we cannot begin to understand it. "The universal mystery of things is but a concrete expression of the supreme mystery of God."[137]

Cusanus and his doctrine spelled the last word of medieval philosophy, and the end of philosophy as a discipline of rational inquiry for two hundred years. The abdication of philosophy did not, of course, mean the end of rational thought but rather its redirection into an entirely new mode if inquiry. The intellectual ferment of the 14th and 15th centuries would pave the way to modern science in the 17th and especially the rationalism of the modern world. But it was most unfortunate for the modern world that when modern empirical science was about to be born, realist and rational metaphysics was the midwife that failed to call. Metaphysics was once the queen of sciences, but after her abdication it was inevitable that positive science would attempt to fill her shoes, to seize the throne metaphysics once occupied. It alone would be left to give an account of reality.

---

[137] Gilson, *Ibid.*, p. 117.

V

The Origins of Unbelief: Descartes and His Legacy

Before the coming of modern science, nothing was left but a generalized skepticism which defined the philosophical attitude of the Renaissance. Montaigne was the certain offspring of that skepticism. He who attributed the disruptions within Christendom to dogmatism, seemed to be at ease with doubt. But man is not naturally a doubting animal; and so it was perhaps inevitable that a man of genius would come along to whom such skepticism was an intolerable burden to be thrown off at all costs. Descartes was that man. Unfortunately, he would begin his great project to restore philosophical certainty and rational metaphysics with the same general philosophical mistake that induced the skepticism he abhorred.

The philosophers and theologians of the 14th century had entered willingly upon the road to skepticism. It was not, admittedly, skepticism that they wanted, but neither was it the truth about the nature of philosophy as it had been convincingly defined by St. Thomas Aquinas. He had defined (we may say, with Leo XIII, for all time) the true relationship between faith and reason, between reason and revelation, theology[138] and philosophy. He demonstrated that while there are two orders of knowledge, the natural or rational and the supernatural or suprarational, one having it's ultimate source in reason, the other in divine revelation, they are *necessarily* in agreement where they *both arrive at the truth* for the truth is and must be one. Unassisted by faith, which possesses the truth and certitude of it by a supernatural gift, reason and thus philosophy is by nature speculative and, does not always arrive at the truth. Hence, the two, while not opposed, are ineluctably in tension. But Ockham and his successors in their pride and restlessness would not keep that tense union for long. Gilson has observed that it is a truism about this type of philosophical mistake that "all attempts to deal with philosophical problems from the point of view, or with the method, of any

---

[138] "[O]ne may err because in matters of faith he makes reason precede faith, instead of faith precede reason, as when someone is willing to believe only what he can discover by reason. It should in fact be just the opposite. Thus Hillary says: 'Begin by believing, inquire, press forward, persevere.'" (*Expositio super librum Boethii De trinitate*, Q. 2, a.1, resp.). Here St Thomas is in complete agreement with St. Augustine: that the right use of reason is "that by which the most wholesome faith is begotten... is nourished, defended, and made strong." (*De Trin.*,XIV,c.i).

other discipline will inevitably result in the destruction of philosophy itself".[139]

Recall here what Gilson observed in an earlier quotation: "pure ideas . . . are born within the mind and from the mind, not as intellectual expressions of *what is*, but as models, or patterns, of what ought to be; hence they are born revolutionists." And pure ideas divorced from our intuitions born first in sense experience of the objectively real, of what is, were the stuff of Descartes' philosophy and so his philosophy was destined to be revolutionary and a disastrous failure, for it would end like Ockham's experiment not in knowledge but an even more profound skepticism.

Descartes was a mathematician who was determined to reorder philosophy according to mathematical principles. He had learned nothing from the mistakes of his predecessors; instead, our young hero who would save philosophy, blundered into the same fundamental error by supposing mathematics to be the key to establishing in philosophy an absolute certainty, eliminating from knowledge anything that was merely probable. "True knowledge alone is necessary; mathematical knowledge is necessary; hence, all knowledge has to be mathematical."[140] Reasoning from such a premise, Descartes persuaded himself that all sciences were one; that human reason

[139] Gilson, *Ibid., The Unity of Philosophic Experience* (New York: Scribners, 1937), p. 120.
[140] *Ibid.,* p.140

operates by the same criteria and principles in every science, but expresses itself differently in each; or, they could at least be so unified under a single method, which, he was convinced, was mathematical. Mathematics is the most evident, because the most abstract, of all the sciences; therefore, any other science can be made as evident if it is rendered equally abstract. Because the objects of mathematical knowledge are essentially quantitative and abstract and for that reason simple, at least as compared to non-quantitative objects, the innumerable objects of philosophical knowledge had to be made commensurate with each other. So, Descartes reduced them all to three: thought, extension, and God and, as objects of our intuition, and made them as simple and immediate as number and space. [141] Descartes could do this because he was no longer dealing with things, the *objective* existence of which is given and necessarily the foundation of any knowledge, but with *ideas*. Behind the whole of Cartesian philosophy and all of modern idealism is the principle that the idea of a thing is identical to the thing itself with respect to all that can be clearly and distinctly known about it.

Descartes' mathematicism, or mathematical rationalism, would effect the beginning of an epistemological revolution in what was the cornerstone of his philosophy: *cogito ergo sum* (I think, hence, I am). To us, the phrase and the conception of knowledge it bespeaks are hackneyed, but in the 16th century it was radically new. Descartes conceived of

---

[141] *Ibid.*, p.144

the human mind as an immaterial substance completely independent of the human body (hence, his mind/body dualism). We can be certain we exist only because we are conscious of the fact. Thus the soul has no relation to the body as it does in the Thomist/Aristotelian concept of "hylomorphism" (the soul inhering the body as its form), because according to Descartes either the soul is part of the material world or it is entirely separate from it. To Descartes there can be no other possibility because he has rejected the realist principles of formal and final causation in the material world which alone make possible purposiveness in nature and therefore any meaning that is not the exclusive invention of the mind. If meaning and purpose in nature are, as implied by Descartes, things which have no known extra-mental reality, then where else could they originate but in the mind? All of this means that our ideas, and thus our understanding of the world, have no correspondence to things, the extramental world, in so far as the mind is incapable of any formative contact with the extramental world as received by the senses. It was not for Descartes as it would later be for Kant that we are not in touch with things as they really are in themselves. Rather, what Descartes concluded is that the mind gets its understanding of reality *primarily* from itself, not the senses, because it directly intuits "such ideas as represent the eternal and unchanging essences: the mind itself, for instance, or God, or the body conceived as pure extension, the triangle, and so on".[142] Meaning and purpose then have their origin in the human

---

[142] *Ibid.*, p. 162

mind not objectively in the order of things themselves. In fact, Man is essentially mind, a "thinking substance"; the body-cum-soul (the hylomorphic union) as conceived by St. Thomist and Aristotle (and everyone in between) has no part in Descartes concept of man's essential being. Man's understanding of reality comes to him directly from his own mind, its innate ideas, from which the mind constructs reality with "mathematical certainty".

These ideas were in a short time received all over Europe and the "mentalism" that gave it birth was the bread and butter of French philosophy until about the 1730s. Descartes' influence was tremendous in an atmosphere rarified of any constructive philosophy. Scholastic philosophy was by then all but exhausted by its own unresolved quarrels and so we may suppose that it was easy for Descartes to convince the greatest minds of his time of scholasticism's ultimate failure to prove God's existence and the immortality of the soul. But he also succeeded in persuading many of them of his own proofs by his own method. Many of these great thinkers were priests or bishops or theologians. By the end of the 17th century, Cartesianism had "become the scholasticism of all those who prided themselves on being up to date in philosophy".[143] But Descartes, with his unshakeable confidence in this method, failed to understand the radically destructive effect upon the mind of his own philosophy.

---

[143] Gilson, *ibid.*, p. 170

Philosophical revolutions, like all revolutions, are destabilizing. They are inherently destructive of established convictions of absolute truth. Cartesianism could be persuasive, but it was destructive of a philosophical tradition that had shaped the western mind. What Cartesians left in its place was a philosophy with its own profound problems and a deep prejudice that scholasticism and the Aristotelian/Thomistic realism that informed it could never solve those problems. Having undermined scholastic philosophy, Cartesianism itself soon became the subject of a reaction that would in turn undermine it, and with much less trouble.

While Descartes' philosophy was wildly popular on the continent, especially in France, few in England, as Voltaire had discovered, read Descartes' writings and those who did thought him a dreamer.[144] It took an Englishman, the "sober and methodical" John Locke, unenchanted by the spell of Cartesian mathematicism, to bring the greater influence of that philosophy to its inevitable demise. It was not that Locke had solved the mind/body problem of Cartesianism; rather, he dissociated mind and body in a different way. His vigorous empiricism effectively rejected Descartes idea of man as an immaterial substance and rejected his doctrine of the mind's innate ideas, thus denying that knowledge is founded on such. The foundation of knowledge was, for Locke, necessarily empirical; we know only what we can experience, for in his view the mind begins as a *tabula rasa*,

---

[144] Cf. *ibid.*, p. 164. See Gilson's footnotes 12 and 13.

blank foolscap, on which everything has yet to be written. But Locke does not mean the same thing by experience that an Aristotelian or Thomistic realist does. He does not mean our perceptions of the external world, but also our awareness of the internal world of the mind, our thoughts, concepts mental images, etc. These all fall under his definition of "idea" which, he claims, derive from both sensation, the observation of the external world, *and* reflection, the observation of our own mental activity.[145] Locke's empiricism led to a quasi-materialist and mechanistic view of reality. If all we know about anything is based exclusively on empirical data, then it is precisely those *metaphysical* realities of a thing (viz., formal and final causation, essence, and substantial being) that are left wholly out of account. I must also say *unnecessarily* left out of account; for no one had ever proven those metaphysical realities to be non-existent (least of all Descartes himself, who rejected these metaphysical concepts, which scholasticism thought to be at the heart of reality, and simply dismissed them as philosophical inventions in favor of an alternative to scholasticism and its "irresolvable problems"). Locke's empiricism reduced reality, in theory at least, to a matter of efficient causation, that is, to a strictly mechanistic concept of how things come into being and change. Thus began that rigorous scientific rationality that would eventually give us at once the marvels of technological production and the horrors of moral disorder.

---

[145] Cf. E. Fesser, *Locke*, (Oxford: Oneworld Publications, 2007), 34-5.

Locke's empirical explanation of the world and our knowledge of it came at a time when the problems of Cartesianism had become embarrassingly evident. Some Frenchmen, Voltaire among them, were ready to listen to Locke. Many in France were the willing heirs of Montaigne's skepticism, which with them became a positive disdain for dogmatism, especially theological dogmatism. Voltaire was a notably passionate promoter of Locke's philosophy especially against Descartes. To destroy Descartes meant the defeat of the last great offensive of theological dogmatism. We must remember that although Descartes hated scholasticism as a philosophical method, he agreed with its theological conclusions and wanted himself to prove them beyond all possible doubt. Descartes tried to demonstrate that incontrovertible proof of the existence of God and the immortality of the soul was to be had by no other means than the innate ideas of the mind. And Locke came along to demonstrate with the same genius and power of conviction that there are no such ideas. What Voltaire particularly rejoiced in, others were greatly distressed by; but the ideas that distressed them they were none the less becoming convinced of. The same people who, under the influence of Descartes, found that they could never again take scholasticism seriously, found they could no longer remain Cartesians. And for some, no doubt, it was difficult to even remain Christian.

Locke's conclusions led him to a hypothetical materialism which Voltaire, a professed materialist, made a great deal of.

Voltaire knew that even if Locke would not explicitly make the materialist argument, but leave it as mere possibility, the clear though implicit argument will nevertheless have (with Voltaire's help) its sure persuasive effect. And it did. The unexpected truth to realize here is that the philosophical revolutionist that bore the greatest responsibility for the contagion of materialism throughout Europe in the 18th century was not the avid materialist Voltaire, nor the cagey materialist Locke, but Descartes himself, the defender of dogmatism. Gilson has (again) put it in a nutshell:

> He had assumed the heavy task of giving a mathematical demonstration of the spirituality of the soul. The better to do it, he had begun by turning the old scholastic soul as the form of the body into a disembodied mind. Now that the Cartesian mind was dead, the body was left without either a mind or a soul.[146]

Descartes, rejecting the substantial integrity of human nature and insisting that mind and body are two really and utterly distinct substances and as such are alien to each other, ruled out of his mathematical demonstration all empirical evidence (it could not otherwise be mathematical). This was certain bait to a brilliant empiricist like Locke to demonstrate in turn that no mind exists, that there are no grounds to be certain that our ideas have any reality, for what constitutes the mind (viz., clear and distinct ideas) there is no empirical

---

[146] Gilson, *ibid.*, p.173.

evidence. By the mid 18th century, materialists like La Mettrie[147] could claim he had been taught his materialism by the demonstrations of Descartes.

Another unforeseen disaster produced by Descartes' divorce of mind and body or matter was the conception of the existence of the material world. Descartes placed everything that is not mind (clear and distinct ideas) in doubt to demonstrate with mathematical certainty the one thing that cannot be doubted, namely, that I doubt, that is, I think, that I am a thinking substance, a mind. But having done so, there was no longer any philosophical certainty that an external world existed. My own existence is assured, but not the existence of anything else. For a soul, which is a spiritual principle united to a body, this problem does not arise. But because in a mind which has no truck with material objects of any sort, that is, nothing it knows to be real comes to it by way of sensations from outside itself, no grounds can ever be found for the demonstration of the existence of a material world. A soul, on the other hand, as Aristotle and St. Thomas conceived it, immediately perceives the existence of material objects or bodies as a certainty that cannot be proved nor is in need of proof – the idea of those real things determined by the forms or essences which are inherent in them and define them arise in the mind only after the initial encounter with the things themselves.[148] It is not that Descartes himself disbelieved in

[147] See La Mettrie's *Man a Machine* (1768)
[148] Cf. Gilson, *op. cit.*, p. 184.

the existence of the material world -- he was no idealist, but his philosophy was, in this way, like a work of fiction that takes on a life of its own and can go even where the philosopher does not deliberately wish to take it or is even aware that it is headed there. The philosopher does not necessarily perfectly understand his own philosophy only the conclusions which he draws from it, which is a very different thing from the philosophy itself. Descartes begins his VIth *Meditation* with, "Nothing further now remains but to inquire whether material things exist"[149]; he could say this with such insouciance because he had no idea, despite warnings from friends, that his demonstrations would produce in every other mind the same conviction they did in his own. Once a demonstration is published, the cat is out of the bag and it becomes a thing completely independent of its author's intentions as it becomes in turn the matter of other fecund and perhaps less prejudiced minds.

Before long, it was evident to the Cartesian school (Leibniz, Spinoza, and Malebranche) that he had failed in his demonstrations regarding mind and matter to explain what for them seemed to be a fact that between mind and matter there was a real connection.[150] God was the only substance left in the Cartesian triad whose existence, on Cartesian principles, was beyond doubt and by which they could then explain everything else. Whatever mysterious force linked mind to matter, God had to be the agent by which we know

---

[149] R. M. Eaton, *Descartes Selections*, Scribner's: New York, 1927, p.145
[150] Cf. *ibid.*, p. 186

that material things exist. If the external world could not be the cause of our knowledge of it because, as Descartes had demonstrated, no action of a material object upon a mind is conceivable, God must be that cause. But if He is the cause of our knowledge of material substances, then He must also produce in us our natural conviction that it is those substances that produce in us the sensations from which the mind derives its knowledge of them. This does not necessarily mean, they insisted, that God is fooling us, which Descartes demonstrated is not the case, but that, while God did put in us that natural conviction, the natural light of reason does not compel us to confirm it, that it is a conviction which we can rationally dismiss as unfounded. Descartes should have come to the same conclusion if he had been as true to his own principles as were some of those who accepted those principles. It was thus decided by his own school that Descartes was wrong or, rather, inconsistent. He had insisted that the existence of the external world was rationally demonstrable, but failed to convince his followers, who, being more Cartesian than Descartes, demonstrated[151] by his own principles that its existence could not be proven.

What all of this metaphysical trouble came to in the end was the idealism of George Berkeley (1685–1753), who concluded – consistent with the Cartesian principles he accepted -- that the material world was a product of the mind, an illusion. Again, Gilson has expressed the problem

---

[151] This was Malebranche's demonstration. Cf. Gilson, *ibid.*, pp.184-197

just right: "Everyone is free to decide whether he shall begin to philosophize as a pure mind; if he should elect to do so the difficulty will be not how to get into the mind but how to get out of it."[152] The fact was that it could not be done, because it cannot be done. Berkeley simply realized the fact and refused even to try.

I have said that Cartesianism was the "scholasticism" of at least seventeenth-century France, and just as with scholasticism, when Cartesianism broke down the results for philosophy and for the civilization of the west were disastrous. Those, like Malebranche, who tried so hard to prop up the tottering Cartesian edifice could not, adjust it how they may, save that system from those who would not accept its principles. The Cartesians had painted themselves and philosophy into a corner. Like Ockham's theologism, but by a very different process of thought, God became the *deus ex machina* by which to save the whole structure of the physical world from impossibility. Certainly, to Malebranche *et alis* God seemed a fixed point in philosophy, an immoveable object in thought; they doubtless felt secure in making God the single cause of the material world, even while confessing their failure to prove the existence of the world so conceived.[153] In Ockham's time, philosophy was not prepared to do without God, but by the 18th century, after successive unresolved crises in philosophy, that was by no means the case. But cut that single thread of causation in

---

[152] *Op. cit.*, p. 196
[153] See Malebranche, *Dialogues on Metaphysics and on Religion*, VII, 5; trans. M. Ginsberg, G. Allen and Unwin: London, 1923. , p183

the world – eliminate God -- and the whole intelligible structure of the world according to the Cartesians falls into meaninglessness.

Of course, Descartes himself, by rejecting Aristotle and Scholasticism, had already brought matters to the brink of meaninglessness. For by isolating the mind from the entire physical and material world, he had made it impossible to rationally account for formal and final causation, without which the world is not intelligible. He thus created the "problem" of causation in modern philosophy. A thing's formal cause is ultimately its essence or that which makes a thing *what* it *is*, or, again, in Scholastic terms, its "substantial form". Thus a thing acts according to its essence or nature and as an agent of change gives to its effects (either immediately or potentially) only what it has to give, that is something of it own essence (certainly not something else's essence), which is why fire ignites and water wets.[154] This is according to the Aristotelian principle of causation mentioned above, that whatever is in the effect, must in some sense be contained in the cause as well. Final causation, which St. Thomas called the "cause of causes", is the kind of causality that answers the question why a thing does what it does and ultimately why it is what it is, that is, to what end or goal is it directed when it is acting as a causal agent, which begs the question of why or to what purpose it exists at all. Aristotle taught that everything acts toward

---

[154] I refer the reader to Edward Feser's excellent explanation of causality in his *The Last Superstition A Refutation of the New Atheism* (St. Augustine Press: South Bend, IN) 2008, 62 ff.

some end or goal according to its nature. It is the nature of the heart and all of its features, ventricles and atria, to pump blood and therefore that is its *purpose* in doing so; and it is in the nature of water to evaporate, condense, precipitate, and collect again cyclically, which it does be*cause* it is water and not, as Hume argued, because that is all we *observe* to happen. Things then are directed toward an end or goal because of what they *are*. This, Aristotle argues, is even true of all inorganic things as well. It is easy to see that without the notion of formal or final causes, even the notions of material and efficient causation (i.e., what underlying stuff a thing is made of and what brings it immediately or potentially into being), do not make any sense. Modern science will allow only for material and efficient causality, contrary to its every statement in which it tacitly assumes formal and final causation. This is true and must be the case because nothing in the whole of the natural order including ourselves is or can be intelligible without assuming formal and final causation. Newton once asked the gauntleted question (among a host of others), challenging the mechanistic view of the world that was overpowering science, "How do motions of the body follow from the will?" [155] How indeed? If, as Descartes left things with his mind/body dualism, the physical or external world is just aimless matter in motion, a machine (his insistence that God is running the machine is no help), then how can the mind, which alone gives us what is real (even God's reality), have

---

[155] Isaac Newton, *Optics*, III, 1, 28 [in Great Books of the Western World (Chicago: Encyclopedia Britannica, 1952), vol. 34, pp.528-29.

any effect upon bodies external to it even the body which a particular mind inhabits? On such a reckoning, the mind is, to use Gilbert Ryle's wry expression, a "ghost in the machine". The mind itself then can have no causal and, hence, teleological or purposive relation to anything outside it. To quote Edward Feser, "[Formal and final causes] are certainly utterly central to, and ineliminable from, our conception of ourselves as rational and freely choosing agents, whose thoughts and actions are directed towards an end beyond themselves."[156]

David Hume was the man who would with unstinting deliberation do the job of eliminating God and causation and do it with such devastating "logic" that he left no stone upon another of Descartes' philosophy, but neither did he spare anything else. Given Descartes' weakness with respect to causation, it was easy work. Hume simply took Locke's hedging empiricism and gave it is head. He baldly exposed the logical conclusions of his radical empiricism, which Locke left merely implicit, laying bare a comprehensive skepticism from which there was apparently no salvation. This was a skepticism so thorough that it utterly striped the world of any meaning to which reason could bear witness, down to the very causality of things. This was not a smiling skepticism like Montaigne's, but a despondent one that moved even Hume to write at the end of his *Treatise of Human Nature*, "I am . . . affrighted and confounded with

---

[156] *Op. cit.*, 71.

that forlorn solitude in which I am placed in my philosophy".[157]

Hume's philosophy saved the mere existence of matter from Berkeley's idealism, but it was a philosophically unintelligible world he advanced (and an incoherent philosophy) in which one thing had no known or rationally demonstrable relation to another outside of what is supplied by certain mental habits of human understanding based on our experience of the world, viz., the customary and the associated as functions of memory. Causation is, on Hume's analysis, merely an abstract idea for which no empirical evidence exists, because we do not experience causation as such only a regularity of effects from which we only infer causality. And since we do not experience causation, Hume argued, it is not a thing reason can demonstrate. All our inductive reasoning regarding our experience of what we call "causation" is derived from custom (i.e., from the repeated experience of the same event following directly another event) and not from the understanding of an objective order in nature. Thus, with Hume, post-realist philosophy comes again full circle; it had moved from skepticism to an ill-founded dogmatism and thence back again to a still deeper skepticism and yet another crisis in philosophy.

With every new crisis comes a new hero who would deliver philosophy from the slough of skepticism. But our

---

[157] Chapter 36, sec. vii.

new hero will only deepen the western mind's alienation from reality. The man is Immanuel Kant. Kant wanted to save philosophy from Hume's dire skepticism, but he was, nevertheless, deeply influenced by Hume's philosophy. It had convinced him of one very important thing that was of tremendous significance to his own philosophy, that metaphysics could no longer be sustained philosophically as a positive knowledge or science. While Kant was content to let metaphysics die, he would not let our knowledge of the sensible world remain in the grip of Hume's pitiless skepticism. That is what mattered to him most. So, unlike Descartes, Kant did not try to reinvent philosophy, but took it as he found it and then did what he could for it. But the only medicine that could cure the patient, namely, Aristotelian- Thomistic metaphysics, Kant himself regarded as so much snake oil.

It would be untrue to say that Kant dismissed metaphysics as of no account; for he believed that man necessarily thinks metaphysically because his moral and religious experience compel him to. But as the primary stage in philosophical knowledge, he gave it a vote of No Confidence. That Descartes' application of mathematics as a method of reasoning to philosophy was dangerous and unworkable, he knew; the abstract definitions of metaphysics could not be an adequate foundation for our knowledge of the world, for being and its properties do not admit of mathematical demonstration. Another method presented itself to Kant.

Europe by the 18th century was already in the throes of a rationalism that was at once profoundly skeptical of philosophical conclusions and increasingly under the spell of Newton, who was apotheosized by the Enlightenment rationalists, and the still new and very successful empirical science. Kant was entirely a man of his age and so was susceptible to its errors (perhaps, as an intellectual, more than most). Natural science having usurped metaphysics as queen, Kant took it for granted that Newton's description of the world was without question the world as it really was. It followed, in Kant's thinking, that no other method than Newton's could be valid. So, Kant was ready without hesitation to substitute as the first stage of philosophical knowledge empirical observation, the method of physical science, for the abstract definitions of Descartes' mathematicism. "The true method of physics is fundamentally the same as that which Newton has introduced into natural science, and which has there yielded such fruitful results."[158] Thus was Kant making the same kind of mistake that was made by Descartes and by Ockham before him, of applying to philosophy a method proper to another discipline. He was not in effect saving philosophy at all, but subordinating it to the judgment of science by making the method of science the standard by which all true knowledge is attained. Kant knew, of course, that metaphysics is no more capable of physical than of mathematical demonstration, but he insisted nevertheless

---

[158] Immanuel Kant, quoted by Gilson, *op. cit.*, p. 227.

that it must be judged by that method and that its judgment was final.

There were of course problems with his philosophy which Kant did not resolve that would precipitate the next crisis in philosophy. They had to do with his principles of understanding. Physics, according to Newton, required the existence of an absolute space and an absolute time; and, on that basis alone, Kant insisted that from our sensible intuition of space and time derive *all* the objects of knowledge given to the understanding. In other words, any object that is not of our spatial and temporal experience cannot be known. All knowledge of any other kind of object is not scientifically valid. Everything else is a mere mental presentation of a *possible* object, that is, only an idea in the mind, corresponding to no known object in reality and therefore the stuff of philosophical speculation.

The problem with Kant's doctrine of understanding is that while it works to explain our sensible experience of the world, it is problematic with respect to our *intellectual* experience or our understanding of sensible experience. Space and time are, he says, themselves mental properties or principles, or "*a priori* forms" as he calls them, which are not derived from things but which we impose upon things in order that the objects in reality become the objects of our knowledge, that we know them to exist.[159] This is very well so far as our sensible experience is concerned. But Kant says

---

[159] Cf. Gilson, *op. cit.*, pp. 230-31

that our understanding is also determined by *a priori* principles, for instance, substance and causality, which he calls "categorical imperatives". It is by these first principles of understanding, according to Kant, that our experience of space and time is intelligible. In other words, because they are *a priori*, they are not drawn from experience at all but *make* it. To use Kant's terminology, they are "transcendent" categories of the mind, that is, they "transcend all the limits of experience and therefore withdraw themselves from all empirical tests".[160] But because they are transcendent and are experienced in the mind only, they cannot be objects of knowledge. In this, far from being Hume's antagonist, Kant agreed with him that our principles of understanding derive from sensible experience alone, and thus the transcendent principles of understanding are themselves not real things and cannot be known as such. To know them is one of the pretensions of metaphysics and it was part of Kant's mission to disabuse metaphysics of all such pretensions.[161] It was Hume's mistake, Kant argued, to have supposed that scientific knowledge was impossible unless the fundamental principles of intelligibility, such as the principle of causality, were strictly empirically known, that is, derived from sensible experience and so can be empirically tested. In this way Kant attempted to save science by shifting the foundations of knowledge "from experience to the intellectual conditions of experience".[162] But to do that he

---

[160] T. M. Greene, *Kant Selections*, Scribners: New York, 1929, p.2
[161] Cf. Gilson, *ibid.*, p. 232
[162] Gilson, *ibid.*

had to debunk metaphysics as empty, consigning it to the realm of illusion while at the same time admitting that it was also necessary because the mind cannot help but draw metaphysical conclusions from our experience.

It was the supreme moment in the history of thought when philosophy willingly and seemingly forever took a back seat to natural science – in effect sold its birthright as a science, for being is no longer an object of real knowledge but of mere speculation, and when philosophy ceases to be about what *is*, of objective, knowable reality, it becomes the source of dangerous illusions. Attempts have been made to revive metaphysics, but until metaphysical realism is again embraced by western thought, metaphysics will lie comatose, unresponsive to every attempt to revive it. And, because the whole course of philosophical thought depends on a sound metaphysics and the course of a civilization depends much on philosophical wisdom, a great deal is at stake.

Kant's "physicism", his attempt to give philosophical knowledge the reliability of physics, had disastrous consequences for ethics for it left no objective, rational justification for morality. But *empirically* there was for Kant no denying the importance of morality to human life. Although convinced that Hume's skepticism had destroyed the metaphysical foundations of morality, Kant was equally convinced by Rousseau, whose ethical writings had a profound influence on him, that without moral conscience, without duty, society was a vicious free-for-all. Backed thus into a corner, Kant felt forced to accept morality as a self-justifying fact, necessary to human existence but rationally, that is empirically, insupportable. So despairing of philosophy to justify moral principles and not willing to dispense with morality as irrational, Kant found his escape from moral skepticism in a kind of rational irrationality, what he called "Practical Reason".

Practical reason, in general, has to do with rational thought directed towards action, especially, for our considerations, moral action. Kant regarded it as including "everything which is possible by or through freedom", everything, that is, that we are free to *decide* is true. This of course, excludes all the objects of physics or mathematics, because their laws are objective and thus determining. In other words, *they* are knowable. The concepts of God, freedom, immortality and the like are necessary but *unknowable*. In the *Critique of Pure Reason*, Kant contends that duty necessarily implies an autonomous free will, which in turn presupposes self-determination and freedom from natural or external necessity. This is because, though primary, Practical Reason is necessarily "impure", because, unlike pure reason, it is not concerned with absolute and universal truths that are demonstrable because empirically knowable. Kant is critical of pure reason, not because he finds it unreliable, but because it excludes too much. That was his problem with Hume's empiricism; it was too exclusive. Kant's idea of Practical Reason is concerned with right and wrong, our knowledge of God and those he believed to be necessary concepts because without them human life would be meaningless. In the 13th century these were known to be demonstrable; but by Kant's day they had to be rescued from a debilitating skepticism. Kant's Practical Reason teaches us what we *ought* to do but provides no demonstration for the *truth* of the rules it dictates. The "ought" is merely our subjective response to our human existence. We all have a moral sense, which Kant referred to as "Duty", by which we know that we have moral obligations to do or not to do certain things. Our moral sense is a fact of our experience and we can know it empirically for it can be objectively observed and described, but the moral truths which direct our moral sense are not demonstrable and so are unknowable. We know the law but not the Law Giver, of whom we have no objective, measurable experience. Practical Reason leads us to postulate that God exists and that there is a perfect moral order (heaven): where there is a law, there must be a law giver, who is necessarily the moral perfection we envision. Real knowledge comes only by scientific, that is empirical, reasoning. We can know nothing of the hidden law giver or any moral perfection, which is no part of our objective experience. All of that belongs to metaphysics, which true science has forever discredited as something closed to proof or disproof. It is useless then for ethics to consult metaphysics; rather, metaphysics must now consult ethics to discover its justification.[163] Kant has turned on its head the foundation of ethics, which has always had its formal justification in a

---

[163] *Ibid.*, p. 235.

known transcendent reality, but if that reality cannot be known and our rational apprehensions of it illusory (so far as pure reason is concerned), then we must resort to the brute fact of the necessity of moral action, of acting in conformity with moral law as ineluctable duty. But to suppose God to exist because our moral experience demands it may be an argument for His existence in the company of other arguments, which presuppose the knowledge of transcendent reality. But alone and weighted with Kantian idealism, that subjective approach to confirm transcendent reality is helpless to free us from our agnosticism. Ethics thus is allowed to dictate its own metaphysics. And "when morality does not flow from what we know, it becomes free to prescribe for us what we ought to believe."[164]   Kant wished to save reason from becoming the battlefield of endless controversy as metaphysical inquiry had become and so jettisoned metaphysics. But the unforeseen result was to shift, by a kind of epistemological legerdemain, the battlefield from metaphysics to ethics. Ethics thus became the No Man's Land of philosophy. Kant did a curious thing when he made Practical Reason primary by raising ethics above metaphysics; because, while Practical Reason is inescapable and moral duty indispensable, it does not, on his own reckoning, confer real knowledge.   And therein lay a more profound problem that bedevils Kantism and, as it is irresolvable, all of modern thought and action, too.

---

[164] Gilson, *Ibid.*, p. 233.

I have already explained how it is a problem in Kant's thought that the first principles of understanding or rational thought, which render our sensible experience intelligible, are not and cannot be themselves derived from that experience and so are not empirically demonstrable. In other words, that which makes knowledge possible cannot itself be an object of knowledge. This is because Kant posited two utterly heterogeneous and, therefore, (in modern philosophy) mutually unrelated sources of knowledge, sense and understanding. He supposed that, though mutually exclusive, without any common root or origin, they successfully work together in the mind when it is doing mathematics or physics. How they could do so, he could not explain. But it was absolutely essential for him that they do, if he was to rescue science from skepticism and keep from falling headlong into idealism.[165] This problem in the *Critique of Pure Reason* was serious enough and provided grist for Kant's critics. But it was a related problem that has made Kant's philosophy the shoals upon which modern thought would shipwreck.

Between the two *Critiques* is an unbridgeable gulf. The *Critique of Pure Reason*, on the one hand, posits a strict necessity operating in nature that is determined by the principle of causality; on the other, the *Critique of Practical Reason* posits an autonomous free will, an essential freedom for self-determination. It appears, then, that man operates in two separate and radically distinct orders, living in the

---

[165] Cf. Gilson, *op. cit.*, pp. 235-38.

natural order, in which everything is determined, but acting in the order of morality where he is free from natural necessity.[166] This would make better sense were there two distinct species of human being. But as this is not the case, the same man is supposed to live in both worlds, the known world of matter in which everything is absolutely determined and the world of morality in which he is free to act as his (practical) reason dictates, to which he thus gives it its intelligibility and meaning, but which he cannot know objectively. You will recall that the principle of causality, what determines everything in nature, is not an object of knowledge but in Kant's reckoning a mere category of the understanding. Theoretical Reason imposes the categories upon our sense data, and the categories in turn render intelligible our experience of material existence. (This, you may remember, was Kant's way out of Hume's radical skepticism.) This process happens necessarily, because of our mind's inability to understand nature without causality. But if we thus make nature to be what it is, then how is it that we also make it to be an obstacle to our moral freedom? Put another way: How is it that Theoretical Reason dictates necessity and Practical Reason freedom? This is the Fact/Value problem, which modern thought so blithely accepts, that lay at the heart of Kant's thought. We may see in this unbridgeable divide between fact and intelligibility a remote consequence of Descartes' radical dualism between mind and body, subject and object, which he had bequeathed to Kant and which Kant did not reject. For Kant,

---

[166] Cf. Gilson, *ibid.*, pp.237-38.

reality was in the end a product of the mind; real objects or the thing in itself (*ding an sich*) exist in the realm of the noumenal, which is cut off from sense experience and so from being known. Theoretical Reason understands reality only by imposing on it the forms of thought by which it can possibly be intelligible; the forms are themselves not knowable but simply given in experience. Such an understanding of reality could never have descended from Aristotelian or Thomistic realism. It could only have descended from Cartesianism. But the antinomies in Kant's philosophy, which Kant did not care to resolve, for it would undo his whole system, nevertheless troubled his disciples.

The huge divide between sense and understanding Kant left begged for someone to bridge it. But bridging it would mean the rapid descent into a degree of philosophical idealism that Kant tried to avoid. Johann Fichte[167] advanced the argument, repudiated by Kant, that it was the Ego, the "I", the essential will of the individual in which sense and understanding were united. The Ego creates nature, brings forth the world of sense and understanding, but can also refashion it by making it ever more intelligible and by so doing becoming ever freer from necessity, from the limitations imposed on it by the material world. And because all Egos make the same world of sense and understanding, it must be that there is One Eternal Infinite Will that makes it so by creating the world in and by our

---

[167] Johann Gottlieb Fichte (1765-1814) published his *Fundamental principles of the Science of Knowledge* in 1794.

minds.[168] Let it just be said that Fichte's solution settled nothing. Far from clearing the air of contradictions, Fichte disputed with his own disciple, Friedrich Schelling[169], over the conclusion he drew from his teacher's philosophy, who disavowed him just as Kant had disavowed Fichte.

The scene is a familiar one by now: philosophy is in metaphysical confusion and someone presents himself as its messiah. This time it's Hegel. Hegel's philosophy I will only briefly describe. Going right to the source of the problem, namely the contradictions or antinomies inherent in his doctrine of Reason, Hegel found his solution in an absolute and eternal Idea which is at once the truth and the whole of reality, which expresses or realizes itself in time and space progressively "through the process of its own development".[170] Nature or the whole is only the external manifestation of the Absolute, the Eternal Idea. And that process of development is Hegel's version dialectic, an eternal process of contradiction and resolution. So, by a kind of perverse master stroke, Hegel not only recognized that the contradictions in philosophy are necessary, he concluded that they are at the very core of reality and so present a true picture of reality.

The Absolute which is aimed at in philosophy is historically manifesting itself from age to age through the

---

[168] Cf. Gilson, *op. cit.*, pp. 241-42.

[169] Friedrich Wilhelm Joseph Schelling (1775-1854) published his *Philosophy of Nature* in 1801.

[170] J. Loewenberg, *Hegel Selections*, (New York: Scribners, 1929), p. 16.

conflict of antitheses. The resolution of each conflict is a unity or synthesis and is the next stage in the self-actualization of the Absolute Idea, which is the truth which is One and the Whole, only to meet the next antithesis and the process continues. The realization of the Idea is for Hegel the "march of God through the world" and, if so, then "the path of the Hegelian God is strewn with ruins."[171] For Hegel's metaphysic was also and primarily a philosophy of history. After almost two centuries of skepticism and, after almost as long a period of critique of Christianity and the Church, Europe (especially Germany) was ready to accept Hegel's dialectic as more than an abstruse and airy philosophical game, but an explanation and principle of historical and political reality.

Hegel insisted that war does not occur as an accident of unresolved differences between hostile parties, but is an element "whereby the ideal character of the particular receives its right and reality".[172] Conflict in history is war between men; and if war is the necessary means by which the ideal state actualizes itself in the world – "receives its right and reality" -- it follows then that war is law. "The military class", says Hegel, "is the class of universality"[173] and the state commands the military class (or *vice versa*). And thus the state is the principle player in the historical process of the dialectic and the soldier in combat is the concrete expression of the dialectical force in the world.

---

[171] Gilson, *ibid.*, p.245.
[172] Hegel, *op. cit.*, p. 464.
[173] *Ibid.*, p.465.

Endless war at every level of existence (neatly dovetailing Darwinian biological and social theory of the struggle and survival of the fittest); such is the result of Kant's ditching metaphysics by confining reason to the sphere of pure science. Of course, Hegel owes nothing else to Kant than the metaphysical vacuum for him to romp in at will.

Few readily admit to the murderousness of Hegel's dialectic. Liberal academics would have us believe that it is a "school of toleration" that teaches a comfortable relativism by which "there is a place for everything because everything is right in its own way."[174] But it would become the philosophical justification for von Bismarck's militarized Prussian state, Marxist-Leninism, German National Socialism, and philosophical Darwinism. When pure science is the only real knowledge and ethics is cut off from any metaphysical foundation (freeing it from any determined bounds but that of conscience), then science becomes either the master of philosophy or its servant. In either case, both are subverted.

The positivism of Auguste Comte (1798–1857) as applied to his sociology was just such a bastardization of pure science, making science do the work of philosophy, and so to serve ends which are incommensurate to it and, from the point of view of pure science, beneath it. Comte was a thoroughgoing materialist and a product of both the French Revolution and eighteenth-century rationalism, especially

---

[174] Gilson, op. cit., pp. 246-47.

the philosophy of Hume, whom he called his "principal precursor in philosophy" [175]

Comte wanted to free human society from all religious and theological conditions, and thus to reorganize it, but on scientific principles. Here, again, the same old mistake. With Descartes it was mathematical principles on which he would make a philosophy that could settle all problems of thought; Kant did the same with physics, and now Comte, with an almost baffling obtuseness in one so brilliant, will do likewise with sociology, a profoundly flawed new philosophy masquerading as a dazzling new science. Like Hegel's historical dialectic of the self realization of the Absolute as the key to understanding, Comte founded his philosophy on a universal law of progress, the "law of the three states", that would be the basis of his whole system of socio-philosophy. Every variety of human knowledge ineluctably progresses from a state of ignorance and superstition, the theological state, to an intermediate state of philosophical or abstract understanding, to the final state of scientific or positive knowledge. In this final state, all of human knowledge would be comprehended in a single homogenous system, reduced to a perfect uniformity, on the basis of which the social cohesion of humanity could be achieved. The problem all along has been that we have not yet reached the scientific stage of human knowledge. By "science" Comte meant that body of knowledge that

---

[175] A Comte, *A General View of Positivism*, trans. by J. H. Bridges, (London: Routledge 1908), p. 7.

objectively represents the real world and which is encompassed by all the positive sciences, from mathematics to biology to sociology. Comte's mission was to usher in that new stage of human understanding. His socio-philosophy was the vehicle by which human knowledge would be reorganized on what he believed were scientific principles and by achieving this solve all philosophical problems. The final result would be a scientific dogma that when commonly accepted would make a new social order.[176]

Man's current problem, as Comte saw it, was how to get from pure science to a new social order. His socio-philosophy was to provide the means. From the perspective of science, the world does not have a unity of its own and the ever growing number and variety of scientific specializations reflect the heterogeneity it finds in the world; rather than unity, the overwhelming tendency in science, despite its own efforts, is toward ever greater disintegration. Such being the fact, Comte's philosophy had to provide the basis for the necessary unity. It was not, he knew, to be found in science itself, for it was not an empirical reality; so, Comte sought it outside science. He had no illusions. He was sure -- had not Kant left no other possibility? -- that the unity or synthesis of all knowledge necessary for the understanding of all reality could not be itself objective or positive knowledge. This profound inconsistency did not trouble Comte any more than it did Kant when he had made the same fatal mistake by giving primacy to Practical

---

[176] *Ibid.*, p. 257.

Reason. Comte knowingly accepted a subjective synthesis as the basis of his vast appropriation of scientific knowledge. All the material of the great dogmas of the future which would address all the social needs of man and reorder society accordingly was to come from science, but the dogma itself had to be philosophical and philosophy, by Comte's time, was regarded as merely speculative.

The aim of Comte's entire project was to redeem man in society and to reorient science to the service of man, for it could not be left to its native tendency to study things indiscriminately. Science cares nothing for man, except as a grand specimen for its investigations into the operations of nature. Science cannot love; it can only know and seek to know more. Comte would make "love" the ultimate foundation of positivism. Thus, philosophy descends again into moralism and moralism is made a religion, the kind of religion you are certain to get without metaphysics. Without metaphysics you are left with a morality that, while it asserts itself, knows nothing beyond itself. This went beyond even Kant who made duty, or our sense of moral obligation, primary while dismissing any objective status for those obligations. In Comte's philosophy, even science itself, which becomes the tool of a purely speculative philosophy, eventually descends into the irrational, into the purely subjective. [177]

---

[177] Cf. A Comte, *op. cit.*, pp. 15, 40.

Any religion requires an object of worship. Since for Comte the promulgations of theology as well as metaphysics were dead letters and few of the educated any longer believed them to be true, he made humanity his positive god or "Great Being". No longer simply the beneficiary of his system, humanity was a positive spiritual power directed by Comte himself as humanity's high priest.

English philosophy was no stranger to Comtean positivism which had its roots in Hume's radical empiricism. A no less powerful mind than John Stuart Mill's had devoted itself to Comte's socio-philosophy. That was in Mill's early career. He later became a severe critic of Comte when Comte, by means of his subjective synthesis, crossed the Rubicon from pure scientific positivism into mere abstract speculation, hence from knowledge to illusion. Mill, under the powerful influence of Locke and Hume, was a thoroughgoing empiricist and thus much in favor of a positive philosophy, which is a philosophy without metaphysics. While he was decidedly agnostic in metaphysics and religion, Mill was not an enemy of religion. But Comte understood what Mill did not: if you give up metaphysics as a rational science and make positive science the only source of real knowledge because the only truly objective knowledge, you cannot keep philosophy as a sort of preserve. And without philosophy, neither can you have meaning, value, goodness, nor any of the things that necessarily define human experience. All these are insupportable by science and so fall by the way and as that happens, as Comte understood, social order becomes impossible. Comte failed to gather more than a few disciples to himself and his new scientific religion, but he had nevertheless seen clearer than most that the profound social crisis of his day, which everyone by the early 19th century was waking up to, had its deepest source in Western culture, that Europe's abandonment of religion as the foundation of social order – its increasing secularization – meant that another religion had to replace it. For Comte acknowledged what was increasingly being denied, that a culture cannot be maintained without religion. Yet he saw, too, that science in its pristine objectivity cannot provide one.

The choice to Mill and his generation seemed to be between philosophy and religion on the one hand, and pure science on the other, between subjective illusion and objective knowledge. With such a choice before him western intellectual man chose science and gave up completely on scientific philosophy and transcendent religion. The former was reduced to speculation on the meaninglessness of existence and the latter considered to be of no other value than subjective comfort for those who could not face the meaninglessness of existence. By this momentous choice European civilization was wedded to modernity.

But for his few disciples, few could take Comte's new dogmatic religion very seriously. Mill's objection was indicative of the general reaction. Yet Comte's positivism lived on as an undercurrent of western thought and scientific socialism was the child modernity gladly adopted.

But the Hegelian Idea was more attractive and adaptable because its kind of supernaturalism was *immanent,* that is, the Absolute Idea was returning dialectically to itself *through man and human institutions.* More than his conclusions, it was Hegel's method that proved most attractive. The Hegelian Idea as a vestige of transcendence or supernaturalism, of course, had to go. The essentially positivist of the 19th century had no use for the quasi-theological Absolute Idea, but the notion of progressive self-realization stuck. It attracted the secular humanist, whose humanism was inimical to the very concept of God and took root in the complete metaphysical and theological vacuum that is modernity.

But nothing yet had come along to make that necessary adaptation of Hegel's method untill Ludwig Feuerbach published his *Essence of Christianity* in 1841, ten years after Hegel's death, followed by his *Essence of Religion* (1845). Feuerbach rejected outright the Absolute Idea and any other kind of supernaturalism. He devoted himself exclusively to the study of man in the same way that the theologian studies God, to divine everything that can be known about the foundation of reality. Man, according to Feuerbach, was the supreme reality, and it was his purpose to convince man that this is so. The Absolute is man himself, who need not look above himself for happiness, but within where be the divine reality. Since there is no transcendent God for man to contend with, it is a matter of the will and intellect in which man needs first to divest himself of all trace of the supernatural. Man's highest realization that God did not create him, but that he created God from his supernatural wishes, and that of all such illusions man must disabuse himself and realize his own supreme nature. Feuerbach, like Comte, thus offers man a new religion which was not atheistic in the classical sense of that word but *anti-theist*, that is, it was not merely without theological faith, it was *hostile* toward it. Comte's religion was a worship of collective man, society; but Feuerbach's was more simple, a starker idolatry, his was the worship of human nature.

Hegel's Idea was haunted by the ghost of a transcendent God, the Absolute Idea being, after all, necessarily unchanging in itself, its historical manifestations notwithstanding. And so Hegel's disciples were left with the vexing problem of reconciling the essentially unchanging Absolute with an ever-changing nature. Feuerbach pulled the thorn by giving them a revolutionary solution, a new philosophical conception of reality that simply dissolved the contradiction between the natural and supernatural and "placed materialism in the throne again".[178] This was not the crude materialism of the 18th century which philosophically denied the existence of God and of any transcendent reality. This new materialism could reticulate in ways the old materialism could not. It was to the old materialism what applied science is to pure, theoretical science. It could be extended from philosophy to biology and to politics. It was not mere positivism or even its single application as Comte

---

[178] Frederick Engels, *Ludwig Feuerbach*, p.28.

had applied it, but the comprehensive ramification of positivism, its application to all human activity. Cardinal Henri deLubac called it "atheist humanism".[179]

To Marx and Engels, this was a great philosophical breakthrough that would for them change their entire direction of thought. As Gilson explained it: "In the doctrine of Hegel, world history is not the history of nature, but of the absolute Idea as expressing itself in nature and in man; now that the Idea itself had vanished, Hegel's dialectic must be understood as the law of the evolution of matter in time, and of all the biological and social phenomena rooted in matter and determined by it."[180] Marx and Engels demonstrated by their intense application of it the breadth of Feuerbach's materialism.

But Marx's dialectical materialism, in which he combined Hegel's dialectic and Feuerbach's materialism, was by no means the only manifestation of Feuerbach's atheist humanism. Darwinian evolution, when masquerading as a universal law, was a form of materialist philosophy that also expressed itself in theories of ethics and economics,[181] and was itself an expression of the idea of Progress that overarched the whole of nineteenth-century thought. Progress was an ineluctable law of history (adapted from Hegel's historicism) and now in the material order of nature

---

[179] See H. deLubac, S.J., *The Drama of Atheist Humanism*, (San Francisco: Ignatius Press, 1995).
[180] *Op. cit.*, p. 284.
[181] See Herbert Spencer, *Principles of Ethics* (1897)

as well, where it manifested itself most notably in the evolution of man from a sub-rational primate unable to control its environment to the homo sapien who in time will, by force of reason through the technological advancement of science, wholly free himself from the limits of nature by a perfect control of his environment. In the idea of Progress, history and biology merge in a single, inexorable march toward the perfection of man.

Man's progress depends on his achieving his autonomy which began with his throwing off the chains of theology and supernaturalism and then those of nature itself. This began, we saw, with the replacing of metaphysics and philosophy with science, and ends with the replacing of science and its unscientific illusions with mere technology as that by which man seeks his autonomy from nature. What modern (and "post-modern") man cannot admit is that the autonomy he seeks is impossible because there is no escaping his real nature and reality was a whole. It was once philosophy's role to rationally inquire into reality, but his tenacious subjectivism gives modern man the illusion of making a reality of his own. This is modern man's great illusion of autonomy. Without philosophy and theology to take account of what exists outside his own mind and beyond mere empirical preoccupations, and thus ignoring the real foundations of revealed religion, modern man has managed with remarkable success to pretend that he and the world he dominates are *what they are not and cannot be*. For two hundred years western man has shaped his civilization to reflect that illusion so that even the culture itself, because culture is an expression of human preoccupations, is disordered and incoherent.

Kant had proclaimed the death of metaphysics, having delivered its *coup de grace,* and thus of any possible objective knowledge of a transcendent order of reality. But he failed to fill, to anyone's satisfaction, the vacancy that was left. Hegel and Comte tried in their different ways to fill it; Hegel, with his dialectic of the Absolute Idea encompassing the entire meaning of past, present, and future reality and progressing to the end of all antinomies, and Comte with his religion of sociology which unites all men and guides them into all truth. Both philosophies were supposed to be the end of philosophy; they were philosophies of history that promised the end of history, the perfection of society, the culmination of a great process, the harbor after the long storm. But it soon became clear after the death of Comte and Hegel that history went on much the same as before. It was obvious that neither had delivered anything like the final word. It was now for modern man to find a way to fend off despair and the loss of the humane civilization which he still valued but did not create and was failing to preserve.

The nineteenth-century dream of evolutionary progress was shattered on the twentieth-century battlefields of the Marne, Ypres, Verdun, and Somme. But in its disillusionment, modernity's bid for autonomy and its antitheist spirit only intensified and was transmitted by a thousand cultural channels as modernity came to terms in its own way with existence in a world without fixed meaning where, in the absence of philosophy as wisdom and knowledge (not, of course the mere academic discipline) and the subjectivization of theology, positive science had become the final arbiter of truth and where material well-being became the primary aim of all civilization and technology its principal hope. The Kantian orientation to duty and the primacy of practical reason were replaced inevitably by a crass social and philosophical materialism. Forfeited to materialism in every form was the specifically Christian civilization and culture that had been ordered, although imperfectly, to a transcendent reality revealed through a sacred tradition, which even its secular powers once at least acknowledged and many revered, and to a natural order that it sought to understand as *received* and thus as objectively existing. Vestiges of that culture yet endure, the Catholic tradition under the auspices of the Church being the greatest reservoir, and, until recent decades, there was yet a strong recollection of it. But that culture is now only a faint historical memory – a curious artifact. It no longer obtains in the structures of society, its public institutions and orthodoxies, its cultural habits and memory, to the extent that when it does examine its Christian past, it completely misconstrues what it claims to understand and be superior to. The study of history is to modern man a means of control; by way of studying the past and alleging to reconstruct it, he uses it to his own ends. It is at worse, a form of propaganda, at best, a way of self-deception. Modern man thereby maintains the illusion he has created of the present, the illusion of his autonomy. Secularization is modern man acting on this illusion.

VI

A Chapter in Answer to Some Objections

One may object that to talk about the death of philosophy in the modern world in untrue, especially when philosophers and students of philosophy abound; departments of philosophy exist in every college and university; and the discipline has been, until perhaps very recently, part of the foundation of the liberal arts education.

In one sense then, it is true to say that philosophy is still very much with us. Since the middle 19th century, there have never been so many philosophers and, especially, professors of philosophy, and most of them publishing like a house afire (there are at least 250 quarterly journals of philosophy in English alone). But, like contraceptive sex, there has been a great deal of activity but no fruit. This frenetic but feckless activity has been aptly called "philosophical inflation". Philosophy has been devalued from a science, and in its present status is no longer the foundation of real knowledge; still less is it any longer the pursuit of wisdom. It has become the sporting ground for highly trained specialists pursuing careers and notoriety in their field. Philosophical inquiry now has almost nothing to do with what everyone else who are not "doing philosophy" actually think and do and so it has become almost worthless.

I say "almost", because there is life yet in modern philosophical endeavor; the western tradition is moribund but not dead. Despite the tremendous effort and technical skill of modern philosophical inquiry, it has "failed to produce a single constructive doctrine, which could act as a rule of public order and private morality."[182] The sterility of modern philosophy is the direct result of the agnosticism and subjectivism at the heart of modernity that Hume and Kant respectively bequeathed to the modern world. Popular distillations of modern philosophical skepticism were eagerly received everywhere as our liberation from (especially religious) dogmatism. But the abandonment of metaphysical realism (and all that follows from it for thought and action) was an incalculable loss to the order of society and to the human heart. In losing the fundamental tenets of long philosophical tradition of the west, we very nearly lost, to use Dante's language from his *Inferno*, the "good of the intellect". Like Dante at the vestibule of his journey through Hell, modern man finds himself "in a dark

---

[182] Gilson, *The Unity of Philosophic Experience* (New York: Scribners, 1937), p. 289.

wood where the right road is wholly lost and gone". For those, like Bertrand Russell, who could see farther than most, even science could not show us the way. Of mathematics itself Russell, the great agnostic and co-author the massive philosophical work, *Principia Mathematica,* said, "mathematics may be defined as the subject in which we never know what we are talking about, or whether what we say is true."[183]

It could also be objected that it is unfair to liberalism to lump it together with all the other diseases of modernity. One might argue that what I have said so far addresses only the intellectual foundations of communism and fascism (and any other apotheosis of the state) and that liberalism has been the professed enemy of these atheistic ideologies, the bane of modern civilization, and has triumphed over them. It may be said then that liberalism has not been part of the problem but a good part of the solution. We are asked to consider its virtues and achievements. Its humanitarian idealism instigated the reform of cruel penal codes, encouraged public education, fought famine and disease, and introduced laws providing for the poor; and, under its auspices, the family came into its own as an independent social unit with legal protection, while at the same time, its

[183] B. Russell, "Recent work on the Principles of Mathematics," *The International Monthly,* Vol. IV (1901), p. 84.

free market principles vastly improved everyone's material condition.[184]

The accomplishments of liberalism cannot be denied. However, it is easy to attribute to liberalism more than it deserves. Liberalism can justly claim little credit for what western societies are proud to call their "moral progress". More about this later, but a few observations are needed here.

Liberalism had two definite salutary elements, its appropriation of Christian morality and its participation in the old humanist culture of the West. But neither of these elements was inherent in liberalism. If it appropriated Christian morality, it did so selectively and with an eye to avoiding any theological considerations. It could partake of the old western humanist culture because that culture was compatible with its aims and because that culture still largely obtained in the mid-19th century; it could not have freed itself, even had it wanted to, from the cultural pattern only then beginning to unravel, in which it developed. Liberalism did not arise out of Christianity (as some Catholic thinkers have supposed) but out of the vestiges of a Christian culture. Nor was it a necessary expression of the old western humanism; it embraced them but as artifacts to be used as instruments for its own purposes. Christopher Dawson regarded liberalism as "sublimated Christianity", a Christianity disabused of the supernatural and ecclesial

---

[184] Cf. Russell Hittinger, "Christopher Dawson on Technology and the Demise of Liberalism" at www.catholiceducation.org.

authority and redirected to secular and material ends. It was
Christianity with a secular humanitarian face. It must be
admitted that liberalism was by no means altogether bad in
its effects, given the forces at work in the 19th century in
Europe. Dawson, who died in 1970, watched the passing of
liberal culture with fear because it was obvious to him what
should be still more obvious to us that what was replacing
the old humanist culture that liberalism inherited and
embraced (with one arm at least) was something far
worse.[185] So long as Liberalism upheld the old humanist and
still fundamentally Christian culture of the west, society
could never be wholly secularized; even though it no longer
embraced the essence of the culture, viz., Christianity, it was
preserving. That was its tragic flaw. For, as Dawson often
observed, Liberalism was too inherently weak to resist the
forces it had to contain – communism, anarchism, nihilism,
all born in the 19th century and which would flourish in the
20th. Even the vigorous and virtuous Liberalism of our
grandfathers' and great grandfathers' eras could not resist
those forces for long because it was empty at the center. It
was essentially Kantian: it extolled moral duty and
conscience and the public good but was agnostic about their
real foundation in a transcendent reality. The liberal wanted
goodness and truth; but as a product of eighteenth-century
rationalism, his concept of goodness and truth was (at best)
purely humanitarian, having no center, which only a

---

[185] See Matthew Arnold, *Culture and Anarchy*. Arnold (1822-1888) was
defending the liberal ideal of the old humanism that was already in decline in
his day

transcendent faith could provide. Liberalism and communism were at bottom on the same side, but in the twilight of philosophy could not see the fact. I am made to think of those lines from Matthew Arnold's poem, "Dover Beach":

> And we are here as on a darkling plain
> Swept with confused alarms of struggle and
> flight,
> Where ignorant armies clash by night.

Such claims are hard to accept if you suppose that Liberalism was essentially Christian. But it was not; Liberalism was only the vestige of Christianity. Of course, a vestige is better than a total absence. While the West was no longer investing in Christianity, liberalism could live off the cultural dividends of a millennium of its spiritual and civilizational achievements. Despite the enormously dangerous climate of the intellectual culture of the early to mid-19th century, the humanist culture that Christianity was largely responsible for creating was still viable. That liberal idealism chose to work with the old humanism rather than against it was its chief virtue. But for all its accumulated capital, the legacy of a Christian civilization, Liberalism was still, a secular religion of progress that fundamentally differed from all the others only in that it rejected the idea that social progress required the coercive power of the state. It was this that set it against the worst trends of the 19th and 20th centuries. Its proponents all being sons of Kant and Hume, Liberalism shared with every other secular intellectual movement of the 19th century the fundamental loss of faith (this despite the participation of many Christians who ennobled it) that was fast shaping a new, thoroughly secular, or, better, desacralized, culture. Its very devotion to progress that led Liberalism eventually to compromise its own principles with those very ideologies that opposed them and thereby abet the dissolution of humanist culture.

It was always the fundamental tenet of liberalism that it is not the power of the state but the liberated human genius that is the fundamental impetus of a flourishing culture, whether it be economic activity or artistic; even religious progress requires that human ingenuity be free of the constraints of overweening authority and custom. But a moral idealism unanchored by at least a philosophical conviction of a real transcendent justice is no match against the raw power of the state and its own formal cultural and intellectual enemies that share its philosophical skepticism. Thus liberalism, to which social and material progress were the primary goals – moral virtue itself as constituent of the common good or justice for its own sake were not its concern – eventually succumbed to the temptation of using the state to its own ends. It is a small step from appropriating the state to being appropriated by the state. When Liberalism became politicized, it became an instrument of the state. The Liberal Party in England and the Progressive Party in America were hardly the realization of what British liberal thinkers like John Stuart Mill and

Thomas Hill Green had envisioned. In Lord Acton's well-worn but little observed maxim, "all power tends to corrupt and absolute power corrupts absolutely."

For the same reason – the exclusive aim of material and social progress as in lieu of and sometimes even opposed to moral progress -- liberalism succumbed to the lure of technology, which was, as Dawson believed, its fatal mistake. Technology did more than anything else to hasten the demise of the older western order and replace it with a technological order. That order is the basis of a thoroughgoing secularism which effaces from cultural life even humane values let alone Christian ones. An old, highly developed, and civilized culture decays slowly; it is a long historical process. So, until the modern technological revolution, western culture was relatively stable and enduring, because cultural conditions so much depend upon men's relationship to their environment. But with modern technology men's relationship to their environment was drastically and suddenly altered. The technological revolution did not come willy-nilly but was deliberate. Western man was already philosophically prepared to embrace so fundamental a change. Technology made it possible for people to live without the ideas and customs of the older humane order. The philosophical revolution changed the way men thought; the technological revolution, which the philosophical revolution made all but inevitable, changed the way men lived.

By technology I do not mean applied science. Although modernity had conferred on modern science the role of being the final arbiter of reality and as such was the willing agent of the technological revolution. Nor do I mean the tools *per se* of applied science; they are only the means to ends which need not be bad (though some, like television, may be too dangerous to achieve the good they are supposed to attain). Dawson understood that the real danger of technology is its systematic application to culture, imposing itself as a substitute for those values which are the foundations of human life. We have exchanged a humane culture for a technological one, the "unbought graces of life" as Russell Kirk called the natural blessings of humane culture, for purely material advantages. In a technological order, the machine, not necessarily but by deliberate application, replaces the human act, in so far as it removes our actions from natural conditions and consequences which act as checks on the destructive forces in human nature and preserve an intimate relationship with our natural environment, to which human nature is partly ordered and which has always been perceived to reflect the order of grace to which also our nature is ordered. We have thus alienated ourselves from the nature of the sexual act – and thus from love and virtue and joy -- by freeing ourselves from the natural consequences of the act with the use of contraceptive technology. By the use of industrial technology we have created unprecedented national wealth but with the result that we have been forced to live in immense urban centers whose wholly artificial environments have almost completely alienated us from a sympathy with and knowledge of our natural (and thus God-given) environment. If the fact of our willing subordination to technology is not obvious from these examples, it should be unmistakable from the emergence of "virtual reality" technology, by which a man submits the whole of his sensible experience of reality to a machine that will recreate it for him according to his fancy, thus relieving him (at least temporarily) of the need to apprehend reality and live in it.

The last quarter of the 20th century saw the beginning of a profound cultural transition from the machine age to an electronic age, as was much written about by Marshall McLuhan and Frederick Wilhelmsen. Both men speculated on the possibilities for a genuine renaissance of western civilization as a consequence of this cultural change. They understood the machine age to have been the ultimate development and manifestation of the dominance of Enlightenment or rationalist principles in the west – the "age of analysis" as Wilhelmsen called it -- and the "electric age" as offering us our freedom from that dominance. But they understood that such an opportunity would have to be deliberately seized upon and while neither was, I think, very hopeful, they clearly saw the possibilities. I will not discuss their hopeful speculations, because those speculations, I believe, have proven, forty years later, to be largely mistaken. We have not seized the opportunity history has offered us.

We cannot say science is responsible for giving us a technological order of culture, for science *as* science is interested only in understanding the material world. But science has undoubtedly been used as the spokesman for a materialist view of existence that allows for the technologies it makes possible to treat the cultural environment in the same way it treats the material environment, a thing to be changed and manipulated at will to exclusively material ends.[186]

So, ultimately, liberalism weakened the traditional society by tethering it to this world with the sable chains of wealth and technology. The older western order was founded upon the belief in and apprehension of a higher transcendent order. That belief was itself founded on an unbroken tradition of philosophical realism that went back to Plato. Ockham broke with that tradition and Hume finally destroyed it. Liberalism, while it valued the old western tradition, did not recognize that tradition's true foundation simply because it did not accept it. Liberalism was not the long lost child of the 12th century returning at last to home and inheritance, but rather was very much the natural child of the 18th and 19th centuries. The foundation of the various reforms that liberalism sought were rooted not in Christianity but in the moralism of Kant, in which ethical values have no known transcendent reality, but are just the necessary tools (the primacy of practical reason) by which men must live their lives. If nineteenth-century or "classical"

---

[186] Cf. R. Hittinger, *op. cit.*

liberalism was short-lived as a powerful player in the development of western civilization, it is because it rested on too weak a foundation to stand up against the powerful forces of change that were afoot in the late 19th and early 20th centuries.

There are those who would say that I am overlooking the fact that liberalism was a tremendous proponent of the freedom of religion. Liberalism, they might argue, may not have been theologically oriented itself, and may even have been as positively agnostic as I have characterized it; but what does that matter if it won for men the civil right to exercise their religious rights?

In answer, let it be kept in mind that religion was being isolated from culture by a deliberate secularization in so far as religious faith was relegated exclusively to subjective experience. As such it was considered the private and, except where it demonstrated its strictly social conscience, ineffectual pursuit of the simple and credulous. In such a milieu, in which liberalism's first principles were squarely positioned, the religious rights it promoted in theory as part of a freeman's civil liberty were nothing more than the freedom to practice with the sanction of natural right *any* religion according to one's conscience and not to any objective truth which it recognized. In practice, however, this meant that those spiritual rights would be observed only to the extent that and so long as society desired to do so and it served the purposes of the state. Nothing inherent in liberalism itself could preserve that social will to maintain religious freedom and there was much in the intellectual climate that militated against it, from which liberalism could not protect the social order because it accepted the philosophical premises which created the anti-theist climate. It was naively supposed that society could enjoy at once the best effects of religious belief and a thoroughgoing secularism in public life for, after all, the principles of liberty demanded it. But Liberalism could not protect for long religious rights when the theological truths that made those rights meaningful were undercut by its own agnosticism. Liberalism could only tolerate religion by privatizing it, confining it to the personal and subjective and so render it harmless and out of the way. It was rather like the way the Victorians regarded young children -- seen but not heard; religion was necessary (people *will* believe these things), but unsuited to the business of real life. Like Victorian children, whose "proper place" was the world of the nursery with its dreams and fairy tales, religious belief was naïve and unsuited to the real world. Though Liberalism was undoubtedly a good and noble rearguard action against the advancing tide of tyranny, anarchy, and antitheism, it was nevertheless sadly inadequate. After the American experiment of over 200 years that put the best of liberal principles to the test, the failure of those principles is all but compelling.

In America and Britain, where the liberal tradition was born and raised, the conviction of Liberalism's consanguinity with Christianity dies especially hard. The embracing of American liberalism by many American Catholics, including many priests and bishops, as exceptional for its compatibility with Christian principles is indicative of a confusion of liberal and Catholic principles. This Americanism is the result (in part) of the supposition that because many of the founders were Christian men, some even devout, it follows that they then founded the nation on Christian principles or at least on principles that are conducive to the flourishing of Christian faith. That supposition betrays a confusion of founder and founding. While few would say America is today a Christian society, the claim that it was intended to be and could be yet if she returns to her founding principles of religious freedom and public virtue is supported by neither the historical documents nor Catholic teaching. The founders may have been, in the main, Christian men, but the principles of government on which they collectively agreed by many unwanted compromises and which remain at the heart of America's public orthodoxy, do not derive from a specifically Christian view of the world or of national polity, not, at least, so far as the Catholic tradition is concerned.

The Church from prudential considerations has for much of her history preferred monarchy, but she prescribes no single form of polity as obligatory for all men at all times. What she has always insisted on whenever she has had anything to say about public order is justice. Whatever the character of American society at the time of the founding, no one disputes that it was an amalgam of variously conceived state polities and regional cultures that had grown out of the rudimentary conditions of their colonial experience, These all were, after a fashion, Christian. The national polity was something else, however. It was forged by political debate and compromise, doubtless, from that colonial experience and that political wisdom we associate with Edmund Burke, but no less and perhaps more profoundly from the abstract principles of Locke's theories of government. These theories derive from his general philosophical conclusions, which, as Professor Feser observed, have exerted a tremendous influence on the modern rejection of moral authority and tradition.

There is the persistent contention, originated by John Courtney Murray (a great scholar and very influential *peritus* at Vatican II in the drafting of *Dignitatus humanae*) and embraced by liberal Catholics, that American liberalism, especially respecting the freedom of religion and its central principle the separation of church and state, was peculiar and to be distinguished from European liberalism as "articles of peace" as opposed to "articles of faith". That is to say, that behind American liberalism's indulgence of religion is nothing more than sound jurisprudence or "good law" allowing for peaceful coexistence, rather than a dogmatic conviction of the abstract principle of pluralism founded on the *theological* idea that all religious claims are of equal value. Murray was sure that the First Amendment in its plain meaning addresses individual consciences only and not the authority of the Church as a divine institution. As such, it implies a thoroughly "sectarian concept of the Church" as nothing more than a "voluntary association of like-minded men"[187] in which "the individual conscience is the ultimate norm of religious belief".[188] This Murray admits to be a "Protestant principle" that Catholics, as *Catholics*, must reject, [189] but which they can readily accept prudentially as *Americans* living in a polity established on principles of tolerance and mutual respect for its peace and security. Despite the unmistakable historical meaning of the First Amendment, Murray and the many who have adopted his point of view insist the Founders and Framers "were not radical theorists' intent on constructing society in accord with the *a priori* demands of a doctrinaire blueprint".[190]

But this conviction is belied by the doctrines of Locke himself. That Locke's philosophy, especially his political theory had a decisive influence on the founding fathers and the framers of the constitution is certain; it is only the precise effects of that influence that are in question. While there is no need to attribute all of Locke's philosophical conclusions to the founders, the influence of certain conclusions on them is unmistakable. His principle of toleration respecting religious liberty is perhaps the most telling and pertinent to our interests here.

---

[187] Cf. Locke, *A Letter Concerning Toleration*, ed. James H. Tully (Indianapolis: Hackett Publishing, 1983) pp. 28, 30.

[188] Cf. Kenneth R. Craycraft, Jr., *The American Myth of Religious Freedom* (Dallas: Spence Publishing Co., 1999) 106-7.

[189] Cf. Murray, *We Hold These Truths: Catholic Reflections on the American Proposition* (New York: Sheed & Ward, 1960) p. 56.

[190] Ibid., 57 as quoted by Craycraft, *ibid.*, 109.

In the teeth of his skeptical empiricism, Locke (unlike the reckless Hume) hedgingly insisted on the existence of God and even the truth of Christianity. But his idea of religious truth was ultimately and practically personal and subjective. Each person, Locke averred, is orthodox unto himself and it follows as night the day that so too is every "church", being, as he conceived it, a voluntary association of those who mutually agree on religious beliefs. The idea of a Church with objective authority beyond its own adherents was repulsive to Locke. Any religious authority must be purely relative, because religious truth itself is not objectively knowable. Hence, Locke declares in no uncertain terms that an "orthodox church which [has] a right of authority over the erroneous and heretical . . . [is] in great and specious words, to say nothing at all. For every church is orthodox to itself; to others, erroneous and heretical."[191] It is obvious here how Locke's empiricism completely governs his idea of religious authority, as it does his idea of religious truth (from which it follows). And from this in turn follows Locke's doctrine of religious liberty.

If a church is a purely natural association of persons according to their individual consciences, that is, their subjective conviction of a set of religious truths, for which there can be no objective certitude, then the right to practice religion is based not on the obligation to God to adhere to the true faith as revealed, but on the absolute freedom of the individual conscience. Thus, can Locke say that toleration

---

[191] Locke, *ibid.*, 32.

and not truth is the "chief charactersitical mark of the true church." Here then from Locke is the principle of pluralism in its nascence that lay at the heart of our public orthodoxy as well as the religious indifferentism inherent in theological modernism. So it is to Locke that we owe, what the late Father Richard John Neuhaus called, the "naked public square", the public life of a society stripped by law of all religious belief, *in order to preserve* religious freedom. There are few illusions more ironic to which many American Catholics adhere with what seems nearly as much conviction as the Faith of the Apostles than the myth of American religious freedom. One doesn't have to be anti-Christian to be an enemy of the Church.

If there be any doubt that this Lockean principle is what the American founders had in mind we have only to look at what Madison, the "Father of the Constitution", had to say regarding religious authority.[192] Madison was a vociferous enemy of any formal cooperation between church and state even to the point of opposing a bill put before the Virginia Legislature in 1784 for the assessment of tax to finance religious instruction in Christian churches. His *Memorial and Remonstrance Against Religious Assessments* (1785), which was written to defeat this bill, "reveals that Madison was hostile to traditional religion and believed in the necessity of keeping religion carefully checked in the public sphere."[193] What drove both Madison and Jefferson was not merely a

---

[192] For a complete rendition of this argument see Craycraft, *op. cit.*,
[193] K. Craycraft, *ibid*, 74.

concern to eschew established religion for the sake of keeping the peace in a society which contains a variety of religious opinion. Rather, it was a personal abhorrence of religious authority as a thing which necessarily enslaves naturally free men. It was, Madison argued, every man's natural (and so inalienable) right to follow the dictates of his conscience "because the opinions of men, *depending only on the evidence presented to their minds,* cannot follow the dictates of other men" (my emphasis).[194] Here as in many another places in his writing on this subject, Madison shows himself to regard the content of religious belief as having nothing more objectively real about it than its persistent presence as a *political* problem.

The imprint of Locke on Madison is unmistakable. He agrees with Locke that the Christian churches are no more than associations for public worship, being just one among many institutions in civil society, and that their separate beliefs have no claim on anyone other than the individual possessing them. It follows from this view that the churches must be subordinate to the state which alone possesses the *objective* authority to command *all* men in its realm. Even the Catholic Church, who claims divine authority, has, on this view, no authority with the state nor any final authority over the individual. With respect to the public life of a society, the Catholic Church is overruled by the state and, in this respect, is a non-entity. Indeed, the greater the claim by the religious authority, the more dangerous it is to be

---

[194] *Memorial and Remonstrance Against Religious Assessments*, 9.

considered. The state accedes the right of liberty to the individual conscience but not to any other authority. Such is Madison's concept of religious liberty that informs the American constitution and the American public orthodoxy.

The separation of church and state in the Lockean view is absolute, and both Jefferson and Madison regarded the "wall of separation" to be necessary to the restoration to man of all his natural rights.[195] Locke himself put it: "the Church itself is a thing absolutely separate and distinct from the commonwealth. The boundaries on both sides are fixed and immovable. He jumbles heaven and earth together, the things most remote and opposite, who mixes these two societies, which are in their original, end, business, and in everything perfectly distinct and infinitely different from each other". Locke could have said nothing more profoundly Protestant. He conceives the relation of grace and nature to be mutually exclusive.

Civil society in the Lockean view is not man's natural condition but only a convention. And so something as alien to civil society as it regards religious tradition, particularly the Catholic tradition whose claims are uniquely profound and far-reaching, can at most be tolerated but not privileged or cooperated with. In civil society, the thing most sacred to Locke and to the Founding Fathers is *liberty*. And liberty, as liberalism defines it, knows no authority but the law and no power but the state. So, any association of men claiming to

---

[195] Cf., Craycraft, *ibid*, 47.

represent a *transcendent* authority is viewed as a necessary threat to liberty so conceived and must be made to heel before the state. A state that has established religious indifference as the dogma of its public orthodoxy is one that will not tolerate any other public attitude to religion. This kind of pluralism is based on a principle of toleration that does not recognize, let alone privilege, the truth. Those Catholics who suppose such a pluralism to be beneficial to the American social order should consider that so far as public life is concerned it subordinates Christian orthodoxy to liberal orthodoxy. But that is precisely what the heresy of Americanism insists upon. And we have only to look as the public life of this country and the disposition of its laws to see that the two orthodoxies, Catholic and liberal, are strangers to each other. And those who argue that the private faith of individuals can reform the laws and public life have not reflected sufficiently on the history of the frustrated pro-life movement or that of almost any other movement of moral reform of the last fifty years that runs counter to liberal orthodoxy.

Murray was much mistaken in calling liberalism's idea of religious liberty "articles of peace" and in advising Catholics to accept it prudentially as such. In truth, they were rather articles of faith, which are demanded by liberal orthodoxy for religionists to accept if they are to have any place in American public life. As Kenneth Craycraft put it so well: "the choice between liberalism and religious orthodoxy is not a choice between reason and dogma; rather it is a choice between competing dogmas".[196]

.

---

[196] *Ibid.*, 25

VII

Discursions: The Culture of Apostasy and the Kingdom of God

The lengthy review of philosophical history in Chapters 4 and 5 showed that what informs the culture of modernity and makes it irreconcilable with the whole of the Christian tradition, lay at its roots, at the level of its conception of itself and of the whole of existence. It was not a mere epiphenomenon of modern culture which was otherwise unaffected. The culture of modernity is *defined* by its apostasy and its apostasy; at its foundation are principles of thought that have estranged it from the ancient and medieval worlds, an estrangement far more profound than that which estranged antiquity from the Middle Ages. These exclusively modern principles of thought are alien to the mind of the Church *because* they are alien to a rational and coherent understanding of reality. The philosophical confusion and derangement we have considered acted like bad genetic material and produced a deformed culture, for men act according to how they think. Thus, modernity was born with a profound birth defect, which, uncorrected, produced over the course of its centuries of formation a Caliban, a grotesquery that to an ancient or medieval man would be unrecognizable a consanguine civilization. I said modernity was "born" even though historically modern civilization is the result of a continuous historical development from the 5th century. But culturally, the civilization we now live in is almost wholly discontinuous with its remote Christian and its even remoter classical pagan past.

Religion lies at the root of any culture; and Christianity is the font of European culture, for Europe did not exist till the Church filled the vacancy the crumbling Empire left in its western territories. Modern European (and American) civilization, and increasingly the older civilizations of the east through colonial experience and commercial importation, or by ideological revolution have adopted and adapted to modernity through a long process of the last hundred years. Modern civilization, for this reason and a host of others, is an entirely new thing in the history of the world.[197] I do not wish to suggest that what produced this cultural revolution in the west was not also a political, economic, and scientific revolution, but these are secondary.

---

[197] Cf. C. Dawson, "The European Revolution" (1954) in *Christianity and European Culture: Selections from the Work of Christopher Dawson*, Washington, DC: Catholic University of America Press, 1996.

The Church and the Culture of Modernity

The world's political, economic, and scientific transformations would not have happened, or would not be the threats to Christian civilization they have become, if not for that more profound transformation at the deepest levels of thought from which these others have sprung.

Nothing about the developments of thought that formed the culture of modernity was necessary or compelling. They were the deliberate contrivances of those thinkers who could have at critical points taken their thinking in quite other directions, but chose not to. In many cases, the intellectual integrity applied was rigorous. So too, perhaps, was their pride. Men like Ockham and Descartes were determined to go wherever their premises led them; and some, like Hume, when they reached those wrenching conclusions were distressed by the ideas they believed they had demonstrated to be truths. Neither was their influence inevitable. Nothing they said was compelling or went unchallenged. But in the decline of Scholasticism were the roots of skepticism and the soil made ready to sow the seeds of modernity. Even as early as Ockham's time, the philosophical milieu in Europe was already beginning to be disordered. Nominalism was a philosophical error that could infect a theologian without immediately altering his theology (Ockham, as I have noted, was theologically orthodox). But eventually, as Nominalism subtly reticulated into the wider non-philosophical world, it would make possible in the order of thought the errors of the Protestant Revolt, which historically was perhaps the single most powerful solvent of the old order of culture in which inhered the old order of thought. Like certain diseases which in early stages do not effect any obvious symptoms, one can be infected with Nominalism or one of its many species and not know it except by a careful philosophical scrutiny which few are likely to perform. Very few ever deliberately choose a philosophy; it is more often an integral part of a complex of other things that one does choose; like a 1000-page Senate bill with all manner of pork barrel riders, it is a "package deal". It is all the more difficult to chose a set of philosophical conclusions if one's philosophical presuppositions, which seasoned the stew that was his education, regard understanding or even apprehending reality to be an impossibility. As Anthony Rizzi has explained, when deliberate philosophy is rejected "a culture, and hence the individuals who make it up, can avoid doing philosophy *consciously*, and thus such a culture can forget that it can indeed and, in many cases, does know. A radical disbelief in the knowability of reality can set in."[198]

What began within the confines of the rarified and secluded world of philosophy, after centuries of mutations and adaptations unchecked because largely unacknowledged, like a featureless gas in the air, became a monstrous unbelief that afflicted an entire civilization. Unchecked, except, I should say, by the Church, who is ever alert to the errors that endanger her children and threaten the just order of civilization. Nominalism did not go

---

[198] Anthony Rizzi, *The Science Before Science*, (Baton Rouge: IAP Press, 2004) 25.

unnoticed even as early as the 13th century. It was condemned as part of a syllabus of philosophical and theological error promulgated by the Bishop of Paris, Stephen Tempier, in 1277, which prohibited the teaching of 219 philosophical and theological theses that were being discussed and disputed in the faculty of arts under his jurisdiction.[199] But while such formal condemnations no doubt mitigate the evil that results from profound intellectual errors, they rarely stop the juggernaut of their influence. I might add, though, that the influence of no one of these deracinated systems of thought we have examined which have helped form the culture of modernity was alone great enough to determine the character of its own age nor of any future age. None of these systems of thought was ever so well or widely received as to be able to gain such influence; each met with considerable critical opposition from various quarters (not just from the Church) and was inevitably, as we have seen, countered by an opposing system. Even the most influential never came close to singly characterizing or wholly dominating anything so complex

---

[199] "Tempier's condemnation is only one of the approximately sixteen lists of censured theses that were issued at the University of Paris during the thirteenth and fourteenth centuries. . . . During the fourteenth century, this Collection grew significantly, so that, in fact, a second, augmented Collection came into existence. . . .The collection of Parisian Articles must have had some kind of official status, and must have circulated among medieval scholars. Bachelors in theology were required by oath not to maintain anything 'in favor of articles that have been condemned at the Roman curia or in Paris.' Moreover, many medieval philosophical and theological texts contain references to and quotations from the 'Parisian articles,' which by no means should always be identified with Tempier's list of condemned articles." Hans Thijssen, "Condemnation of 1277" in *Stanford Encyclopedia of Philosophy* (internet edition), 2003.

and varied as the mind of their age. The old humanist culture of Europe still, to a large extent, unified European thought and that unity was not readily broken. Not, at least, until the late 18th Century when the Age of Reason or the "Enlightenment" was fully fledged. It has been so called because it stood in opposition to the allegedly superstitious "darkness" that preceded it, which has been called (perhaps contemptuously) the "Age of Faith". Certainly, by the French Revolution the unity of the old world was visibly shattered. But its undoing was the result of the cumulative force of these philosophical betrayals. Their errors became in their general effect -- an inability to think in accordance with reality -- the very air most educated men breathed. Even for that man who sets himself squarely against the prevailing climate of opinion, a tough-minded "conservative" who condemns the intellectual trends of modern civilization, even this man may not know how much he has himself been shaped by the ubiquitous culture of modernity, unconscious of what lines he himself has drawn in the sand against *any* principle that would encroach upon his freedom to determine what (as distinct from *whether*) he will believe.

If anything is obvious from our survey it is that modern philosophy has been a continual progress of disintegration, of growing fragmentation and confusion. Not to be missed in all of this is that what was lost was our understanding of reality, our ability, given the prejudices of modern thought, to understand it objectively. In the late medieval debate over realism and nominalism, St. Thomas was the premier advocate for *realism*; his articulation of realist metaphysics is the most complete in a philosophical tradition which reaches back to Aristotle and Plato, that is, the foundations of western thought and thus of Christian *philosophy*. And while the Church never forsook realism, nor forgot her servant, whom Leo XIII declared the Common Doctor of the Church, St Thomas's influence in philosophy waned with the fortunes of Scholasticism and Aristotelian philosophy in general after the 16th century. He was eventually thrown into the common grave with every other scholastic and, because theology and philosophy were growing estranged, was largely unheeded outside of theological circles. Not until 1879 did the Church attempt to restore Thomistic philosophy when Leo XIII in *Aeterni Patris* declared him "the prince and master of all Scholastic doctors" and in 1880, designated him patron of all Catholic universities, academies, colleges, and schools throughout the world. Although none of the problems that have dogged modern philosophy since the 16th century obtain in the metaphysical realism of St. Thomas, philosophy never again embraced it. It is as Gilson has observed that "men are most anxious to find truth, but very reluctant to accept it."[200] Always at the root of our philosophical difficulties are other problems, spiritual or moral. The truth, even when the mind clearly understands it, does not always appeal to the heart that *prefers* the falsehood. Truth, it may be said (without intending to assert the primacy of the will over the intellect), does not compel, but has to be *chosen*.

---

[200] *Loc. cit.*, p. 61

The realist tradition teaches that our knowledge of reality begins in the senses and that from sensible knowledge we proceed by abstraction to intellectual knowledge. Until Ockham, it was always understood that by this process we come into contact with and understand reality. And it was precisely this realist understanding of our knowing reality that Ockham had abandoned. His nominalism continued to undermine and eventually produce the philosophical skepticism that would precipitate the work of Descartes who then begat modern philosophy. Descartes with his *cogito ergo sum* as the first principle supposing that knowledge of reality begins in the mind, turned the process of knowing on its head and forever changed the way we think about reality and our relation to it.

It should also be obvious that, as broadly varied and even contradictory as were the philosophical movements that gave us modernity, they yet are all of a piece, like the unity of a play or novel. What is common to all of them is that each has played its part in the steady drift away from a Christian conception of the world. Thus Engels, the materialist, can claim the heritage of Ockham, the nominalist, calling nominalism "the first form of materialism":

> . . . materialism is the natural-born son of Great Britain. The British schoolman, Duns Scotus, had already asked, 'whether it was impossible for matter to think'. In order to effect this

miracle, he took refuge in God's omnipotence; i.e., he made theology preach materialism. Moreover, he was a nominalist. Nominalism, the first form of materialism, is chiefly found among the English schoolmen.[201]

Lenin endorsed Engel's attribution,[202] even as he also describes Hegel's system as a more immediate source of his materialism. If Ockham's dogmatic theologism is the ancestor of the dogmatic materialist ideologies, however ironic and improbable that may seem on the face of it, we may be sure that from Descartes, Locke, Hume, and Kant, came the more popular agnosticism that spread across liberal Europe and America in the 19th century in the beguiling form of secular liberalism.

Philosophically, all that separates the ideological materialist and the liberal agnostic is the materialist's dogmatism. So, after the fall of the Soviet regime in Russia and Eastern Europe, little at bottom changed; confusion and moral and political disorder have followed political liberty not justice. Remember: agnosticism, or religious and philosophical skepticism, was once the demon to be exorcised, but it is now and has been for more than 150 years a comfortable intellectual virtue. Now it is only in politics that we allow dogmatism; we call it ideology. While its

---

[201] Friedrich Engels, *Ludwig Feuerbach and the Outcome of Classical German Philosophy*, p. 84. Although Engels names Scotus not Ockham, Gilson (Cf. *loc. cit.*, p. 285) believes he confused Ockham and Scotus, both nominalists, but Ockham was the Englishman, Scotus as Scotsman.
[202] Cf. Gilson, *ibid.*, p.285

philosophical agnosticism allowed liberalism to be very tolerant and broadminded politically, begetting the pluralism, we so much honor today, it was a barrier to any direct and specifically Christian influence from the Church or the many (largely Protestant) Christians who labored to realize its ideals. The liberal agnostic could admire religion but only in so far as its morality coincided with his own ethical and social ideals and only from a distance. The Christian and the liberal agnostic could work together because they both accepted the immediate ends of their social doctrine and because their profound theological differences could be ignored in order to achieve those ends. But like the religiously mixed marriage, in which the question "In whose religion will the children be brought up?" is blithely ignored by the newlyweds till it becomes a destructive problem, the ultimate consequences to society of a secularized ethic were left unconsidered until the problems it created threatened the social order and then only a minority of Christians considered it. With her accustomed prescience, the Church under Pius IX (*Qui Primus, Syllabus of Errors*) saw the issue clearly, that Christian civilization and all the goods that obtain from it were at stake, even while most Evangelical Christians, who had "privatized" their theology and regarded the state and society as *necessarily* secular, did not.

The Church understood that what lay behind nineteenth-century agnosticism was the legacy of the Enlightenment, the friend of "liberty" but not of the Church or transcendent religion. The Enlightenment's hallmark was the apotheosis of positive reason, and, as we have seen, this could be so even while the foundations of reason and of science were being undermined philosophically, as science and philosophy parted ways when modern empirical science was enthroned as the deposit of true knowledge, and philosophy (thanks to Kant) willingly accepted the role of court jester, the only one at court who could say anything to anyone, even the king, because no one took him seriously. Hume had made the bed to lie in for both the hard materialist and the so-called agnostic, the half-hearted materialist, who would have his cake (morality – hiding behind Kant's moralism) and eat it too. Science, thus, for a while, was absolute monarch. The Enlightenment mind placed its supreme confidence in reason and its principles as well as their scientific application. Alasdair MacIntyre has identified this apotheosis of reason as the "encyclopedist tradition".[203] But, of course, that it was a tradition and, therefore, one among other traditions of rational inquiry is precisely what Enlightenment rationalists or encyclopedists would have denied. They were dogmatically confident that the Enlightenment standard of rationality was the only standard by which everything that could be known was known or would be known given time and diligent application. Nietzsche, who rebelled against the entire Enlightenment tradition, attacked it assumptions and exposed its inconsistencies and hypocrisy. Thus was born

---

[203] *Three Rival Versions of Moral Inquiry*, (Notre Dame: University of Notre Dame Press, 1990).

"post-modernism", which has signed the death certificate on reason and science. For at least 150 years, the encyclopedist tradition had been the sum and substance of the western academic milieu, but over the last thirty years in the Humanities at least, post-modernist principles (what MacIntyre calls the "genealogical tradition" and whose great patriarch was Nietzsche), have come largely to dominate. So, agnosticism, after all, has at least one dogma, that reason as applied by modern positivist scientific standards of rationality could achieve all that could be known, that it could encompass reality. This Enlightenment mentality, however, dies hard for it is thought to be the foundation of many of our dearest social and intellectual values and so still prevails in the more conservative institutions. In the waning of scholastic theology in the 20th century, the Enlightenment mentality had gained in influence even among Catholic scholars and intellectuals to the extent that by the time of the Council, there was a great though unpublicized struggle between those who had come largely (perhaps for most without being fully aware) to understand Christianity and the Church according to the Enlightenment or rationalist principles and those who remained faithful to the scholastic tradition, which, though supremely rational does not subordinate faith to reason.[204] We have already observed

---

[204] Cf. Jeremy Driscoll's book review of Aidan Nichol's *Looking at the Liturgy: A Critical Review of Its Contemporary Form*, (San Francisco: Ignatius Press, 1996) in *First Things*, Vol. 73, May 1997, pp. 52-3: "The ideas that led to the ritual reforms of the Second Vatican Council—and are still driving further reform— did not spring brand-new from the deliberations of the Council. They have historical pedigrees, often quite long, and some of those pedigrees ought to give us pause. Nichols presents some of the little-known work of Waldemar

some of the effects of the influence of the Enlightenment faction in *Gaudium et Spes*.

The influence of the culture of modernity and specifically of modern thought on Catholic thought I want to touch on here but will discuss more fully in a later chapter. That influence is exceedingly subtle, complex, and even tortuous, but its main threads, as twisted as they are, may be discerned. If the principles of Enlightenment rationalism have infected Catholic thought and scholarship in the post-conciliar era, it was a recrudescence of its original effects in the Church of the 18th century which is evident in the demands of the heretical Synod of Pistoia (1786).[205] We are inclined to think that such "modern" problems as the demystification of Catholic theology, liturgical innovation, and the wish to democratize the Magisterium or at least to reduce papal authority have been opinions current only since Vatican II. But these, while not as ascendant as in our era, were nevertheless current in the 18th century under the influence of a pervasive deism and heresies such as

---

Trapp in *Vorgeschichte und Ursprung der liturgischen Bewegung* (1940), claiming, 'Trapp's study makes it abundantly clear that the origins of the liturgical movement lie in the eighteenth-century Enlightenment.'" On the scholastic side, the evidence of an active faction lay in the "Ottaviani Intervention" mentioned above and the united support for the papal election of Cardinal Siri over Cardinal Roncalli (Pope John XXIII).

[205] Pius VI commissioned four bishops, assisted by theologians of the secular clergy, to examine the Pistorian enactments, and deputed a congregation of cardinals and bishops to pass judgment on them. They condemned the synod and stigmatized eighty-five of its propositions as erroneous and dangerous. Pius VI on 28 August, 1794, dealt the death-blow to the influence of the synod and of Jansenism in Italy in his Bull *Auctorem Fidei*.

Jansenism, Gallicanism, and Febronianism.[206] The fact of their influence presents the question of how these ideas infected Catholic thought.

There were many causes, but I am here concerned with only one: the prevailing interpretation in post-Tridentine scholasticism of St. Thomas on nature and grace, which I have mentioned earlier and which, I suggest, is the most profound and far-reaching cause. It has much to do with the theological difficulties of the conciliar texts and the theological confusion after the Council. As I have said before, this is a profound subject and the stuff of trained theologians. My purpose here is only to indicate the problem and its difficulty and where stand the main lines of demarcation between modern and Catholic thought.

The modern debate over the supernatural in Catholic theology has much to do with how St. Thomas is to be understood. Until Vatican II, the common understanding of the supernatural, or grace and its relation to nature, has been based on the interpretations of the famous sixteenth-century theologians, the Dominican, Thomas de Vio Cardinal Cajetan (1469–1534) and the Jesuit, Francisco Suarez who followed Cajetan. By the late 19th century, Cajetan's commentary on St. Thomas' *Summa Theologiae* was so well

---

[206] Febronianism was a powerful movement within the Church in Germany, in the latter part of the 18th century, directed towards the nationalizing of Catholicism, the restriction of the power of the papacy in favor of that of the episcopate, and the reunion of the dissident churches with Catholic Christendom. It was thus, in its main tendencies, the equivalent of what in France is known as Gallicanism.

established in Catholic theology that in the critical Latin edition commissioned by Leo XIII, his commentary was set at the bottom of each page of the text. According to Cajetan, St. Thomas taught that nature and grace were mutually exclusive orders of being, nature operated at one level and grace or supernature operated above it. When God created the natural order, He did not order it, including man, to any other than purely natural ends. This means that man has no natural desire for God. The desire for God is superimposed gratuitously by an intervention of supernatural grace. Unfallen man enjoyed in his unbroken communion with God a continuous flow of grace. But this grace was necessarily *extrinsic* to his natural state, which was unendowed by grace and, if left to itself, would have no knowledge or desire for God or the divine. Cajetan knew, and what was soon defined by the Council of Trent, that man was created in grace, a "state of holiness and justice", and so understood that man cannot be happy in his natural state, that is, without grace, that man was destined for the Beatific Vision. But he posited the abstraction of a hypothetical state of "pure nature", operating in parallel with supernatural grace, in order to avoid the logical difficulty he faced in the teeth of the simple doctrine that man was created in grace and thus ordered to the supernatural. If, he thought, that man *simply* possessed in the order of creation a soul disposed to God and heaven, then it must be that grace could not be gratuitous, that God would then be forced by justice to gratify that natural desire in man. God cannot be compelled, so the doctrine of man's relation to grace must be *qualified*. Hypothetically then, the faculties of the human soul did not *necessarily* have a capacity for grace. Cajetan was thus forced by his own presuppositions to conclude two mutually exclusive ends of man. He presupposed that the predilection for God obtains in the will, that it is, therefore, a *moral* desire. He clearly saw the danger of Pelagianism in the notion that man is disposed to grace as an act of the will. It is interesting that Cajetan's Commentary was at the time of its publication thought problematic,[207] but so overwhelming was its influence that his dualistic understanding of nature and grace passed unchallenged and with little scrutiny until the theologian, Henri Cardinal de Lubac, criticized it in his book, *Surnaturel* (1946)[208], and Etienne Gilson, the philosophical historian, strongly opposed this aspect of Cajetan's interpretation of St. Thomas' work[209].

De Lubac convincingly argued that no such understanding of the relation between nature and the supernatural ever obtained in Catholic theology until the High Middle Ages.

---

[207] Dominic Soto, the famous Thomist of the Council of Trent said Cajetan's "gloss destroys the text. It is torturous" as quoted by de Lubac in E. Gilson's *Letters of Etienne Gilson to Henri de Lubac*, San Francisco: Ignatius Press, 1987, p. 101, note 3.

[208] After Pius XII's encyclical, *Humani Generis* (1950), de Lubac published a revised edition of *Surnaturel* in two volumes, which were published in English as *Augustinianism and Modern Theology* and *The Mystery of the Supernatural* (1967).

[209] Gilson accuses Cajetan of distorting St. Thomas in his commentaries, calling them "corruptorium Thomae" (the corruption of Thomas). See *Letters of Etienne Gilson to Henri de Lubac*, p. 92. See also Ralph McInerny, *Praeambula Fidei: Thomism and the God of the Philosophers*, (Washington D.C.: Catholic University of America Press, 2006), 39 ff. for a critical view of Gilson's critique of Cajetan.

The distinction had always been between the natural and the moral. He cites the difficulties the Church had, using Cajetan's doctrine, in answering the Jansensts, whose distortion of St. Augustine's doctrine of grace led them to consider human nature incapable of any virtue (very like the Calvinist doctrine of Total Depravity). More dangerous still, behind Cajetan's consequent dualism of nature and grace, and thus of philosophy and theology and of reason and faith, lies the incipient error of nominalism. What Cajetan encountered in St. Thomas was the elucidation of a paradox, the mystery of grace, which to his neo-scholastic mind, without (we may presume) the subtlety or humility of St. Thomas', was inadmissible. Hence, he insisted on the gratuitousness of grace, that grace was necessarily God's action toward us and not ours toward God, that we received it but only *passively*. De Lubac equally insisted on the gratuitousness of grace, but, rejecting the thin-air abstraction of a "pure nature", accepted in its paradoxical simplicity the Church's own insistence that man's highest end and the fulfillment of his nature comes with the Beatific Vision, for which St Thomas claims throughout the Summa that there is in man a *desideratum naturale*. De Lubac read St. Thomas to mean precisely what he wrote, for nowhere does Thomas posit a "pure nature". Whatismore, St. Thomas does not locate the natural desire for beatitude in the will as does Cajetan, but in the intellect.[210] Being innate to the intellect,

---

[210] Cf. *Summa Contra Gentiles*, Lib. 3, Cp. 57, n.4: "Supra probatum est quod omnis intellectus naturaliter desiderat divinae substantiae visionem. Naturale autem desiderium non potest esse inane. Quilibet igitur intellectus creatus potest pervenire ad divinae substantiae visionem, non impediente

the *desideratum naturale,* is manifest not in moral choice but in an inchoate or indeterminate orientation to the truth, by which the intellect cannot perfectly rest till it finds its ultimate satisfaction in God, Who is Truth. It is only a potentiality or capacity of the intellect; it cannot positively direct it, for that is an act of extrinsic grace necessitated by man's fallen condition. But even before the fall, man could no more attain his end as man *de natura* than he could take himself out of existence; his end as is his being is dependent on God. Nature is ordered to grace. And thus is the Catholic understanding of the nature and foundation of culture.

De Lubac further argued that Cajetan's interpretation which posited an autonomous natural order is a primary source of modern secular humanism.[211] If nature is pure or self-sufficient and grace is utterly alien and thus wholly adventitious or extrinsic to it, then culture is properly secular and thus, naturally autonomous of all spiritual values, which bear no necessary relation to it. Society, on this reckoning, can, hypothetically, achieve a purely natural perfection without ever acknowledging God's law or authority. Of course, there is no need to assume that Cajetan believe this implication of his idea.

De Lubac's critique of Cajetan's reading of St. Thomas was devastating to its influence in Catholic theology and

---

inferioritate naturae." (*Every intelligence naturally desires the vision of the divine substance. But a natural desire cannot be in vain. Any and every created intelligence then can arrive at the vision of the divine substance; and inferiority of nature is no impediment.*)

[211] Cf. Peter. J. Leithart, "Henri de Lubac: A Brief Introduction" at Leithart.com.

inadvertently to Thomistic theology as a whole. Unfortunately, what de Lubac proposed as a solution to the problem of nature and grace never filled the hole he had uncovered in Cajetan's argument. That is, de Lubac succeeded in persuading theologians that Cajetan was wrong, but his own theory of the mystery of the supernatural never prevailed. It had its own problems, brushing dangerously as it does with nominalism and Pelagianism, and it had influential rivals. One of these rival views was that of the German theologian, Karl Rahner who took up where de Lubac left off.

What de Lubac only implied in his theology, Rahner boldly posited a third element between nature and grace, the supernatural finality imprinted upon our nature. To nature and grace he positively added this third reality wholly distinct from the other two as they are from each other, the "supernatural existential". This is nature called to grace. But, strangely, though he agreed with de Lubac's critique of Cajetan, Rahner retained the concept of pure nature if only as a hypothetical postulate and thereby came far closer to nominalism than did de Lubac. It is significant that Rahner does not claim that a "pure nature" really exists, but calls it a "remainder concept" (*Restbegriff*), while insisting that it is "necessary and objectively justified".[212] How, one has to ask, can what is admitted to be not real be "necessary and objectively justified"? This shows the unmistakable mark of

---

[212] K. Rahner, *Karl Rahner: Theologian of the Graced Search for Meaning*, ed., by Geoffrey Kelly. Minneapolis: Fortress Press, 1992, p.114.

Kantian epistemology upon Rahner's thought. That a mere idea, a thing without extra-mental existence, can be made the foundation of a theology that purports to explain *objective* reality, is a philosophical confusion that comes only from the abandonment of realist metaphysics. Rahner was not unfamiliar with Thomistic theology, but he thought that to give St. Thomas a more "authentic" reading and to present to the modern world a "meaningful" theology, he had to use the insights of modern philosophies, such as that of the Kantian Joseph Maréchal and the existentialist Martin Heidegger.

It is from such influences, especially Maréchal's, and not St Thomas', that Rahner acquired such insights as that *"every* [my emphasis] act of human understanding contains within it an orientation toward infinite Being as the *a priori* condition of that understanding."[213] Thus, our authentically human and fundamental capacity for God, Rahner claims, is at once wholly "existential" and "supernatural" and unconditional, and, therefore, not dependent upon our choosing grace or willingly cooperating with it. No doubt Rahner is trying to take into account the actual subjectivity of our experience of grace, but his Kantian premises lead him astray into naturalizing the supernatural.

By integrating nature and grace in this way, Rahner's doctrine is even more dangerous than Cajetan's rendering them extrinsic to each other. Ironically, in Rahner's theology,

---

[213] S. Joel Garver, "Rahner and de Lubac on Nature and Grace", at www.joelgaver.com, p. 3.

which intends to mix nature and grace in the "supernatural existential" they are conceptually more separate than in Cajetan's. Rahner fell into the opposite error of confusing the two by rendering nature as unconditionally and inherently "graced". The history of salvation, in Rahner's theology, is the playing out of "something which was already present in its fullness from the outset".[214] If Cajetan's extrinsicism, his dualistic conception of nature and grace, with its implicit nominalism, has been in some measure responsible for secular humanism, (which, we must remember, began not with the 19th century and the secularization of society but with the Renaissance and its secularization of the Liberal Arts),[215] Rahner's integralism, as I have already observed, encouraged the same thing. By naturalizing the supernatural, the distinction between sacred and secular breaks down. If the supernatural is operative in every existential act, then all our acts, cultural, political, and intellectual, are privileged with autonomous values and

---

[214] Rahner, *Foundations of the Christian Faith*, trans. by Willima Dych, New York: Crossroad Pub., 1978, as quoted and cited by S. J. Garver, *loc. cit.*, pp. 12, 19.

[215] To trace that secularization as far back as we might, we would have to lay some of the responsibility at the door of the medieval Scholastics themselves, whose purely intellectual orientation to Sacred Tradition and an almost obsessive preoccupation with logic and dialectical argument had led them to nominalism. This was Ockham's milieu, remember, and Cajetan's two centuries later. To this danger and weakness, monastic theologians, such as St. Bernard often attested. (Cf. Jean Leclercq, O.S.B., *The Love of Learning and the Desire for God A Study of Monastic Culture*, New York: Fordham University Press, 1961, chapter 9.) It might also be noted that it was the very dialectical method of the scholastics, the *questio disputata*, that in no small measure protected them from error in so far as every assertion was subject to rigorous review and scrutiny and had thereby to be defended. But the virtuous argument does not necessarily lead to truth nor bespeak moral virtue.

knowledge and thus privileged against any external authority – even the Church -- because the supernatural order, the order of grace, loses it supremacy and uniqueness. The Church becomes in our cultural experience a useful but unnecessary institution, which, while it is more directly focused on the life of grace, is no more privileged to it than any other institution. If this is not an explicit tenet of Rahner's integralism, it is certainly its tendency. We have witnessed in the wake of Vatican II the secularization of the Mass in the name of "enculturation" and ecumenism, the movement to democratize the Magisterium in the name of "collegiality", the blurring of the secular and religious, the lay and the sacerdotal, and the confusion of liberal principles of social and economic order with those of Catholic social doctrine.

Both de Lubac's and Rahner's theories of grace tend (intentionally or unintentionally) to obviate the gratuitousness of grace, that it necessarily comes from *outside* ourselves, from God and not by any other necessity than His goodness, His own perfect nature. All of their complexes of qualifications and disclaimers notwithstanding, they tend to locate the desire for God inherent in human nature in the will. Perhaps more than their conclusions, these theologians' more fundamental error is their intellectual overreaching by attempting to *break* the seal of mystery on the relation of nature and grace as distinct from merely *penetrating* it as was, for example, St. Bonaventure's ambition. In this, Rahner is guiltier than de

Lubac[216]. But then de Lubac's insistence on the mystery of the supernatural did not stop him from trying to rationalize it in terms however qualified and use it in his arsenal for the debunking of the entire scholastic tradition; and Rahner, with less humility and as hair-splitting as the most ardent scholastic, was, it seems, intent on removing the mystery.

To their theology we may apply the same criticism that medieval monastic schools, with their more spiritual and literary tradition of theology, made of the scholasticism of the urban cathedral schools and their preoccupation with mere logic. Monastic theologians like St. Bernard of Clairvaux, Hugh of St. Victor, and William of St. Thierry often observed a lack of respect for the mystery of sacred doctrine among the Schoolmen with their "hyperdialectic". Even one of their own, Peter Cantor, complained that scholastics could treat God's word as if it were just another of the liberal or mechanical arts, making theology a matter of mere technique.[217] Monastic culture with its exclusive orientation to the spiritual life and, therefore, to all that will facilitate the desire for and final enjoyment of God in Heaven, were naturally afraid of the obvious tendencies of the secular (i.e., non-religious) learning of the schools that could be so absorbed by the procedures of disputation as to

---

[216] De Lubac showed himself an obedient son of the Church when he revised his *Surnaturel* in response to Pius XII's encyclical *Humani Generis* (1950) that emphatically affirmed the gratuitousness of grace which his work had left rather nebulous.
[217] Cf. Jean Leclercq, O.S.B., *The Love of Learning and the Desire for God, A Study of Monastic Culture*, New York: Fordham University Press, 1961, pp 250-51.

almost mistake it for a value of its own. Without denying the propriety of studying theology outside the monastic experience which they regarded as a "school of charity", they were keenly aware of the dangers of the professional study of Divine truth as encouraging a spirit of selfish ambition for reputation and preferment that would be anxious to break the seal of mystery of sacred doctrine and "penetrate it as if by forcible entry".[218]

This they saw as an abuse of dialectics not as something inherent to it. The monastics were not in competition with the scholastics to see whose theological method would prevail, for they often used the scholastic method themselves but were able to transcend it. The monastic theologians carefully observed the principle of "holy simplicity", which, far from excluding knowledge, sought it through prayer, holiness of life, and a rigorous adherence to tradition, namely their monastic tradition and the Fathers of the Church upon whom their own was founded. As William of St. Thierry put it, "Holy simplicity is an unchanging will in pursuit of a changeless good."[219] Simplicity's necessary virtue is humility, which in the secular theologian as in the monastic draws back the mind from the labyrinth of speculation to its single and principal quest to seek God. If the will is fundamentally turned toward God, the intellect cannot stray far from Him. There was no question in their minds of the necessity of grace to illuminate the intellect in

---

[218] J. Leclercq, *loc. cit.* p.252
[219] Quoted by J. Leclercq, *loc. cit.*, p.254.

the pursuit of theological truth. In that quest, humility is a virtue of the first order, allowing the intellect, while seeking to see into the divine mysteries, to shun hubris (Abelard's great fault). The danger feared from abuse of the scholastic method was not only for the spiritual welfare of the scholastic, but for the doctrine it was supposed to elucidate. Theological speculation in the 12th century was beginning to exceed the limits of rational inquiry set by faith by trying to make the divine mysteries heel to reason, forgetting that they are transcendent truths. The danger was an incipient naturalism or, as in William of Ockham's case, a distorting theologism. St. Bernard's great dispute with Abelard, for example, was not over abuse of his method but the conclusions to which he was led by it. We might suppose St. Thomas with his magnificent *Summa* also falls under St, Bernard's censure; it would have seemed a tremendous display of human pride. But St. Bernard (1090 – 1153), who was "wisely unlearned" as well as "learnedly ignorant", would have seen that St. Thomas, who came almost a century after him, using the same method (though with many more resources, some of which, like Aristotle's metaphysics, he would not have approved), avoided the deviations of Abelard.[220] Still, St. Thomas's own holiness notwithstanding, we do well to remember that even the Angelic Doctor could not see the truth of the Immaculate Conception. The tendency of some scholastics was to turn St. Anselm's great maxim, *fides quarens intellectum,* on its head, making reason preeminent rather than allowing

---

[220] Cf. Leclercq, *ibid.*, p. 258.

understanding to seek the truth by humble submission to the final mysteries of the Faith and not by rational inquiry alone.

I have tried to show in the forgoing discussion of nature and grace how profound and profoundly distorting were some of the theological ideas operating upon and among the Council Fathers and in *Gaudium et Spes* in particular, and which went largely unexamined and which affected how they understood the modern world and the culture of modernity. All this explains to some extent why the fathers failed to demonstrate any theological understanding of culture. Caught between a distorting neo-scholastic interpretation of grace and an at least equally distorting modern correction of that error, it seems hardly likely that the Council Fathers would speak clearly and cogently about culture and secularism. What I have identified are two opposing views of the problem of nature and grace, from neo-Scholasticism and from modern theology, both of which assent, one by implication only and the other by direct assertion, to the secularization of society, the natural world being wholly self-sufficient either because it is a realm unto itself, unrelated to any transcendent reality, or because it is itself inherently graced.

Bad theology was nothing new in the Church, but the great danger from the modernists in the Council, what indeed *made* them *modernists* and not simply mistaken, was their insistence upon sweeping away tradition to make way for their theories. In their attempts to correct the mistakes of tradition or to accommodate modern thought, they thought outside any tradition and so were unaccountable to any established principles of thought. It is the distinctive character of modernity that it sets itself against tradition and eventually destroys it. This is at bottom why the Popes of the 19th and early 20th centuries set themselves against modernity. They understood, and especially Leo XIII, that modernity had infected the very springs of our understanding and were changing the way we viewed reality. What *is* was increasingly confused with what *I think*. What saved neo-scholasticism from the worst tendency of its own mistakes is that it remained within an intellectual tradition that could mitigate those errors by subjecting them to a sympathetic interrogation. But modernism made its own errors the grounds for destroying tradition. Cajetan, and Suarez after him, remained Aristotelian realists and thus essentially within the Scholastic tradition. We cannot say the same of Rahner or Maréchal (de Lubac is, I find, much more complex and ambivalent). The metaphysical realism of the Scholastic tradition, especially as developed by St. Thomas, on which the whole of Christian philosophical understanding is based, has long been in danger of being irretrievably lost. The consequences of that loss would be ruinous to the Church and to civilization.

Hence, when, before the council, the Church spoke to the modern world, she spoke as a critic. If she condemned more than advised, she did so because the modern world had not yet been thoroughly enculturated with these errors of thought. But all round her, the social order was changing rapidly driven by these errors and it was imperative that she not only admonish but condemn them while it was still possible for the world to turn around and undo the damage. The moment was critical. In the mid-19th century, it was still only the second (and in some places only the first) generation to have been born into the culture of marginalized Christianity and thus to have lived and breathed modernity their whole lives. Much of modern thought still tasted like apostasy. It was time – if indeed it was not already too late -- for the Church to strike. She had by then no power over secular society to impose her will by interdict (which always had, in any case, to be freely complied with). Yet for the many who would be imposed on to their considerable detriment by the de-Christianized state, it may be said that it would have been good for all had the Church imposed her will by her acknowledged authority. Those who do not know the good to be chosen cannot be said to be really free to choose it. Better that the good be imposed as a condition of common life, for it to be feely chosen once understood, than that the good be altogether lost and with it any possible freedom to choose it.

Because today the infection of Catholic thought with the errors of modern philosophy has become all but mortal, the counsels of Leo XIII in *Aeterni Patris* (1879) and of John Paul II in *Fides et Ratio* (1998) all the more important to us. And this is true whether it be a result of a rejection of scholastic thought or of the attempt to correct a defective scholasticism.

Both encyclicals, but especially *Aeterni Patris*, attempt to restore traditional Catholic philosophy. The "Christian philosophy" they recommend is not a specific set of tenets (John Paul II, in *Fides et Ratio*, denied that there is any specifically Christian philosophy in that sense); it rather a kind of method – the best method of philosophizing – that unites the study of philosophy, which loves and seeks the truth, with a Christian's proper docility to the truth that has been revealed to us. Far from being mutually exclusive, between faith and reason is a "bond of friendship" by which each is aided by the other.[221] Christian philosophy is the work of the spiritual as well as the intellectual man. St. Thomas and St. Bonaventura, the greatest of the thirteenth-century masters, were both. As great as their learning and intellectual abilities were, their profound wisdom was only possible through the cooperation of these abilities of natural order with their religious experience through prayer in the order of grace – *orando quam disputando*.[222] Thierry of Chartres said of "philosophy" that it is the "love of wisdom and wisdom is the integral comprehension of truth: without love it cannot be attained, or at best it is barely attained."[223]

With respect to metaphysics, the traditional philosophy of the Church has been realist and, since St. Thomas, Thomistic. This is why Leo XIII in *Aeterni Patris* prescribed the restoration of the doctrine of St. Thomas as preeminent in

---

[221] Cf. E. Gilson, *The Church Speaks to the Modern World: The Social Teachings of Leo XIII*, New York: Doubleday Image Books, 1958, p. 8.
[222] St. Bernard, *De consideratione*, V, 32, PL. 182:808.
[223] Quoted by J. Leclercq, *loc. cit.*, p. 263

the Catholic tradition. Leo XIII saw this restoration to be of the first importance. He did not prescribe it as an intellectual formality, a kind of shibboleth by which one could identify himself as an educated Catholic, but which was otherwise hopelessly impractical in the modern world. Rather, Pope Leo XIII considered it as the only solid basis on which a restoration of a just political and social order could be realized, because metaphysical realism lay at the heart of both the western philosophical tradition and Scholasticism, its (at least historically speaking) culmination. And both have their culmination in the work of St. Thomas. Metaphysical realism, Leo clearly understood, is not merely one among many possible theories by which to speculate about reality; it is, in its broad outlines, rather a *discovery* (apparently only in the western tradition) of the necessary foundations of being. And with respect to knowing, metaphysical realism involves a fundamental and necessary presumption that our senses are our primary contact with reality and that it is that presumption that makes all discovery possible. Without a realist foundation, nothing in St. Thomas' teaching whether it be on the divine origin of all authority, law, or any fundamental principle of political justice, would be coherent. All other alternatives lead ultimately to some form of subjectivism which is the destruction of all true science or systems of genuine knowledge.

Leo XIII in his encyclicals took care not only to prescribe the return to metaphysical realism, but also to delineate and denounce the fundamental errors in speculative and practical philosophy that have proceeded from its abandonment. I have already given a general account of those errors, but Leo XIII identified in his encyclicals their underlying principle. Let us call it the Principle of Autonomy. In speculative philosophy, modernity has insisted on the autonomy of reason, resulting in naturalism with respect to the order of existence and rationalism in the order of human knowledge. In practical philosophy (i.e., ethics and political philosophy), it has been the autonomy of the will, the refusal to submit man's moral freedom and political authority to the higher authority of God, which in turn has entailed a rejection of the divine law and inevitably its derivative, the natural law. Leo XIII called this political and ethical manifestation of the Principle of Autonomy "liberalism". Whatever benefits we may justly acknowledge liberalism has conferred on the modern world, whatever virtues it may ostensibly demonstrate, at the bottom of all its accomplishments and social idealism is its refusal to acknowledge God's supreme authority either in the abstract or, especially, in the divine authority of His Church. Liberalism made both the individual's will and conscience in ethics and the democratic will in politics, higher than divine authority.

The Principle of Autonomy forms the foundation of the whole structure of modern culture. It gives the lie to the argument that secularization was the only solution to the religious wars of the 17th century that embroiled Europe, especially Germany, for thirty years and scarred her for many more. Those conflicts, it should be recognized, were as much political as religious (if not more so), though they were the direct result of the Protestant revolt against the authority of the Church. But for that revolt, which destroyed the spiritual and political unity of Europe, no such war would have occurred. The claim -- founded upon this unhappy period of conflict in Europe's history (a history of conflicts), that religion is a divisive element in culture is a mere stalking horse. For religion, perhaps more even than language, is the most profoundly *unifying* element in culture. A culture that excludes religion from its common life has no deep unifying principle. The disintegration of Europe into vicious nation-states, each bent on aggression or on protecting itself from its neighbor's, cannot be laid at the feet of religion. The wars of the Middle Ages were petty by comparison with those of post-Reformation Europe. The movement to secularize European society, which took two hundred years, was motivated by the desire to be free of the spiritual *as well as* the temporal authority of the Church. No doubt, its liberation began with opposing the Church's temporal authority in the politics of Europe which she held until the latter 19th century, and which she had retained, wisely or unwisely, from her medieval powers. But the growing alienation in Europe from the mind of the Church during the 17th to the 19th centuries eventuated in an equal resentment of her spiritual authority. Even where the motion for liberation seemed simply political as in Italy, in the mid-19th century, behind it was a powerful anti-religious sentiment.[224] This fact Pius IX learned the hard way, when, upon his election as Pope, after having freed all political prisoners, appointed many laymen to positions of high office in government, and introduced many political reforms in concession to the political opposition (all of which earned him his early reputation as a liberal) was thanked with a revolution that forced him to flee Rome in November of 1848.

Secularization was the achievement of cultural autonomy from divine authority. It had already, by the mid-19th century, been an intellectual *fait accompli*, but it was necessary then to realize the idea in society. This was the explicit motive for Comte's sociolatry, which would completely reorder society, and certainly Marx and Engle's in founding the Communist movement. We see the principle of autonomy in every form of secularization: explicit in the religious philosophy of Feuerbach and lying just beneath the surface of the social and political ideals of liberalism. Everywhere the priest is succeeded by the intellectual as guardian of the higher tradition of western culture. In the order of knowledge, science becomes the sole arbiter of truth. Technological change, driven by scientific rationalism and cultural materialism, added tremendous force to secularization. Technological renovation requires continuous change in social and cultural habits and forms, and makes a traditionary society impossible. And where

---

[224] The great Italian patriot and revolutionary, Giuseppe Mazzini (d. 1872), was a confirmed deist, who rejected Christianity, preferring Thomas Paine's "religion of humanity."

tradition is weak so too is religion. For the strength of a culture is the strength of its traditions and those traditions have always been fundamentally religious, until, that is, the culture of modernity.

Though it has for some time been generally (though not well) understood that religion plays an important role in the early development of any culture, the illusion continues to prevail that modern western culture has progressed beyond the need for religion. It is supposed that, while historically religion had some direct influence in the Christian Middle Ages, it was an aberrative interruption in the progressive development toward modern civilization. Hence, the originally disparaging term of "middle" given to that period by the fifteen-century Renaissance humanists who disregarded, in their devotion to classical civilization, the Christian civilization that both succeeded it and largely preserved it in its own humanist tradition and in which these new humanists still lived and worked. It is a peculiarly modern assumption that religion is operative only in the primitive or pre-scientific stages of cultural development, its childhood. We owe this strong prejudice to Comte's now ubiquitous idea of the Three Ages of Man and to modern anthropology which has uncritically adopted it. But this again is modernity's Principle of Autonomy operating. If religion belongs to the infant stages of cultural development and if, as it is supposed, modern man has reached his maturity, then, like the man who leaves his father's house and authority to assume his own life by his own livelihood, modern man has matriculated into his autonomy from religious authority, which was always founded on "superstitions" which his "matured" mind no longer accepts nor needs because he now understands the world and makes it his own.

Throughout Christopher Dawson's historical work, he demonstrates the integral relationship between culture and religion. In his book, *Religion and Culture*, Dawson doubts "whether a culture which has once possessed . . . a spiritual class or order that has been the guardian of a sacred tradition of culture can dispense with it without becoming impoverished and disoriented."[225] T. S. Eliot, upon whom Dawson had a profound influence, even more strongly asserts that culture is "essentially the incarnation (so to speak) of the religion of a people".[226] The west's de-Christianized culture is not merely at odds with itself; it is at odds with reality. It has replaced its intellectual and spiritual foundations of realist (Aristotelian-Thomist) metaphysics and the revealed truth of Christian theology with nothing more that a farrago of ideas and beliefs succeeding one another in a continuous revolution in their utter failure to order thought and human society.

---

[225] C. Dawson, *Religion and Culture*, London: Sheed & Ward, 1949, p. 106.

[226] Eliot, *Notes Toward the Definition of Culture*, New York: Harcourt, 1949, p. 27. For an excellent discussion of Dawson's influence on Eliot's critique of modern culture, see Benjamin G. Lockerd, Jr., "Nature and Religion in the Cultural Criticism of T. S. Eliot," *Modern Studies in English Language and Literature*, vol. 51, no. 1 (Feb. 2007): pp. 327-359.

The Church and the Culture of Modernity

Modernity holds the belief that a culture can be reconstructed, because it supposes that culture is nothing more than the product of material conditions, whether natural or by human atrifice. In its grand illusion of spiritual autonomy, modernity denies that religious tradition originates ultimately in the objective reality of human nature in its relationship to the natural world and to the spiritual realities which overarch it and ultimately govern it. There may be no surprise in saying that the truth of the nature of culture is just the opposite of modern belief, that the spiritual life of culture creates its material expressions,[227] and thus the vitality of a culture is intimately and profoundly bound up with its religion.[228]

For this reason culture is necessarily sacral (again, to be sharply distinguished from *sacred*). I have already explained how we necessarily "sign" culture with meaning, because culture is the ineluctable product of our human creaturely experience in the order of existence. But, as we have observed, that order is not "pure nature" it is impinged upon continuously and profoundly conditioned by God's act of creation – and thus ordered to grace -- by that which is "above" it, those spiritual realities, which a culture ignores at its peril. The whole natural order, and culture specifically, then, cannot be neutral toward religion. That it can be neutral is the modern illusion which the culture of modernity and specifically liberalism has created and which

---

[227] Cf. Lockerd, *loc. cit.*
[228] Cf. Dawson, *Progress and Religion: An Historical Inquiry*, London: Sheed & Ward, 1931, p.232.

is the effective cause of our discontents, of the west's severe cultural decline and social disintegration. It is then a fatal mistake to suppose that the secular belongs to itself, that it need or should not be sacralized but rather kept free of religious content and values. It is one thing to recognize modernity to be a cultural and historical fact, which the Church has always done; it is quite another to recognize it as *normative*, as prescriptive of what is normal in the development of a civilization. If the conditions of modernity are not normative, the question, then, for the Church is: What is to be sacralized? The simple answer is: everything. The Church's evangelical mission is to "restore all things in Christ". This is not to propose a chiliastic view of the world or of the Church's mission, it is simply a recognition that nothing is *by nature* unrelated to grace or irrelevant to man's finality as God's creature created for Himself and to enjoy Him forever. Hence, St. Thomas' axiom: "Grace does not destroy nature but perfects it".[229]

It is an error equal and opposite to the error of secularism to suppose this to mean that culture should be rendered sacred. Dawson observed that in primitive societies the distinction between sacred and secular does not exist and that it is a sign of a highly developed civilization that its culture and religion are distinct. "The higher religions, and especially Christianity, involve a certain dualism from the nature of their spiritual claims."[230] But what are distinct are

---

[229] *Summa Theologiae*, 1.1.8.2.
[230] Dawson, *Religion and Culture*, London : Sheed & Ward, 1949, p.113.

not necessarily unrelated. The elements of a culture, while they are not themselves sacred, can be infused with the sacral and thus be rendered as signs of transcendent reality. In this way, a culture can still be secular in the sense that it is not sacred but not secularized. The "certain dualism" obtains nevertheless and must be considered.

The root of this dualism between the world (*saeculum*) and the spiritual order that ultimately governs it St. Augustine located in the human will: man's spiritual autonomy and power to choose his own good by either subordinating his will to the divine order or by declaring with Lucifer *"Non serviam"*. In the latter choice, he sets himself up as autonomous being and cuts himself off from Him Who gave him this power to *choose* independently but not to *be* independent. Thus, St. Augustine averred that what lay beneath the whole of human history are two opposing tendencies of will that "produce two kinds of men and two types of society".[231] These tendencies ultimately develop two "cities", the one established and built by love of God that seeks spiritual beatitude, the other by the love of self that leads inevitably to the contempt of God. This may seem, on the face of it, a gross simplification of history that would put St. Augustine in with Tertullian and the Donatists, as though he condemns as evil the state and all secular civilization. It is rather the case that St. Augustine was an historical realist; from his consideration of history he distinguished himself

---

[231] Dawson, "St. Augustine and the City of God" in *Dynamics of World History*, edit., by John J. Mulloy, La Salle: Sherwood & Sugden, 1992, p. 310.

from Eusebius with his political idealism, and Prudentius, who extolled Rome and the Empire, and those philosophers who accepted Cicero's thesis that the state operates fundamentally with justice. Rome was to St. Augustine always the "second Babylon"[232] and the much-touted blessings of Roman law to society he knew to have been secured by countless acts of injustice to individuals.[233] But he could have deduced the same from the doctrine of original sin. And for that reason we find St, Augustine's judgment to be consistent with the whole tradition of Catholic social teaching. Thus, we find Blessed John Henry Newman expressing the same opinion and the same unmistakable contempt of the world, the City of Man:

> Earthly kingdoms are founded, not in justice, but in injustice. They are created by the sword, by robbery, cruelty, perjury, craft, and fraud. There never was a kingdom, except Christ's, which was not conceived and born, nurtured and educated, in sin. There never was a state but was committed to acts and maxims which it is its crime to maintain, and its ruin to abandon. What monarchy is there but began in invasion or usurpation? What revolution has been effected without self-will, violence, or hypocrisy? What popular government but is not blown about by every wind, as if it had no conscience and no responsibilities? What

---

[232] Dawson, *ibid.*, p.307
[233] Cf. *De Civitate Dei*, XIX, vi.

dominion of the few but is selfish and unscrupulous? Where is military strength without the passion for war? Where is trade without the love of filthy lucre, which is the root of all evil?[234]

Newman no more than St. Augustine regarded the secular as a non-moral sphere. Rather, both understood that it is Christianity that makes good citizens, that the same spiritual and moral realities which Christianity enjoins man to observe and obey, are as necessary to their secular activities and social relations as they are to any hermetic existence. They are in truth the only possible remedies to the ills of society. There are no purely secular solutions.

St. Augustine's dualism and thus his condemnation of the Earthly City, the secular order of the world, is strictly an historical view. That is, what he condemns are the actual historical manifestations of that City according to its inherent tendency. In his larger metaphysical view of the created order, which came to him from purely Hellenic sources, St. Augustine was nearer to Origin than Tertullian or Tyconius[235]. He admitted that the Earthly City also had its place in the universal rational order, in which God orders all things in His Providence in a universal harmony which to the human mind is ultimately incomprehensible.[236] St. Augustine's philosophic universalism is in fact the central

---

[234] Newman, "Sanctity the Token of Christian Empire" at www.newmanreader.org , under "Works", Sermon 17.
[235]Tyconius was a Donatist.
[236] Cf. Dawson, *loc. cit.*, p. 315.

theme of his *City of God* and is what distinguishes him from the old apocalyptic tradition that awaited a concrete millennial kingdom established at the end of history. The Earthly City then is not an equal and opposite realm against which the City of God struggles to establish itself in the world. Rather, the Earthly City is the existential disorder and confusion of man's experience in a natural order vitiated by sin, but within a universal order under the Divine Providence by which all things adhere in a spiritual unity and which directs the entire created order towards its ultimate goal.[237] Thus the City of God is the greater thing, of which the Earthly City is only a corruption; it is coextensive with the order of the spiritual creation, whose operations are, again, beyond our ken. The City of God is an eternal and transcendent society whose visible manifestation is the Church, whose citizenship we share with the angels, whose King is Truth, whose law is love, and which will endure forever.[238]

If then St. Augustine allows for the Earthly City, it is as an historic reality, which his realism does not permit him to deny. They are not two eternal static orders predestined from the beginning to be what they are. As Dawson observed of Augustine's conception of history, "the true history of the human race is to be found in the process of enlightenment and salvation by which human nature is liberated and restored to spiritual freedom."[239] Augustine

---

[237] Cf. *Ibid.* p. 316.
[238] Cf. *Ibid.*
[239] Dawson, *Ibid.*, p.320.

did not accept the idea of secular progress, but supposed the Earthly City to be essentially unprogressive, in so far as it operated on its own principles, though he was not unaware of the tremendous material advantages of life in the Empire. But in so far as the Church exists and operates in history and represents and wields in prescribed ways the unseen power of the transcendent spiritual order, in so far as she is the point at which that eternal and transcendent order inserts itself into the mundane sensible world, progress toward a just (though not perfect) society is possible. However, this can come only by a subordination of the one order to the demands of the other. The Blessed Newman described the Church as the earthly manifestation of the Kingdom of God, an "imperial power", a "counter kingdom"[240] that

> claimed to rule over those whom hitherto this world's governments ruled over without rival; and if this world's governments would not themselves acknowledge and submit to its rule, and rule under and according to its laws, it "broke in pieces" those governments—not by carnal weapons, but by Divine Power—"without hands," to use the Prophet Daniel's language. Or, as another Prophet expresses it, "The nation and kingdom that will not serve thee

---

[240] Newman, "The Christian Church an Imperial Power" at www.newmanreader.org, Sermon 16.

shall perish; yea, those nations shall be utterly wasted."[241]

The hierarchical Church is not merely one of many institutions that help to order and preserve a just society; it is itself a spiritual society and to whose spiritual authority the kingdoms of the world must submit or lose their mooring to truth and thus to reality itself. Newman in his uncompromising way makes this clear:

> . . . He [God] has spread and diffused abroad a spiritual and regenerate kingdom far and wide, and this has encroached in a blessed way upon the world. But it is only in proportion as things that be are brought into this kingdom, and made subservient to it; it is only as kings and princes, nobles and rulers, men of business and men of letters, the craftsman, and the trader, and the labourer, humble themselves to Christ's Church, and (in the language of the prophet Isaiah) "bow down to her with their faces toward the earth, and lick up the dust of her feet," [Isa. xlix. 23] that the world becomes living and spiritual, and a fit object of love and a resting-place to the Christian.[242]

If the hierarchical Church is the visible manifestation of the Kingdom of God, then as such she is superior to the state, which makes scandalous the claim of the

---

[241] Ibid.
[242] Newman, "The Church and the World", Ibid., Sermon 8.

modern state that she is subordinate to it. But the Church nevertheless finds herself the *de facto* subject of the modern state, not because her proper authority is the lesser, but because the modern state is oriented to power rather than authority. This is why power and authority are so easily confused in the modern state. The principle of the Rule of Law has been helpful in avoiding that confusion in the modern world but it has proven ineffectual against the overpowering tendency to legal positivism. That the Church, with her supreme moral authority, should be a dynamic social power is a conception of the Church that St. Augustine introduced and is often mistaken for the medieval theocratic ideal, which conceived the *plenitudo potestatis* to be proper to the Church over all of Christendom. But though Augustine's conception may very well have led to that ideal, it does not necessarily entail it nor obviate or weaken the more moderate conception of the Church as the supreme moral authority *within* the political order over which the state retains supreme authority. The higher aims of the Church which at once transcend and assist the purposes of the state remain outside its authority. Augustine's conception places the state's authority in its proper relation to the Church's higher authority. How that relation is worked out is, of course, necessarily problematic given the power and inevitable ambitions of the state, but if Augustine conceives the Church to be a dynamic social power, it is only by her direct and indirect influence over and not by her control of the state.

Nor does his conception of the Earthly City deprive cultural life in the secular order of any possible spiritual significance. St. Augustine would have welcomed the modern idea of grace penetrating culture with meaning by sign and symbol and thus sacralizing it; it was after all he who in his *de Doctrina Christiana* wrote the first treatise on semiotics.[243] On this understanding of grace operating through nature, there is no mistaking the relative importance of the spiritual and material element in life. And far from the Donatist and later Protestant conception of secularity as unredeemable by grace, the Augustinian conception affirms moral freedom and responsibility in the social order. The difference Christianity made in western civilization becomes obvious when compared to its influence in the East. The state there was sacred and omnipotent; the individual had no rights, being utterly subservient to the state and thus rendered completely passive. The Eastern hierarchical Church, which had wedded itself to the state, was helpless to change this old oriental ideal. But St. Augustine decisively broke with it, denying the state any divinity and seeking the principle of social order in the human will,[244] thereby leading the West toward the social ideal of moral freedom and responsibility that makes it peculiar among world civilizations. In this way, the Church recognizes both the otherworldliness of the Kingdom of God and her own responsibility as its this-worldly

---

[243] *De Doctrina Christiana*, Books I-III.
[244] Cf. Dawson, *loc. cit.*, p. 325.

manifestation. Hence, the Christian civilization of the European Middle Ages was a great advance for the secular order but only under the spiritual auspices of the Church. But any historical acquaintance with the medieval civilization of Europe (as opposed to certain idealizations of it) makes unlikely any mistaking it for the Kingdom itself. Even at the height of her social influence and integration in the 12th and 13th centuries, the Church struggled everywhere against moral and intellectual opposition. She was yet occupying foreign territory, ever the pilgrim; she was, as she always must be, at odds with the world and when not, at odds with herself. She conquers only under the sign of the Cross and a crucified King.

Even in a Christian society, there must be a tension between the spiritual aims of the Church who orients all her thought and activity to a Heavenly Kingdom, and the immediate and thus merely terrestrial aims of the secular order. But even those aims, when properly ordered to the good (*bonum*) of man, cooperates in the spiritual ends of man bound up necessarily as they are in the universal good (*bonum universalis*) which is God Himself. Man's supreme good, Goodness Himself (*Summum Bonum*), is He Who made man and all other goods for him. Ultimately, therefore, the distinction between sacred and secular, nature and grace is a purely terrestrial one; in the kingdom of Heaven, Christ's eternal kingdom, no such distinctions can obtain, for all things shall have been brought into Christ and what has not shall have been burnt up like rubbish.

The Church and the Culture of Modernity

Whatever the prudential considerations the Church must make in her response to the modern world, and they are many, the Church must approach the modern world with a full understanding of the root and flower of the culture of modernity – *a fleur de mal*. She must understand that it is not and cannot be "neutral" with respect to her own spiritual claims on man. We do not normally regard a culture as being in a state of apostasy, but that is the best description of a completely secularized culture. It is an easy passage for the prejudiced or simply uncritical mind, from the necessary acceptance of the mere fact of secularization as a thing to be managed and the prudential considerations that follow, to an acceptance of the thing itself as necessary. Many in the Church understand modernity in its strict chronological sense and do not admit any prejudicial sense of the word; modernity is not bad, it is just different and therefore indifferent to the claims of the Church. These would argue that the secular and the sacred, religious faith and experience and social life are properly mutually exclusive realms except where they intersect in the moral life. Even then however, any connection between religion and morality must in the pluralist society be left out of public consideration. Modernity, they will admit, presents certain problems for the Church. Modern life with its consumer materialism can be distracting from spiritual or religious occupations and with its greater sexual "freedom" can even be dangerous. But these are moral problems and can be dealt with on that level. Even pronounced evils like abortion are ultimately only moral evils and not different in kind from those of other ages. As such, they are mere aberrations of what is at bottom a normal culture. But culture cannot be indifferent or neutral to religion, for religion is at its foundation and western culture, contrary to the illusion it has created for itself, is no exception. The West's abrogation of its religious roots in Christianity is a true *auto da fe*.

It does not require any argument to claim that culture necessarily reflects a given people's view of the world. Neither does it require any argument to assert that a religious view of the world is natural to man; he realizes without thought or contrivance that spiritual realities exist beyond his powers to create or manipulate. Modern man regards himself as an exception: he has reached, by his own estimation, the maturity of his species; he can see through the superstitious illusions that dominated primitive, ancient, and medieval man and which kept him in thrall; he now bravely sees the world as it is and that he is alone and its supreme power and authority. His philosophy has persuaded him that physical nature is the only power beyond man's control and that science will conquer even that. All other realities are within him, of his own creation, or of no account because unknowable or mere superstition. But the fundamental problem of the modern world, apart from original sin which afflicts man in every age, is precisely that modern man's view of reality is profoundly false. Here is the tragic irony of modern man, that in his hubris he should believe he sees more clearly than his predecessors when in fact his own understanding of the world and of himself is so obviously benighted and fractured. This was the faith of modern man, especially in the nineteenth-century; the events of the 20th century destroyed a large measure of that faith. But as there has been nothing to replace it in the post-modern world except a nihilistic cynicism, our institutions still try against a rising tide of irrationalism to maintain the illusion that human reason alone is the great doctor of all our ills. All the old rhetoric of democratic liberalism and Enlightenment rationalism rings embarrassingly hollow now. The modern view of the world still obtains, but as a sort of habit, like an alcoholic who continues to drink long after he has lost the pleasure of it, feeling only the debilitating effects of his addiction.

And so the secularized culture and civilization that has grown out of the modern view of the world is fundamentally at odds with reality. It is also fundamentally at odds with itself, because western civilization developed from Christianity, and even its classical sources, as we have seen, are closer philosophically to Christianity than to modernity.

The culture of modernity is the flower of that philosophical rebellion against classical metaphysics which began in the 13th century with Ockham; was made general in the 16th by Descartes, and which with Kant in the 18th century ushered in a new regime, philosophy having been dethroned and decapitated and the reign of science begun. The supreme casualty of that rebellion was not only the unity of Christendom but Christianity itself. Protestantism was philosophically as well as theologically and politically a consequence of that rebellion – the nominalism of Ockham had done its work. Protestantism is at once a corruption of Christianity and the inevitable theological result of the abandonment of the Scholastic tradition in philosophy, which alone moored western thought to realism. Without it, the protestant sects were rudderless in an increasingly turbulent and turgid sea of skepticism. The Reformers dealt with the problem by an inherent fideism, but that was no solution and Reformed theology's own kind of subjectivism made it all too susceptible to modern thought to which Protestantism has largely succumbed. After the Protestant Revolt, Christianity would never again speak with one voice and European civilization would suffer terribly for it, falling as it did into theological confusion that led to a profound and pervasive spiritual rebellion.

Europe's apostasy in turn produced the culture of modernity and so spiritually defines it. To understand the culture of modernity fundamentally it is necessary to regard it as the culture of apostasy and as such, modernity does not merely obscure or distract from Christian ends. It is hostile to them and destructive of them (even if not being intentionally so), because it developed out of a rejection of all transcendent reality and then of Jesus Christ Himself as Savior of man. The culture of modernity has sloughed off all religion as it had first sloughed off metaphysics. And even under liberal regimes where religious freedom has been allowed, according to political expedience as the right of the individual as a private pursuit, (hence, placing his religion on the same par with his private vices), religion has been allowed no *public* status. England's establishment of religion in the Church of England was strictly Erastian, making the Church an arm of the State and thereby deeply secularizing it in all but form.

What was originally strictly a deliberate theological decision, became in time an uncritical cultural habit. One doesn't any longer choose unbelief by and large, but is born into it with out any apparent choice. The apostasy is cultural in that we live and breathe it; it is in our institutions, social life, literature, art, language. There is no separating it from what we were as a culture. Now only remnants of that culture can be found as odd artifacts in the ruins of an ancient and now almost unintelligible civilization.

As a result, there is no common intellectual tradition between the Church and modernity from which to understand one another, so profoundly disjointed are they. They are mutually exclusive views of the world and man, and so any attempt to accommodate modernity is extremely dangerous. As Alasdair MacIntyre has made clear, there is no neutral ground of rationality on which each can dispute the other's claims. That was the fond illusion of the Enlightenment, and the Church has struggled and struggles mortally now against its sweet incantation. The Church cannot afford to abandon her intellectual tradition simply because the modern world no longer accepts it as "meaningful" or "relevant", for the truth cannot be known and understood except within her own tradition of theological, spiritual wisdom, which is the gift of Christ to His Church through the Holy Spirit. This is true too of her and philosophical wisdom. Even though non-dogmatic, the Catholic intellectual tradition has not been a purely human enterprise, for the Church has kept careful watch over the development of her intellectual life, which she has always subjected to the scrutiny of revealed truth. Catholics must not be embarrassed by the status this fact confers upon her nor accept the status the modern world gives her; she is in the world but not one among equals. Our Lord, even when torn and bleeding before Pilate, about to be sentenced as a criminal to an ignominious death, did not pretend to be other than He was, King of Heaven and Earth.

The well, let us admit, is poisoned. This is not to say that modernity cannot be used like a solvent, but only that it cannot be *ingested* like wholesome food. The Church must appropriate but not assimilate modernity as many have supposed who believe that *aggiornamento* means embracing the modern world as though the Church could benefit by its instruction. Any prudent rapprochement with modernity must be premised on the fact that it is an apostate culture. Such a recognition automatically makes any "opening of windows" suspect at best. It certainly alters the tactics of rapprochement, for it understands that it was not the Church that forsook the modern world, but the modern world that forsook the Church. The Church had, since the French Revolution, certainly been extremely critical, but the hostility has all been the other way. Conversion, therefore, must be all one-sided; there can be no meeting modernity halfway.

The culture of apostasy is not an abstraction to denote the outcome of a series of philosophical errors nor is it a rhetorical expression to lend gravity to a merely intellectual objection. This culture is the outcome of an historical development that is writ large over three centuries of historical, intellectual, and cultural development. It is the actual condition of thought and expression, of sign and symbol, of social and economic exchange in Europe and America today and increasingly throughout the world. It began, as I have recounted, as a series of philosophical mistakes; but, as ideas have consequences, as thought forms action, so these formal errors of thought were the seed to the substantial changes that have revolutionized the very order of society. It bears certain primary, unmistakable, and ineradicable characteristics: secularization, denial of transcendent authority, naturalism, moral relativism. These are qualities which cannot be neutral with respect to religion and especially Christianity. Rather, these fundamental characteristics of modernity presuppose a radical hostility, for they are antitheses of a Christian, and especially a Catholic, view of reality. Europe did not reject Christianity on strictly disinterested, rational grounds. The truth is not so simple.

Kant explains in his *Was ist Aufklärung* (*What is the Enlightenment?*) that man has reached a stage in his growing up in which he is ready finally to fling off the shackles of external authority. He can now begin to think for himself, to assume the responsibilities of manhood. Till now the guardians of thought, the intellectual authorities have kept us in our childhood, telling us what to think, what is good and bad, right and wrong. But men are now ready to shake off this oppressive despotism and make a free and unhampered use of their reason, first of all against their oppressors, the enemies of reason.[245] The oppressors are, of course, all or primarily religious authority. The way to emancipation now lay open, but Kant understood that intellectual reform was to be a slow but steady process before Reason assumed the throne Authority occupied. Of course, in the Kantian understanding of Practical Reason as the primary use of reason and the act in which man realizes his essential freedom, it is not Reason per se that is enthroned but private judgment. In this way, modern man contested for his autonomy with any authority that would impinge upon his moral and intellectual freedom.

In the intellectual order, the resultant conflict was a *cause célèbre* that occupied the fevered attention of the educated classes. It was the main topic of letters from all over Europe, the talk of the press, and an ever present theme of topical literature.[246]   Here is how the historian, Paul Hazard, describes it:

---

[245] Cf. Paul Hazard, *European Thought in the Eighteenth Century from Montesquieu to Lessing*, London: Hollis & Carter, 1954, pp. 31-33.
[246] *Ibid*, p.47

The era of vague discontents, of local rebellions, of heresies and schisms, so much deadwood that could be cut away to preserve the life of the tree – those times were past. Now it was a case of striking at the root of the tree itself. It was not a matter of an isolated revolt, here or there, of the insurgence of an individual, or a group, of a controversy between rival theologians; it was nothing short of an attempt to achieve the total defeat, the complete annihilation of religion that was now the object of the campaign, backed by a firm determination to see it through.[247]

Under attack was not religion *per se* but *revealed* religion and, hence, dogmatic religion. What autonomous reason and private judgment cannot abide is the proposition that there are claims upon man's intellect and will that are absolute and that these claims have a supernatural origin. The social, cultural, and political effect of the conflict, the like of which the world had never seen and which continued long after it ceased to be a "hot" issue in the salons, coffee houses, and press rooms of Europe, was the modern world and the culture of apostasy.

The term "culture of apostasy", though accurate to denote the essential character of modernity in relation to Christianity, at this point requires some qualification. So far, I have treated "apostasy" as the operative term, but it should

---

[247] *Ibid*, p.45.

be evident by now that "culture" is equally operative in that it is the condition in which the apostasy obtains in the modern world. There are two things to note here about the term "*culture* of apostasy". First, that the effect referred to is specifically cultural and not *personal* apostasy. Second, that since the 18th century when the revolution of thought and feeling became ubiquitous and popular, what began as personal apostasy in key individuals of tremendous intellectual and social influence became in time cultural by a process of secularization. In becoming cultural and thus no longer individual it ceased to be a personal and, therefore, necessarily *conscious* rejection of Christianity. By the middle of the 20th century, a generation was being raised and formally educated, in Europe and England at least, but to a large extent in the American educated classes as well, without any knowledge or understanding of the specific propositions of the Christian religion – an entirely new social and cultural reality. This new situation in the history of man is a culture of apostasy that has become a culture of unbelief. It would do well to somewhat refine this idea of the culture of apostasy and how it is related to what I call the "culture of unbelief", for how it is understood will determine in no small way how the Church relates to modernity.

Apostasy is formally a complete and deliberate defection from allegiance to a set of principles and beliefs. Such a defection is no longer deliberate and conscious but inherited, without knowledge or choice, by the individual simply by being native to a culture which prejudicially excludes those principles and beliefs. In that case, we can no longer regard the problem in the same way that a strictly personal and, therefore, deliberate apostasy would demand. Apostasy has settled into the unconscious background of life and thus has become a kind of privation of belief, akin to pagan unbelief, but different. It is essentially different in that the culture of modernity itself, unlike classical civilization, is exclusionary of a religious view and understanding of reality to a degree that makes it hostile in subtle and more profound ways than was pagan culture. In fact, we may say that classical pagan culture, for reasons I have already examined, was not necessarily hostile to Christianity; it was rather the *state* that regarded it as an enemy to be destroyed. When Christianity was formally legalized, there were few cultural obstacles (the moral ones were still considerable) for the average person to overcome in embracing the Faith. It would certainly be an oversimplification to say that for the ancient pagan in the classical world it was a mere matter of exchanging his formal gods for the one true God, that for him changing religions was like changing clothes. But such an oversimplification is at least consistent with the truth that classical paganism *recognized transcendent reality* which made the Christian proposition far less strange and unpalatable.

It is easy to see that any person whose conscious life has been wholly formed by the culture of modernity, that is, by specifically modern values, modes of thought, moral understanding, and social experience, all of which preclude, obstruct, or subvert any awareness of any reality outside of modern conditions and structures, is at a serious disadvantage in believing Christian truth. It would not do then to treat him as though his unbelief were the result of a careful deliberation of what he sufficiently comprehends and has rejected as either unconvincing or undesirable. We can no longer suppose that kind of unbelief to prevail in the modern world. I do not mean to suggest, however, that his unbelief is necessarily *innocent* – an invincible ignorance. It is a truism that seekers find, but many who have both opportunity and ability have not the least curiosity in even the truth of their existence. Still, modern man stands in a different and more difficult relation to faith than did man in any other age.

The truth of faith cannot be definitively proved (for then it would be knowledge and not faith) by rational argument and this is any believer's predicament, but especially modern man's. His closed conception of reality, that has become the foundation of his thought and thus the way he subjectively experiences the world, has presented to him an almost insurmountable hurdle. For what is objectively presented to him passes through the mill of his own subjectivity by which his senses, his intellect, and ultimately his will are captivated. Modern man has rendered himself *incommunicado* to reality. Hence, what Karl Rahner called modern man's experience of the "silence of God in the world", perfectly describes it as a "genuine and powerful experience" [248] of a world-view into which God does not fit. Man's own exercise of reason can thus lead him nowhere; all of his arguments proceed from false premises that are the windowless prison of his experience.

Josef Pieper has carefully defined all belief as the acceptance of something unconditionally as real and true on the testimony of someone else who understands the matter out of his own knowledge.[249] "This someone, the witness, authority, is the 'principal thing,' since *without* his testimony the matter would not be believed at all."[250] For the religious believer, the Someone is of course God Himself Who has revealed Himself, His own Being and Works, which are normally hidden from man. God is then both the witness and the content of religious belief. To the unbeliever, especially the modern rationalist, this is an outrageous demand: he is asked to accept as real and true, a set of facts which he can in no way examine. He is referred to a witness who never meets him directly, as one meets his human friends, but who nevertheless requires of him a kind of absolute and unconditional assent that he is called to give in no other case.[251]

But as religious belief is impossible without belief in revelation, so a belief in revelation can be supported only on

---

[248] Rahner, *Theological Investigations*, (London, Baltimore and New York), 1961-92, vol. 3, p.462.
[249] Cf. J. Pieper, *Belief and Faith A Philosophical Tract*, Chicago: Regnery 1965, p.52.
[250] Pieper, *ibid.*, p. 52.
[251] *Ibid.*, p. 56-7.

the ground that God has actually spoken in a way that man can receive and understand. It is not an idea or a principle in question, but a fact of history and a fact of human nature. It is a fact of history because "the Word became flesh and dwelt among us"; and it is a fact of human nature because it is natural for man to "hear" the voice of God, to receive and understand at some level His revelation. Communication can only fully take place when the person for whom it is meant hears and receives it. Man is in a unique metaphysical situation to do so.

Revelation in the strict sense of God's speaking directly to man is something man is uniquely capable of hearing. Just as the human mind, which is a receptivity to being, is naturally open to the material reality of the world because it has a faculty for receiving that reality, so does it also have a natural, inherent faculty for receiving divine speech. Otherwise, as Pieper points out, belief could not justly be demanded of men.[252] This receptivity to those realities beyond the natural order which God alone communicates to man is not itself supernatural; although a form of that vital communication is what we call "Grace" which also the soul is by nature capable of receiving. This means that it is, in a real sense, natural to believe in revelation as it is natural to receive it. And so it is not unreasonable for the Church to expect modern man to believe in the fact of revelation (still less, its possibility). At the same time, it is necessary to understand why modern man refuses to believe. If the

---

[252] *Ibid.*, p. 60.

modern mind is to be confronted effectively, it is necessary to be alert to the conditions that produce or encourage its disbelief in the *possibility* of divine speech. It is necessary to understand the modern mind's inability to receive *any objective* truth across the great Kantian divide between the empirical world that can be known and the "numinous" that cannot.

The great dilemma of modern man is that modernity, his culture and civilization of unbelief, continually distracts his attention from the fullness of reality as well as distorts his view of it. For it is very difficult to look at one's culture objectively unless there is another culture that one knows to which he can oppose it. The old humane culture that obtained in the west until the First World War provided that necessary foil to the culture of modernity. Modernity's failure to see reality, let alone the transcendent reality as revealed, is not a matter of ignorance but a deep, barely conscious, *prejudice*, which when challenged can become hostility. Yet it is not a prejudice most men have chosen but in all likelihood inherited; it is the very air they breathe. As with anyone who does not *want* to believe a thing, there is "an infinitude of hidden, often barely discernable modes of shutting the mind and heart."[253] But modern man has remodeled his entire civilization to secure himself against any realization of transcendence. The ubiquitous mediation in every aspect of life of his technology, his forms of political and social organization, his very modes of thought from his

---

[253] *Ibid.*, p.62.

philosophical preoccupations to his concepts of history all work together in a dense network to prevent any other reality breaking through. The conditions of modern life almost compel his inattention. It has been a relatively blithe ignorance he's imposed upon himself, for against the great upheavals of modern civilization, its wars, social disintegration, and profound philosophical confusion and despair, man's greatest compensation has been the unprecedented and almost universal material contentment he has achieved for himself. He has no greater distraction from reality than the desperate reality of (at least) maintaining that contentment.

Intellectually, modern man's most effective inadvertence, reserved for those who *will* "know" but not believe, has been his retreat into agnosticism. Respecting religious faith, agnosticism is not an intellectual position at all, but an attitude that one "stands toward the self-revealing God, in the situation of an independent partner, equal in rank, who may be 'interested' or not as he pleases."[254] He supposes that he may wait quietly in comfortable neutrality till which time any proofs should come his way to convince him that God has actually spoken. But it is precisely when faced with the claims of God's Revelation, with the teachings of the Church, that he may not remain neutral (hence, the great importance in the modern world of the preaching mission of the Church). Man does not stand before God as an arbitrator who can, as the Blessed Newman expressed it "test the

---

[254] *Ibid.*, p.65.

Almighty in a passionless judicial fashion, with total lack of bias, with sober minds."[255] It is the fatal error of Enlightenment rationalism, as I have already observed, that the truth is only to be found by stepping outside of every tradition of thought to then reason your way to it by naked logic and "the facts", to think, to quote Newman again, "truth may be approached *without homage*."[256] Agnosticism is not a position the Church need respect except as a tragic fact of modern man.

Other philosophical positions are more respectable because they are more philosophical. The twentieth-century philosopher, Karl Jaspers, is representative of a common type of modern thought that disputes the Christian intellectual tradition. Jaspers is profoundly Kantian in that he defines belief as "the certainty of truth which I cannot prove in the same way as scientific knowledge of finite things may be proved."[257] Yet, in Jaspers' thought as in Kant's, religious belief is not despised because it is not founded in knowledge. He calls it variously "the substance of personal life", "the fulfilling and motivating element in the depth of man", the foundation . . . of our thinking", and "the indispensable source of all genuine philosophizing".[258] But in spite of the importance Jaspers assigns to religious belief,

---

[255] J. H. Newman, "Faith and Reason" in *Oxford University Sermons*, (London, 1880), p198.
[256] *Ibid.*
[257] K. Jaspers, *Philosophy of Existence*, trans. R. F. Grabau, (Philadelphia: University of Pennsylvania Press, 1971), as quoted by Pieper, *loc. cit.*, pp. 66-7.
[258] Quoted by Pieper, *ibid.* p. 67 from Jaspers' *Der Philosophische Glaube*, Zurich: Artemis-Verlag, 1948. English edition: *The Perennial Scope of Philosophy*, trans. by Ralph Manheim, (New York: Philosophical Library), 1949.

he declares that because the objects of religious belief are not items of knowledge, being not scientifically demonstrable, they have no specific content to which the believer can hold. If they are supposed to be true, it is only because we adopt them as such. But then what is to prevent us from adopting a different set of beliefs that we prefer? The decision then to embrace religious belief is purely existential and thus, objectively, it is the believing itself that matters not the content of belief. Thus, no authority, no "knowing witness", as Pieper terms it, need be accepted, and for the mature mind, for the philosopher, it must not be accepted, for in his rejection is all his freedom and dignity. Although the common person, even in the exercise of his radical freedom, does not realize that the dogmatic content of his religious beliefs is an illusion, the philosopher necessarily does know and rejects it. He will "cling to no authority, nowhere receive truth as dogma, nor owe his salvation to any historically handed-down revelation".[259] So, for all of Jaspers' existentialist affirmation of the *experience* of religious belief, it amounts in the end to a negation of belief itself. Jaspers admirably represents modern man's rejection of the Enlightenment rationalism's hubristic rejection of religious belief, but he is still philosophically at sea. Modernity will accept God but only on its own terms; it will never accept a God Who has spoken to man objectively nor any divinely ordained authority by which His revelation is mediated. Modernity may even grow doubtful of the blessings of

---

[259] K. Jaspers, *Philosophy*, trans. E. B. Ashton, (Chicago: Chicago University Press), 1969–1971.

secularism, but it will not find within itself any alternative. The Church must point modern man the way out of the prison of modernity. Those who think modernity is fresh air for a Church that has shut out the modern world have been shut in too long.

As Pieper as pointed out, there are many approaches to a belief in a God Who reveals Himself to man; St. Augustine, Pascal, Blessed John Henry Newman, and Simone Weil are figures, whose paths to faith are representative of many others of a kindred spirit of all times and places.[260] Pieper has very helpfully explained how, if modern man is willing, a way can be shown out of his prison to belief in revelation.[261] The willingness alone is doubtless the most difficult step, for its impediments are specifically moral and spiritual. But considering just the intellectual difficulties, two of the principal ones need to be addressed before any progress can be made. The first is the difficulty of the conception of revelation as an event in time and place in which God speaks audibly to man. This is made worse by anthropomorphic explanations that are no longer viable because the modern imagination cannot accept them, at least not at the outset, for to the malformed intellect they present too many of their own impediments to understanding. St. Thomas's broad definition of revelation, which far from being merely "medieval", could be particularly helpful to typically modern misapprehensions of what the Church

---

[260] Cf. Pieper, op cit., pp.84-5.
[261] See Pieper, ibid. pp. 78-85, whose explanation I follow closely.

means by revelation. In the *Summa Contra Gentiles*, St Thomas explains that it "is simply the communication of a spiritual inner light whereby human cognition is enabled to observe something that would otherwise remain in darkness."[262] By this conception it is understood that at the innermost core of this process of divine act of communication is something mysterious, which defies, at least for the modern consciousness, the pictorial imagination. What then the modern man is invited to accept is neither a rational abstraction nor is it, though inscrutable, a meaningless conundrum, but a kind of "in-spiration" by which God, Who is disposed to reveal Himself, communicates to man.

The other impediment for modern man to accepting divine revelation is the problem of tradition and authority, for what is communicated to the original recipients must then be diffused through time by the agency of an authority for all men to receive it. Less inscrutable than the initiation of this process, which is the revelation itself, the process of diffusion is what Pieper calls a "pattern of emanation". This corresponds to what we can readily imagine occurs naturally and as a matter of course when mankind acquires some hitherto unknown truth. We are familiar with the pattern of emanation as it occurs in the hard sciences. Modern physics, for instance, discovers an aspect of reality

---

[262] Pieper's rendition of St. Thomas' "*Revelatio fit quondam interiori et intelligibili lumine mentem elevante ad percipiendum ea, ad quae per lumen naturale intellectus pertingere non potest.*" *Summa Contra Gentiles*, III, 154 as cited by Pieper, p.78 n.6.

which was previously unknown. This new knowledge is then passed on to others in a variety of ways: it is discussed, even disputed, among other physicists; books are published and university courses taught; it becomes the subject of school curricula and eventually of general knowledge or acceptance. As the new knowledge devolves to lower and lower levels of comprehension, in a word, to the "public", we are further and further from the clarity and precision of the original discovery. At the bottom rung, the plain, educated person will have a more or less vague notion of the reality discovered. Even so, he properly participates in the truth of the primary discoverer.

An important difference between the two realms of belief is that in the case of revelation there is a spiritual dimension which permits a greater or lesser proximity to the source of revelation, viz., God, by something other than intellectual capacity. The saints have not always been very bright people. Hence, partaking of the divine truth revealed to the initial inspired recipient should not be confined to the intellectual plane. And for this reason, its diffusion is still more assured for even the simple can receive it. The statement, "I believe what the Church believes", the modern skeptic would regard as nonsensical. It appears to be what he would call "blind faith". But what he finds unintelligent, irrelevant, and imprecise in the realm of religious belief, he accepts uncritically in any other field. What is called "blind faith" is more subtly and precisely understood by the Scholastic concept of *fides implicita*. If, as a well-educated man, to use Pieper's example, he were asked his opinion of the debate in modern physics over wave versus particle theory, he would refer to what he had been taught on the subject and may even site the more learned conclusions of well-known physicists. In doing so he would be sharing in some way in the knowledge of those physicists. In the same way, according to the principle of *fides implicita*, the simple or half-instructed minds can have a share in the revealed truth they have embraced. Thus is the unity of all true believers for they are tied by faith one to another by their acceptance of the authority of those who know at first hand, the Incarnate Word Himself and then His Apostles, and from that connection back to the Prime Author Himself, God the Father. The Church has for this reason always made the broadest application of this concept and insisted on the unity of all those who have accepted sacred tradition.

But none of this will avail at all unless modern man is first disabused of his metaphysical prejudices. He must see again that the created universe is an order of which he is only a creature, though the most significant one. Otherwise, he will never see how or why revelation is even possible. He must understand that unlike investigating facts of nature, God's communication to man is a matter of a "particular and fundamental facet of his existence"[263], for which a "scientific" objectivity is of less use. For it is not primarily an affair of the head, but of the whole person. There can be, therefore, none of his modern biases, but a "receptivity and

---

[263] Pieper, *ibid.* p. 83.

attentiveness extending to the depths of his soul."[264] What is demanded of modern man in shaking off his modernity is first and foremost humility. Humility is the prime quality of philosophic wonder at the fundamental mystery of reality which modern scientific man has lost and post-modernism scorns with its bemused cynicism at modernity's failure.

No one, perhaps, is a more illustrative example of a modern's escape from modernity than St. Edith Stein.[265] She began as a practicing Jew, later turning to atheism, then, in the midst of her career as a philosopher, she converted to Catholicism and at the same time entered the Carmelite Order. Her conversion was not a spiritual escape from irresolvable philosophical problems; it was the *solution* to those problems. Becoming a Catholic meant, she understood, embracing traditional realist metaphysics. She and Martin Heidegger, the 20th century's most influential German philosopher, were both students of Edmund Husserl's Phenomenology and both abandoned it; but Heidegger (raised a Catholic), as we know, became a Nazi, having gone on to deconstruct traditional metaphysics; Stein was martyred in a Nazi concentration camp. Stein perceived the limitations in Husserl's phenomenology, which approached realism but did not go far enough and finally left it behind. Edith Stein's conversion was not the result of a slow development of thought but rather of a profound willingness (amounting to compulsion) to receive the truth

---

[264] Pieper, *ibid.*
[265] See Alasdair. McIntyre, *Edith Stein: A Philosophical Prologue 1913-1922*, (Lanham, MD: Rowman & Littlefield Publishers), 2005.

and understand it, even if understanding came only after the fact – *fides quarens intellectus*. She was as a philosopher open to reality at the deepest part of her being -- not just at the level of rationality, practicing philosophy with her whole person by integrating thought and life. She thought through the theoretical and practical questions of philosophy in order to adopt a corresponding way of living, to live *in* the truth, so that when she found the Truth she had no other reasonable choice but to follow Him. The life of St. Edith Stein seems to confirm St. Thomas' dictum that philosophy is the handmaid of theology.

In Divine revelation, God reveals Himself, and so is both the content of the message and its Witness (the Incarnate Word). Thus in rejecting revelation, modern man rejects reality itself. He has stopped his ears to God's speaking to him and will not partake of His reality. Modern man has insisted on making his own reality by insisting on his own understanding of the reality he perceives and that there can be nothing else; he prefers to be alone and to receive nothing from God. He treats Divine revelation as a kind of "announcement of a report on reality"[266] and dismisses it as a crude primitive artifact of a pre-rational age. But it is really the imparting of Reality Itself, for it is God imparting Himself to man, of which man cannot afford not to partake. And in order to partake he must believe. "If God has really spoken, it is not only good to believe Him; rather, the act of

---

[266] Pieper, *loc. cit.*, p. 90

believing generates those things which in fact are goodness and perfection for man."[267]

Contrary to the received or popular interpretation of *Gaudium et Spes*, the Church's effort before the Council to address modernity was precise and very much to the point. For it was not the modern world (chronologically speaking) she turned from, but modernity. She did not argue with it, she did not negotiate for acceptable terms; she knew with what she was dealing, an implacable and irreconcilable enemy, and she condemned it. It has been said that the Church condemned what she did not understand, stuck as she was in medieval delusions about reality. But only she with her "medieval delusions" could point out to the modern world its errors. If you distinguish between the Church's prudential (and sometimes imprudent) reactions to the modern world's rejection of her temporal power and her responses to that world's rejection of her spiritual authority, it is clear that she understood the modern world better than it understood itself. Her very condemnations were instructive and only an initial attempt to correct her rebellious children – to save them from their own stupidity before irreparable harm was done to countless souls and to an entire civilization. Pope Leo XIII understood that beyond condemnation, it was necessary to communicate to the modern man the truths he had rejected, not merely by arguing for mere propositions but to help him see the fullness of reality, the true order of things, which he was

---

[267] *Ibid.*, p. 91

losing sight of. Far from a mere debate over abstract propositions, what he envisioned, I think, was a Catholic culture that could re-enculturate and thereby resacralize the culture of Europe (at least) with a Christian culture reinvigorated (at bottom) by the traditional realism of St Thomas that imbrues all fifty million words of his immense body of writing. This was to be done through education, by the restoration of Catholic philosophy naturally through Catholic schools, colleges, and universities.

Christopher Dawson understood that the intellectual effect can happen only within a cultural and social context. He thus urged the study of the process of Christian culture "from its spiritual and theological roots, through its organic historical growth to its cultural fruits"[268] and insisted that education in the broadest sense of the word was necessary to enculturation as the chief means by which a culture can be transmitted over time. The cultural process by which this philosophical wisdom is to be recovered and preserved must take place within social institutions, which, if not themselves preserved, the cultural renewal becomes all but impossible. The present danger is the complete disintegration of those institutions.

We are thus on the horns of a dilemma: the philosophical wisdom cannot be recovered without the necessary cultural institutions and those very institutions are crumbling without that wisdom to support them. In the face of that

---

[268] C. Dawson, *The Crisis of Western Education*, (New York: Sheed & Ward), 1961, p.155.

dilemma, the Church has chosen not to prescind from culture. She knows the intellectual milieu of the 13th century has long passed into the so-called "dustbin of history" so that intellectual abstraction alone is of little use. It seems, as I have suggested above, that the Council fathers were under the influence (as were many in the Church before them) of the mistaken premise of the Enlightenment's encyclopedist frame of mind, that man is a "naked reasoner" whose rationality is independent of the particular bonds of moral and religious tradition, that the very essence of rationality is its objectivity, its freedom from all other allegiances than to reason itself, universal, impersonal, and disinterested. It follows from such a premise that there is a traditionless body of knowledge to be had and that modernity was a neutral, disinterested player, who like the Church is unafraid of truth wherever it may be found, and thus could be engaged on any intellectual field. It could accept modernity's rules of engagement for those rules were the necessary terms of objective rational investigation apart from which one was guilty of a distorting bias. On such terms, modernity could not help but prevail; for to debate from the Catholic tradition was regarded as an inadmissible prejudice and to debate outside the tradition was to effectively abandon it.

It was, I think, by observing rationalism's rules of engagement that the approach to modernity in *Gaudium et Spes* is finally incoherent, despite the many important truths it, *in passim*, articulates. That fact also accounts for why it omits any assessment of the Church's formal rejection of modernity, as though the Church had never addressed the matter. This omission is all the more surprising because it has been the Church's explicit judgment that all modern solutions to philosophical problems from Descartes to Hegel had failed and this judgment has defined the tenor of Catholic thought for a hundred years, from the *Syllabus of Errors* (Pius IX), to *Humani Generis* (Pius XII).[269] It is also why *Gaudium et Spes* seems to look benignly upon modernity, willing to admit it without serious scrutiny. And it is certainly why it altogether fails to see the importance of culture, because culture, except in the abstract, is not something one can be objective about; "it is the womb", as Russell Hittinger aptly described it, "of which all our thinking is formed."[270] Modernity had already been vetted and rejected. It had been the settled opinion of the Church that modernity was at odds with Catholic tradition; she had recommended the basic structure of the Thomistic theory of knowledge, rooted as it is in a realist metaphysic, and the Thomistic understanding of nature and grace, as the foundation for any enduring solution to the problems of the modern world. But it was perhaps convenient to ignore the precedent, for to have seriously considered that critique would have made *Gaudium et Spes* a rather different document.

---

[269] Cf. R.R. Reno, "Theology After the Revolution" a review of *Twentieth-Century Catholic Theologians: From Chenu to Ratzinger* by Fergus Kerr in *First Things*, May 2007.
[270] Russell Hittinger, "Christopher Dawson: A View from the Social Sciences" published on www.catholiceducation.org, p.3.

VIII

Modernity, Theology, and the Catholic Tradition

The present state of theological pluralism in the Church, the result of the wholesale rejection of the scholastic tradition and particularly of Thomism by the Church's dominant theological culture, is certainly a tremendous and complex problem which we would do well to try to understand. The ability of the Church to communicate the Gospel to the modern world depends much on her theological culture. Fractured and debilitated as that culture is by the poison of modern thought, it has seriously reduced the Church's ability to speak coherently to the modern world, which is already ill-disposed to listen with an open mind.

The period of anti-modernism, 1850 to 1950, was a ferment of Catholic thought and action, which makes it all the more curious and lamentable that many of the more salutary resources of that era were not drawn upon at the Council. That oversight is so odd as to be almost paradoxical when one considers the products of that ferment it did employ.

A number of brilliant theologians of the latter part of that era, like Henri de Lubac, Bernard Lonergan, Hans Urs Von Balthasar, and Yves Congar *inter alis*, were severe critics of the dominant neo-scholastic theology and their writings had considerable influence at the Council. Neo-scholastic theology, as de Lubac observed, was itself a kind of proto-modernism, that while supposed to be the enemy of modernism, it was itself deeply and subtly compromised by its dualist understanding of nature and grace.[271] But this, I think, is an overstatement of the case. A magnitude of difference stands between a theological orientation that openly embraces modernity and one which has inadvertently left itself in certain fundamental ways defenseless against it. A man with a limp who tries to hurriedly cross a street in heavy traffic is surely imprudent; if he stands still in the dark in the middle of the road he is crazy. It must be admitted that some of the theologians who aggressively criticized the standard Thomistic theology of their day did not dispute the central judgments of the regnant theology but only the philosophical arguments on

---

[271] See R.R. Reno, "Theology After the Revolution" a review of *Twentieth-Century Catholic Theologians: From Chenu to Ratzinger* by Fergus Kerr in *First Things*. May 2007.

which many of those conclusions were based as well its failure to account for historical development (it was Newman's attempt, you'll remember, a generation earlier to give such an account in his *An Essay on the Development of Christian Doctrine* (1845) that brought him so much grief from the ultra-conservative quarter in the Church). Lonergan and de Lubac, for example, were Thomists, but were disgruntled by the rigid and desiccated thing many (by no means all) of the neo-scholastic theological manuals from which they were taught had made of it. So their theologies, while attempting to be Thomistic, were speculative and exploratory and, therefore, eccentric, expanding the range and exploring the possibilities of Thomism. In this way they were loyal sons of the Church, trying to advance the theological project of understanding and exploring the relation between the articles of Sacred Doctrine and their fullest meaning. But these theologians made the fatal error of undermining the very theological culture in which alone their work made sense, for the meaning of their work is almost unintelligible apart from the standard scholastic theological framework and vocabulary in which their work obtains. The more they were opposed and misunderstood in the neo-scholastic milieu of the Church at the time, the more preoccupied they became with promoting their theologies and still more with denouncing and debunking the flawed neo-scholastic opposition, which, we may suppose, was not in every case very cogent or helpful. It would have been bad enough had they simply been dismissed, for the Church would have lost some profound insights; but their failure to show how their work fit into the broad framework of classical theology that neo-Scholasticism provided almost assured the misconstruction of their work as heretical by the mavens of neo-Scholasticism and, by others, as the theological grounds for the revolution they looked to foment in the Church. In the hands of the Church's real enemies, their theological eccentricities became the instruments of the genuine heterodoxies of a powerful faction of modernists that was present at the Council and who, in their fervor to renew what they considered a moribund Church, would renovate Catholic theology and dismantle Catholic tradition.

Indeed, some of these theologians were themselves thoroughgoing modernists, but others, like Lonergan, de Lubac, and Balthazar, who had no designs to destroy or undermine Catholic tradition but to renew it and deepen it, were modernist only in the sense that they explored modern thought and derived from it what they considered valuable insights for the Church. Given even that in their speculations they sometimes wandered from orthodoxy, they did not stand against the magisterial authority of the Church by insisting (publicly, at least) on them as the truth of the matter (as did others, e.g., Charles Curran and Hans Küng). Of the state of Church's theological culture after the Council, they were more likely to lament the changes that brought them about than favor them. Their greatest mistake was their one-sidedness. They neglected to acknowledge the need for the foundational theology which gave their exploratory theologies significance. That mistake was fatal to the post-conciliar generation of theologians, to whom their innovations were meat and drink, as though an adequate substitute for a standard theology. The result was the destruction of the old theological culture, without which the novel insights could not be properly assessed. In the old theological culture, some of these insights would have been correctly judged as tangential to orthodoxy; but in the disordered milieu that followed the Council and in which its directives were implemented they became triumphant shibboleths of a "new Church".

But the fault lay most heavily on those in the Church who were all too ready to dismiss indiscriminately whatever smacked of neo-scholasticism and to embrace whatever was new and brilliant and modern. Karl Rahner was the one ironic exception in this generation of theologians who did attempt to expound the novel ideas of his transcendental theology in continuity with neo-scholasticism. By patiently working within the system, Rahner could see his modernisms work their way by a willing theological establishment into the textbook system through which they would be taught and thus subvert that old system to serve a completely new direction in theology – a "Rahnerian consensus" – after the Council.[272] Rahner's "misbegotten, post-Kantian, faux scholasticism"[273] may now be largely seen as a failure, but the damage it wrought to an entire

---

[272] Cf. R.R. Reno, *ibid.*
[273] *Ibid.*

generation of Catholic thought has been done and it will be a long time before it is undone.

The misdirection of these theologians and the misappropriation of their work by the enemies (witting and unwitting) of Catholic tradition debilitated the Church's effort to speak to the modern world. Rather than help the Church out of a theological "complacency", it fomented theological disorder and confusion and engendered entrenched political factions of "progressives" and "traditionalists" and, later, "neo-Catholics" that warred with each other, embarrassing the Church's ability to speak with one voice. Whatever good these theologians' work can do to deepen the Church's theological understanding and reformulate her dialogue with the modern world cannot be realized until a scholastic synthesis with its "systematic clarity and comprehensiveness"[274] has been recovered and rejuvenated. The only remedy is to resuscitate what was the living tradition of Scholasticism through the work of its greatest theologian and the Church's greatest intellectual benefactor, St. Thomas Aquinas. But if Scholastic tradition is to be revived, it will help to understand the provenances of the theological modernism that overwhelmed it.

The philosophical sources of modernity, as we have seen, run deep and are widely reticulated, but, in the main, they run along the channel of metaphysical skepticism that fed the roots of a dechristianized European culture that bore

---

[274] *Ibid.*

such varied and poisonous fruits as characterized the intellectual milieus of the 19th and 20th centuries. Many who rejected or looked askance at the Church's critique of modernity were nonetheless themselves critical of its intellectual derangement. They saw the unwholesome results of the failure of the regnant German idealism of the 19th century: nihilism and determinism. And it was along this channel of metaphysical skepticism or, more precisely, Kantian epistemology, that modernity infected Catholic thought.

By the end of the 19th century, it was evident in the moral decay and philosophical despair of the *fin de siecle* that by the demise of metaphysics and the hegemony of Enlightenment scientific rationalism, the spiritual dimension of human experience had been too long neglected. This was the period of the young manhood of Jacques Maritain who, with his wife, Raïssa, made a pact to commit suicide together if they could not within a year discover some deeper meaning to life, having lost almost all philosophical hope. Into this desolation came Henri Bergson who appeared to many, including the Maritains, to save metaphysics from the determinism of positivism and rationalism, thereby making a place for the spiritual dimension of human experience for modern man. It was to the Maritians and many others an antidote to despair.

But Bergson did not save metaphysics; he only reintroduced it into philosophical speculation. Kant had effectively killed metaphysics, which was then helpless against Empiricism and Idealism; and Bergson's metaphysics was a child of Kant – at least epistemologically. Bergson's reinvigorating metaphysics at the end of the 19th century was rather like reanimating a cadaver. it was, for that desperate time, a remarkable show that set some, like the Maritains, thinking in a direction which led them ultimately to Thomistic realism and the Church. But unfortunately, it also set a number of others already in the Church, who were disgruntled with her apparently ineffectual response to modernity, in the wrong direction.

Bergson's main goal was to demonstrate that being is necessarily elusive (though not illusory) to the concepts of the discursive intellect.[275] Becoming has, in Bergson's thought, priority over being; reality is the undifferentiated and dynamic flux of the *élan vital* that permeates the universe, to which the discursive intellect is hopelessly out of touch. The operations of the discursive intellect on this vital force, on our direct experience of the dynamic flux of reality, is then like a vivisection, killing the living process of that force to preserve it as a labeled specimen. As we do this, we create for ourselves a differentiated series of static, discrete, quantified, "things" – profoundly unrelated to our living experience. In this way, the intellect gives a false impression of *being* as most important; but being is not what we experience and "know". Rather, it is the dynamic process of *becoming*. The Kantian Bergson insisted that the dynamic

---

[275] Cf. Richard Peddicord, O.P., *The Sacred Monster of Thomism, An Introduction of the Life and Legacy of Reginald Garrigou-Lagrange*, (South Bend: St Augustine Press), 2005, p.57.

process called "reality" cannot be known objectively but only intuited. Intuition, he thought, is a kind of non-conceptual knowledge that is rather more like instinct than intellect.[276] On such a reckoning, understanding reality is primarily a matter of looking inward not outward.

Such thinking seemed to a number of Catholic thinkers, like the Frenchmen, Édouard Le Roy and Maurice Blondel, to put metaphysics at last on a modern footing. Scholastic metaphysics, they thought, was (at best) a useless instrument with which to understand religious truth, especially for communicating that truth to a world that had long been, as they thought, disabused of Scholasticism's philosophical foundations. As Le Roy and Blondel saw it, the Church offered the world her conceptually formulated dogma and the world scoffed. Bergsonian metaphysics freed them of all such useless baggage, providing the philosophical means of locating the foundation of Catholic dogma in religious experience. The true value of the Church's doctrine was not in their objective truth or falsehood as determined by either discursive thought or by objective revelation, but by the practical needs of religious experience apprehended by non-conceptual intuition.[277] Hence, religious experience is something more profound – more real – than mere dogma, which, being formulated in mere concepts, cannot touch the reality of God revealing Himself to man.

---

[276] Cf. *Ibid.*
[277] Cf. *Ibid.*, pp. 56-60.

Maurice Blondel[278] was profoundly influenced by Bergson's philosophy, as were many of his generation in and outside the Church, who believed that Bergson spoke for their time better that anyone else. Under Bergson's influence, Blondel was persuaded that philosophy must receive its impulses from action, that is, from actual experience as opposed to pure thought. Truth could not be found in abstract thought unless concepts and ideas were considered in their proper context, the dynamic action of the concrete subject. This is because he regarded will and not intellect to be the primary faculty of truth and being. One had first to act upon a truth – to experience it – before he could know it.[279] In this way, is Blondel's thought informed by one of the distinguishing features of Kant's philosophy and theology, immanentism.

Blondel, having foresworn the Scholastic tradition of philosophy and with it Thomistic realism, he had also foresworn the classical definition of truth: the conformity of the mind to reality-- *aedequatio rei et intellectus*, grounded in the convertibility of truth and being. Truth is about being, about what *is*. The senses directly apprehend the real and through the intellect one knows it as real, knows it to *be*. In this way, there is an "aedequation" between the intellect and reality. Truth is apprehended when the judgment of intellect successfully "adequates" the real as real. When the intellect fails to conform to the way things really *are* (that is, to *being*),

---

[278] b.1861- d.1949.
[279] See Blondel's, *Action (1893): Essay on a Critique of Life and a Science of Practice*, tr., Oliva Blanchette, (South Bend: Univ., Notre Dame Pr.), 2003.

a falsehood obtains. His distaste for Scholasticism and especially the rationalism he supposed it to be deeply marred by, led Blondel to operate by a definition of truth founded on a completely different principle: the aedequation of intellect and *life*. On this principle, which Bergson had worked out, Blondel supposed that truth was to be discovered in experience primarily not in thought, that is in the relation of thought to being. Our experience of life and especially of God is where the truth, living and dynamic, is to be discovered. This is not to say that Blondel discounted the Church's dogma. On the contrary, he believed them profoundly. Rather, he subordinated dogma to religious experience as something inadequate to express the fullness of truth. The truth has to be *lived*, to be fully apprehended, not merely thought; it is the "aedequation of intellect and life". Just as the classical definition asserts that truth is apprehended by intellect conforming to being – what *is*, Blondel's immanentist definition asserts that truth is apprehended by intellect apprehending *becoming*, that is, our subjective experience of being.

Blondel was, it is understood, a devout Catholic and was trying to provide his contemporaries with an effective apologetic for the faith that would render it relevant and intelligible to the modern mind. The classical apologetic proofs of the truth of Christianity with their reliance on miracles and the historically verified credibility of Christianity's witnesses, he discarded as irrelevant to modern man, favoring instead an anthropological approach by way of man's inherent desires and needs that favored the existential over the rational. Blondel attempted to demonstrate that the doctrines of Christianity were true because they are rooted in the elemental expressions and longings of the human heart, the "dynamics of human consciousness", viz., hope, love, etc.[280]. As Blondel himself wrote:

> Objective justifications of Christianity based on strictly intellectual arguments would have little effect. For the contemporary difficulties with Christian Revelation did not concern its reasonableness but rather its relevance to human life.[281]

Only a transcendent, personal God, he thought, could account for the deepest existential phenomena of human beings.

So much is true, but the merit of this anthropological approach to apologetics was undermined by Blondel's coming at the nature of man the wrong way around. One has to begin with God and His revelation of man to man if one is to understand human nature existentially or otherwise. Blondel's mistake was, therefore, not merely tactical but profoundly philosophical. However good were Blondel's intentions, they were thoroughly undermined by the Kantian anti-realist principle of immanence that he

---

[280] Peddicord, *op. cit.*, p. 62-63.
[281] Quoted by Peddicord, Ibid., p.62-63.

adopted. He took the principle in its most useful application directly from Friedrich Schleiermacher, who has been called the father of modern Protestant theology for his attempt to reconcile orthodox Protestant theology with Enlightenment principle. Schleiermacher accepted Kant's *a priori* agnosticism that speculative reason could not have any knowledge of God or of the world of things in themselves and so he in turn concluded that "the religious sentiment of a wholly immanent human consciousness" was the only possible foundation on which to establish Christian faith.[282] And with this conclusion Blondel wholeheartedly agreed.

Under the strong influence of Bergson that led him to Schleiermacher, Blondel then insisted that we can believe in the possibility of a historical supernatural Revelation only because of an existential need perceived in human consciousness for its own fulfillment; hence no *objective* grounds exist for believing in God's Revelation.[283] Frederick Coplestone explained Blondel's idea: ". . . man must rediscover God from within, not indeed as an object which can be found by introspection but by coming to see that *the Transcendent is the goal of his thought and will*" (italics mine).[284] Of course, to disbelieve in objective grounds for divine Revelation is not to disbelieve in Revelation itself, but from there it is only a short step. Blondel's rejection of those

---

[282] Ibid., p.63.
[283] Ibid.
[284] F. Coplestone, *A History of Philosophy*, vol. 9: "Maine de Biran to Sartre," Part II: "Bergson to Sartre" (Garden City, NY: Doubleday, 1974), p.19.

grounds had helped others to take that short step, which he may have refused to take himself.

Rather than persuading the modern unbeliever, Blondel's theory of action had the effect of undermining the faith of an unsuspecting generation of young Catholic theologians by the insinuation of Kantian immanentism or subjectivism into Catholic thought. What Blondel chose as his primary tactic or method of approach to the modern man with the Catholic faith became dangerously close to a *doctrine* by which the Catholic faith was to be judged. Certainly, it became a means which modern thought employed to dismiss orthodox Christianity.

Perhaps that was its appeal to Blondel: to turn the weapons of modern thought into instruments of truth, like swords into ploughshares. He wanted the modern world to accept the Catholic faith he fervently held, but believing the difficulty to be a mutual misunderstanding rather than a profound alienation, he accepted modernity's terms for a rapprochement. He assumed that modern philosophy was neutral ground and so could provide the best approach for reasoning with modern disbelief. Of course, he was wrong and the Church is still living with the consequences of that mistake. Pius XII warned in 1950 in *Humani generis* of the dangers using modern philosophy in Catholic theology:

In theology, some want to reduce to a minimum the meaning of dogmas; and to free dogma itself from terminology long established in the Church and from philosophical concepts held by Catholic teachers, to bring about a return in the explanation of Catholic doctrine to the way of speaking used in Holy Scripture and by the Fathers of the Church. They cherish the hope that when dogma is stripped of the elements which they hold to be extrinsic to divine revelation, it will compare advantageously with the dogmatic opinions of those who are separated from the unity of the Church and that in this way they will gradually arrive at a mutual assimilation of Catholic dogma with the tenets of the dissidents.

Moreover, they assert that when Catholic doctrine has been reduced to this condition, a way will be found to satisfy modern needs, that will permit of dogma being expressed also by the concepts of modern philosophy, whether of immanentism or idealism or existentialism or any other system. Some more audacious affirm that this can and must be done, because they hold that the mysteries of faith are never expressed by truly adequate concepts but only by approximate and ever

changeable notions, in which the truth is to
some extent expressed, but is necessarily
distorted.[285]

The effect of Blondel's influence on Catholic thought was
the idea that Grace was no longer gratuitous to nature, no
longer extrinsic, but immanent, at least with regard to
human nature. For if all human action, thought and will, are
naturally directed to the Transcendent, then God is always
and everywhere acting in man, who is always moving
naturally toward God and he has only to *realize* the fact. This
is not an elaboration of St. Augustine's famous dictum,
"Thou hast made us for Thyself and our hearts are restless
until they rest in Thee", which supposes man's restlessness
to be an *absence* of grace. Blondel's principle of immanence
gives us rather that grace is always already present in
human nature, not just in the order of the intellect but also
and especially in that of the will, and is only *assisted* by
God's supernatural grace. In this way, Blondel's "method"
loses or at best blurs the distinction between grace and
nature. We have already noticed how the loss of the
distinction was worked out in certain aspects of Karl
Rahner's theology.

When a thinker's influence is under discussion his
intentions, real or supposed, are all but irrelevant. Blondel's
use of the principle of immanentism was powerfully

---

[285] *Humani Generis*, An Encyclical Letter Concerning Some False Opinions
Which Threaten to Undermine the Foundations of Catholic Doctrine, August
12, 1950, 14-15.

influential in the destruction of the concept of the supernatural order in much of post-Conciliar Catholic theology. His confidence that, on modern philosophical principles, Christianity could be rendered intelligible to modern man was shared by the likes of Loisy, Laberthonnier, Tyrell, von Hügel, and many others who traduced scholasticism's ability to articulate the truth of the faith. This confidence was at the heart of theological modernism. Modernism we may define as "the attempt to synthesize the basic truths of religion and the methods and assumptions of modern thought."[286] Defined as such, modernism is understood as the subtly reticulated thing it is, a disease that has no specific locus, like the HIV virus that debilitates the immune system and thereby renders the body defenseless against any and all infections and diseases. For very good reason did Pope St. Pius X call modernism the "synthesis of all heresies".[287] It is so called because it is characterized by a set of premises which, as we have seen, is at odds at the profoundest level with the traditions of human wisdom that prevailed up to the 17th century. To the modernists, modern man's rejection of Christianity was entirely the fault of a hopelessly entrenched, abstract, and desiccated theological tradition that was incapable of addressing his concerns. Yet, while there is some truth to the modernists' attribution of a "fortress mentality" (for good and ill) to the Church's behavior toward the modern world

---

[286] Peddicord, op. cit., p. 68.
[287] See Pope St. Pius X, Pascndi dominici gregis (1907) n. 5 on the difficulty of coming to a clear-cut definition of Modernism and for his own precise definition.

up to the Second Vatican Council, the modernist disregard for the inherent the dangers of modernity is like a suicidal man who *will* stand in traffic and resents anyone who tries to rescue him. But then the modernist is blind to those dangers; he does not believe that the first principles of modern thought are alien to Catholic principles and destructive of Catholic doctrine and so need to be defended. He resents the Church's interventions against modernism to rescue him because he doesn't believe he *needs* rescuing or that there is anything to be rescued from.

Immanentism was itself, as I have suggested, only a symptom of the modernist's conformity to modern thought at a still deeper level. At the bottom of all true theological modernism is the rejection of the realist principle of *aedequatio rei et intellectus*, the mind's conformity to reality. That rejection is the error at the root of modern philosophy from its nascence in Ockham's nominalism to its coming of age in Kant's metaphysical agnosticism. If the guardians of the Church's orthodoxy, like Reginald Garrigou-Lagrange, O.P. attacked the likes of Bergson and Blondel, it was because their influence was the main channel of modern philosophical principle, especially Kantian, into Catholic theological thought.

The errors of modern thought were not likely to remain confined to the rarified domain of the speculation of a few thinkers in the Church, but would certainly corrupt Catholic thought at every level if not discovered and refuted and their proponents disciplined. Garrigou-Lagrange understood, as did Pius X, that if the Catholic tradition of metaphysics is abandoned so inevitably would the Catholic system of ethics be abandoned with it. For there could be no rational immunity from the various diseases of modern thought if ethics is left without any sufficient ontological foundation. It must follow from a rejection of (Thomistic) metaphysical realism that our conception of the good has no foundation in being; and if it has no foundation in being, it can have no foundation in truth either, for the principle of the convertibility of truth and being is intrinsic to the perennial thought of the Church. If the good cannot be known as objectively real, it cannot be the object of knowledge but the stuff of mere shifting sentiment and desire. However firmly the early pioneering modernists may have held to the doctrine of the Church (and not all were as devout as Blondel), the philosophical principles from which their theological speculations proceeded undermined it. Faith without reason will wither on the vine.

Pieper[288] makes very clear the teaching of St. Thomas that what is first of all required of man before he can even perceive the good let alone perform it is that he *know* it. This can be so only if "the good presupposes the true." Blondel was right to suppose that mere rationality is insufficient, not only in respect of determining the will, but with respect to the work of the intellect too. "The first act of the will', says St. Thomas, 'is not due to the direction of reason, but to the

---

[288] See J. Pieper, *The Four Cardinal Virtues*, (New York: Harcourt, Brace & World, 1965), 23 – 25.

instigation of nature or of a higher cause."[289] But although God has made man for Himself and in His image and thus ineluctably oriented man to Himself (we may call this a kind of "grace" inherent in human nature by virtue of creation and thus a thing still given, even gratuitous), it remains that "the truth is the good of our knowing mind, upon which the mind fixes itself by nature."[290] In other words, while man is compelled by his nature in the order of intellect to know the truth of real things (this does not mean he necessarily unerringly finds it), it is not granted the mind to follow only its own light to the truth, that is by its own autonomous freedom. Yet, in so far as the mind can be enlightened by reason alone, the principle remains, which Blondel et al. denied, that the good of man consists in being in accord with reason, *bonum hominis est secundum rationem esse*.[291] And it must be added here in fairness to Blondel that "reason" comprises all modes perceiving reality not only the discursive. But let us also note with Pieper that "above all the *'reason'* of Christians perceives also the realities of faith" (my emphasis).[292] And as those realities are *objective*, so must our rational perception of them be.

To deny this is to fall prey to a kind of ethical voluntarism or pragmatism (Kant's legacy) which separates moral action from its roots in the cognition of reality. Immanentists suppose that by a philosophy of action à la Blondel one is

---

[289] Ibid., 23.
[290] Ibid.
[291] Ibid., 24.
[292] Ibid.

directed to the vital force behind man's knowledge of the truth. But in so far as they make volition and action as the primary mode of man's knowledge of God and the good, they have pulled the plug on the real dynamic of man's knowing, which is the mind's innate relation to being, to the real, and, hence, to knowledge of the truth (through pure cognition as well as and in conjunction with other modes of knowing). For this reason, Thomists have maintained that truth is determined formally by the mind's judgment in a process that begins necessarily in the direct apprehension of the real and, therefore, that the foundation of the ethical life is "reason perfected in the cognition of truth".[293]

The front-line opponents of modernism like Garrigou-LaGrange, who wished to debate modernists like Blondel, found them as obstinate as themselves. Behind all their arguments was a fundamental preference for Kant over St. Thomas or simply a rejection of Thomism, which amounted to much the same thing. Scholasticism was the real *bête noire* of the modernists. But Thomism in the 20th century comes in different varieties and some prefered a Thomism which has little to do with the Scholastic tradition.

The theologian, Marie-Dominique Chenu, O.P. (1895-1990), introduced the idea of the "historical Thomas" as distinct from the *faux* Thomas of Scholasticism's invention, a distortion, he insisted, of many centuries of misinterpretation. The genuine Thomas, according to

---

[293] Cf., Pieper, Ibid., 9.

Chenu's method of historical interpretation, was a creature of the 13th century. In the same way, according to the modernist's historical-critical method of biblical interpretation (as in that of the Jesus Seminar scholars), that Jesus -- whatever we may believe Him to be by *faith* – was *historically* a product of first-century Palestine. On this view, St. Thomas cannot be correctly understood outside of his historical context. The danger of Chenu's historicist method of interpreting Thomas was the same as the biblical method's interpretation of Jesus, that is, of rendering Thomism a dead artifact, a fossil of the Middle Ages. Whatever Chenu wanted to do for Thomism by his method, this was its effect, for it removed Thomism from any consideration of the truth or falsity of its propositions especially excluding the entire tradition of Thomist interpretation. The only thing of concern, then, to be demonstrated was whether or not a given position of the Thomist tradition would have been held explicitly by St. Thomas himself according to very strict historical criteria. Chenu was very adept at such demonstrations and rarely considered whether the position in question was true or false.[294]

What Chenu intended by his method, it appears, was to undermine what he called "Baroque Scholasticism",[295] by calling into question the truth of the principles of neo-Thomist philosophy at the root of "the official theological

---

[294] Cf., Peddicord, *op. cit.*, 109
[295] Cf., ibid. 106

ethos of Roman Catholicism". And given the highly charged atmosphere that prevailed since the publication of Pius X's encyclical, *Pascendi Dominici Gregis,* (1907), Rome's fierce reaction to Chenu's manifesto of sorts, *Une ecole de theologie*[296], from the heart of the Dominican order at Le Saulchoir, was understandable. Rome was clearly baited.

The neo-Thomist defenders of the scholastic tradition treated St. Thomas as the source of a "living tradition", of thought transmitted chiefly by the great Dominican commentators of the 16th century, theologians such as John of St. Thomas, Bañez, and Cajetan. The tradition was more than the words of St. Thomas but a body of wisdom acquired from their profound study and thus historical considerations were not their primary concern. The more important question for the neo-Thomist has always been whether a proposition follows directly from what St. Thomas wrote and thus attributable to Thomas -- *ad mentem sanci Thomae* -- and not whether St. Thomas explicitly said it or whether it can be demonstrated to be historically situated in his time and place and milieu. On such a principle (as old at least as the Middle Ages), it is reasonable to attribute to your authority that which you learned by direct study of him. But the principle, of course, does not justify misrepresentation or contradiction of the authority, which would negate the principle itself, nor does it presume inerrancy either in the author or in the tradition. Chenu et al.

---

[296] Chenu, Marie-Dominique, O.P. *Le Saulchoir: Une école de la théologie.* Paris: Etiolles, 1937. Reprinted in Une école de la théologie: Le Saulchoir, ed. G. Alberigo. Paris: Cerf, 1985.

criticized the scholastic tradition for its failure to understand the importance of history for theology – a *"candide ignorance de l'histoire"*.[297] While these critics doubtless had identified a fault in the tradition, they failed in an equal or greater degree to appreciate the dangers of historicism in their use of historical principles in theology. Some traditional Thomists, notably Etienne Gilson, were critical of the tradition for paying too little attention to the historical propositions of St. Thomas, but in pointing out the weakness of the tradition they did not reject it.

A tradition can be mistaken. Even Sacred Tradition, with the exception of its dogmatic teaching, is not infallible, though the fact does not diminish its authority. It is possible for an intellectual tradition to grow senescent and feeble-minded even moribund, not because it is old but because it is no longer intellectually vital. T.S. Eliot said of tradition that it cannot be inherited but must be obtained by great labor.[298] There are dangers, he observed, in maintaining a tradition: of "confusing the vital and the unessential, the real and sentimental", and of supposing tradition to be

---

[297] The better of the traditional Thomists, such as Garrigou-Lagrange, were in no way ignorant of the importance history to St. Thomas' method. Garrigou-Lagrange himself observed that Thomas, unlike Descartes, was deeply rooted in a variety of historical traditions of thought that included the Church Fathers, Doctors of the Church, and classical philosophy and made recourse to the history of errors in his objections. (Cf., Peddicord, *op. cit.*, 111 n.)

[298] Although Eliot was speaking of cultural not theological tradition, the principle nevertheless applies. Cf. "Tradition and the Individual Talent" in *The Sacred Wood: Essays on Poetry and Criticism* (London: Methune), 1920.

immutable or hostile to all change.[299] I might add to these the danger of insularity, of supposing that anything outside the tradition is wholly alien and of no value. These are dangers which obtain in any tradition and have been observed in neo-scholasticism by its friends as well as its enemies.

It is well known that the methods of teaching Thomistic theology and philosophy in many seminaries and universities in the Catholic world were, in general, rigid and mechanical, incommensurably inferior to the intellectual energy and acumen of the Common Doctor himself. The tradition had grown moribund in spite of (perhaps in some ways because of) the neo-scholastics' attempts to revive it. But the modernists and those influenced by them preferred to kill the patient than cure him. Garrigou-Lagrange himself must have been aware of the problem when he admonished his fellow Thomists that "one cannot follow St. Thomas by falling into a material literalism". But Garrigou-Lagrange understood, as did Pope St. Pius X, that for Thomism to remain true to St. Thomas and to the intellectual foundations of Catholic thought, certain basic theses must be acknowledged and adhered to. Hence, were the Twenty-four Thomistic Theses defended and insisted upon by Rome.[300] It may be, as many have argued, that the enforcement of

---

[299] T.S. Eliot, *After Strange Gods: A Primer of Modern Heresy* (New York: Harcourt Brace and Company), 1934, 18-19.

[300] "We admonish professors to bear well in mind that they cannot set aside St. Thomas, especially in metaphysical questions, without grave disadvantage". --Pope St. Pius X (1903-1914), *Pascendi Dominici Gregis*, September 8, 1907. The Theses were issued by Pope Pius X in 1914.

scholastic Thomism by this means was imprudent, but the abandonment of these theses in the teaching of Catholic philosophy and theology was immeasurably more so. They were the metaphysical basis of Catholic thought.

The opponents of the scholastic tradition of Thomism would have neither the baby nor the bathwater. They would have St. Thomas, but their Thomas would be the creation of a historicism born of philosophical principles that Thomas himself would have rejected. Their Thomas was a prisoner of his historical time and place. This, of course, *did nothing to make Thomism relevant to modern man.* For many who wished to make it relevant, it was necessary to redefine the essence of Thomism. This was largely the doing of the Dominican theologian, Edward Schillebeeckx (b. 1914 -), who maintained that the content of St. Thomas' theology was of "altogether secondary importance to his method and approach".[301] The Thomistic method was supposed to be not merely eclectic in one's sources, which St. Thomas undoubtedly was, but especially adaptive to the prevailing trends of thought. This assumes that St. Thomas adapted his thought to (especially) Aristotle's in order to render Christian thought up to date and in alignment with the best philosophy available. But this was *precisely the reverse of what Thomas was about.* Rather than adapting Christian thought to

---

[301] Cf. Romano Amerio, *Iota Unum, A Study of Changes in the Catholic Church in the 20th Century*, tr., Rev. Fr. John P. Parsons, (Kansas City, KS: Sarto House) 1996, 533. Schillebeeckx's admitted respect for St. Thomas' "method" strikes me as somewhat disingenuous or, at best, misleading; for Thomas' method was the scholastic dialectic of *disputationes* which could not be more alien to the modern modes of philosophical analysis.

Aristotle's, he was adapting Aristotle *inter alles* to Christian thought, taking whatever was useful, that is, whatever was true, to construct a Christian system of thought, founded not on any pagan philosophy, which nevertheless was indispensable, but ultimately on divine Revelation. It is a common misunderstanding to say that Aquinas "baptized" Aristotle; but it was rather more of a *conquest* than a baptism. St. Thomas appropriated all that was useful in the pagan philosopher to articulate and elucidate the whole tradition of Christian thought.

Modernity has long alienated faith from reason and as a result theology has been rendered irrelevant to science, now considered the sole repository of truth (in so far as the post-modern world still believes in the concept). But to St. Thomas, philosophy, while it was by definition a purely rational knowledge, was not on Christian grounds autonomous from theology which necessarily presupposes divine revelation. It was the essence of St. Thomas' project to, as Gilson, puts it, "explain how natural philosophy can enter into theology without destroying its unity."[302] St. Thomas stressed the fact that what God revealed to us in Scripture remains a unity even while it speaks of other things than God, natural things, men, animals, etc., knowledge of which does not transcend natural reason but are its proper objects. So, far from bringing Christian theology up to date by making it Aristotelian or by trying to

---

[302] E. Gilson, *The Philosophy of St. Thomas Aquinas*, (Random House: New York) 1956, 14

demonstrate that Aristotle's philosophy was Christian, both of which imply a divorce of theology from philosophy, Thomas was acting on the Christian principle that the truth is one. This principle is itself premised upon the fact that the organic knowledge of all things is ultimately related to God because it actually exists in God's knowledge of Himself.[303] Thus while its proper object is God and its source God's revelation of Himself, theology (as Thomas understood its purpose) directs all natural knowledge to the supernatural knowledge we have of God by revelation. Only on that ground did he appropriate the truths in Aristotle's philosophy to serve Sacred Science, under which he understood all philosophy to fall. It was not to serve any *independent* philosophical aim to explain the nature of things.

Certainly, if at the heart of Thomism there is no system of discrete theses but a mere methodological outlook, it could readily be adapted to modern thought, always assuming of course that modern thought holds the trump card in any dispute over Catholic doctrine. But to approach modern thought on that assumption is to try to get eggs from the fox. To make Thomism a mirror of modern thought is in effect a rejection of Thomism as it is a rejection of traditional philosophy.

The evidence of this rejection and its effects was clear even during the Council. Thomism, which enjoyed under the auspices of *Aeterni Patris* privileged accommodations in the

---

[303] Cf. Gilson, ibid.

course of philosophical studies in the Church's Program of Studies (*ratio studiorum*) for its seminaries, was effectually demoted to steerage class by Vatican II through the total silence of consiliar texts on *Aeterni Patris* and Thomism itself.[304] *Optatam Totius*, the Council's decree on the intellectual formation of the clergy, says nothing about Thomism, but mentions only the "perennially valid philosophical patrimony".[305] And the content of that patrimony was being settled not by the scholastic tradition but by the new philosophical pluralism.

Whatever else may be said of modern philosophy, or philosophical inquiry since Descartes, it is neither valid nor a patrimony, for it does not express traditional Catholic thought nor in any way constitute a Christian philosophy. While it is an open question what a Christian philosophy may be, it cannot be said that modern philosophy, which has demonstrably been at odds with Catholic principles and dogma, is any such thing. Neither does it constitute a tradition, for if "patrimony" means anything, it bespeaks a traditionary body of thought however variegated by conflicts between points of view. The history of modern philosophy has been a long series, not of a continuous development grounded on a fundamental unity, but of continuous revolution, one philosophical system radically overturning the next. It is unified only in the negative, in its rejection of metaphysical realism. Far from a unified view of

---

[304] Cf. Romano Amerio, *Iota Unum* (tr., Fr. John P. Parsons), (Kansas City, Missouri: Sarto House), 1996, p. 536.
[305] *Optatam Totius*, 15.

reality, its "pluralism" demonstrates rather a conceptual farrago. Whatever insights modern philosophy offers Christian thought, they are no more than *disiecta membra*, disjointed truths that form no consistent body of thought that has any part in the Church's perennial heritage. Thomism is the crown of the scholastic tradition, but also of the whole of the perennial inheritance of Catholic thought from the Fathers on down, in which the scholastic tradition itself, however imperfectly, participated. If a tradition is ever a prison, and for some it has been, it was never such for St. Thomas, who, like all greatly skilled thinkers in a tradition, saw beyond it, but could do so only by means of it, by looking out from its summit.

The rejection of St. Thomas' principles and fundamental notions can hardly be said to be a true and fruitful fidelity to the Common Doctor of the Church. The new pluralism attempted to make St. Thomas just one more fish in the pond by the audacious claim that St Thomas' own method demands that the true "Thomist" adapt his thought to the prevailing philosophies of the time. To suppose that St. Thomas himself was a pluralist of this type is to suppose a great deal about him that is simply not true, but one falsehood in particular is especially distorting; it is that he did not work within a tradition but was a kind of "free radical" among the immense variety of his sources.

The philosophical pluralism embraced by the Catholic theological community since the Council rejects the unity, as well as the principles, of thought that characterized scholasticism in favor of modern philosophical principles. It is an indifferentism that is hostile to the very idea of a perennially valid tradition of thought. It does not admit the possibility of philosophical certitude, having accepted the impossibility of a *science* of theology or the objective knowledge of transcendent reality. In so far as it has a right to the name at all, it is a disordered pluralism. True pluralism admits of a variety of points of view *within a tradition* because it is only within the continuity of a traditional mode of thought that any fruitful reasoning can take place. Outside is only a mob-like confusion of ideas, jostling, fighting one another unintelligibly; it is Babel.

It is a false notion of tradition that supposes it precludes conflict. The Christian theological tradition has been far from monolithic, but has always contained a considerable variety of theological schools and modes of thought, the Johannine, the Pauline, the Alexandrine, Augustinian, Thomist, Franciscan, etc. This is true not least of all in the putative uniformity of the High Middle Ages, where scholasticism, though dominant, vied with a variety of other schools. Within scholasticism itself were a number of contending elements: realists, nominalists, Averroists, the neo-Platonic Aristotelians. Medieval Scholasticism went far to preserve by its own pluralism the fullness of the Christian theological tradition. A "living tradition", Alasdair MacIntyre explains, is "an historically extended, socially embodied argument".[306] Michael Polanyi agrees that a "dynamic tradition", as he calls it, requires the possibility of internal dissent, even while the dissenter is rooted, as is the dissent itself, in a given tradition.[307] The terms of participation in a tradition are at once fiduciary *and* rational. Polanyi explains that all knowledge proceeds initially from belief, that is from an implicit trust in uncritically received convictions inherited from the linguistic, cultural, and historical realities in which one is embedded.[308] Thus, there is in any healthy participation in a tradition a necessary tension between submission to authority and a critical attention to all that one receives from that authority. In such a participation there is no room for fideism, which adherents of a tradition, especially in the Church, have often been accused of in the modern world. And as for the tension that inevitably obtains in a tradition between authority and the critical mind (both of which, by the way, may occur in the same person, St Thomas being an excellent example), far from being deleterious as is supposed by the modern disposition to (especially) intellectual authority, is, actually productive.

The two enemies of tradition in the modern world and thus enemies of Catholic principle have been and continue to be the rationalist objectivism of Enlightenment

---

[306] MacIntyre, *After Virtue: A Study in Moral Theory* (University of Notre Dame Press, 1984, 2nd edn.), 222.
[307] Cf. Mark T. Mitchell, "Michael Polanyi, Alasdair MacIntyre, and the Role of Tradition" in *Humanitas* 19, 1-2 (Spring-Fall 2006), 6.
[308] Ibid., 7

presumption or the subjectivism of post-modernism's despair -- the consequence of the prior presumption. The Enlightenment supposed that reason was opposed to tradition and vice versa. But the Enlightenment's epistemological objectivist demands, that all knowledge is the direct result of the application of a strict scientific methodology, was insupportable. Nietzsche's just critique of the Enlightenment rationalism's presumption was so far just as it declared its presumed objectivism a sham, a convenient falsehood uncritically and almost universally accepted. Reason was supposed to be unconditionally neutral ground and so necessarily independent of all traditions, that is of any received knowledge, of all cultural prejudice, most especially religious belief. But, as McIntyre has argued, "[w]e, whoever we are, can only begin enquiry from the vantage point afforded by our relationship to some specific social and intellectual past through which we have affiliated ourselves to some specific tradition of enquiry".[309] It is manifestly a fiction to suppose that knowledge can occur in a vacuum; that anyone can at once remain rational and question *all* of his premises. But the Enlightenment maintained the fiction that it could be done and the illusion that it was in fact doing it.

For nearly two hundred years Europe was thus almost entirely under the illusion of a great hoax, that scientific or empirical knowledge was the only real knowledge and all

---

[309] A. McIntyre, *Whose Justice? Which Rationality?* (Notre Dame: University of Notre Dame Press) 1988, 152

other claims were necessarily fraudulent. The same gave the idea of Progress its inevitability and from it made a religion of modernity. And even those who rejected the more outrageous tenets of the religion of modernity, were infected by its far subtler principles of thought that infected the intellectual air they breathed. Modernity is a formidable enemy to faith and morals even in its present senility and decrepitude, but in those heady days when scientific thought could credibly promise a new Eden, it is was all but irresistible. Even those like Blondel who rejected scientific rationalism and its disappointing blandishments, were nonetheless prey to the spirit of modernity, that modern thought was necessarily an advance on whatever traditional rationale it opposed. Thus could Kant be preferred to St. Thomas and, even for these critics of rationalism, the certitudes of empirical science could in a breath wipe away the certitudes of faith.

Thus many modernist theologians, even those with the best of intentions, were prey to a false dilemma; they presumed that modern thought was obligatory to any intellectually responsible person, because it superseded any tradition that contradicted it; and correspondingly they supposed tradition to be necessarily hidebound and destructive of intellectual honesty and objectivity, for they had accepted, along with most men of their age, the Enlightenment fiction of the absolute objectivity of reason. It was this epistemological fiction that, more than anything else, led them to reject not only the concept of tradition, but more importantly the corresponding concept of authority, without which tradition has no force or continuity. The Enlightenment "encyclopedist tradition" (as MacIntyre calls it[310]) had learned from Kant that if one is to be rational he has to emancipate himself from all authority.[311] But the "heresy" of its objectivism (that all genuine rational inquiry occurs in a "vacuum" of total factual objectivity, unaffected by anything other than "reason" alone) infected not only the overt modernist who was inclined to jettison the scholastic tradition of Thomism, but, ironically, also many in the Church who sought to preserve it.

Long before the theological trends of thought we call "modernism", the influence of Enlightenment thought was already infecting Catholic thought by way of apologists' attempts to defend the ancient religion from the attacks of its Enlightenment critics on their own terms by using modern science and modern philosophy, which they had imbibed in the waning of scholasticism. Cartesian philosophy, we will recall, was taught in universities throughout Europe. This was so, even while it lost its influence at the highest levels of philosophical inquiry. Its popularity was largely due to its complete rejection of scholasticism. This made it very appealing to Protestants, who, perhaps more than many Catholics at that time, rejoiced in its demise. The influence of Christian Wolff (1679 – 1754), a disciple of Leibniz, who wrote a comprehensive course of Philosophy that was the

---

[310] See Chapter 7.
[311] Cf. McIntyre, *Three Rival Versions of Moral Inquiry*, (Notre Dame: University of Notre Dame Press, 1989), 64.

standard text in many German universities, had effected the separation of experimental science from rational philosophy.[312]

Hence, theologians of every Christian denomination in the early 19th century struggled to make some accommodation with the triumphant rationalism of the Enlightenment by reformulating the central Christian doctrines to render them acceptable according to the canons of that intellectual culture.[313] In Catholic theological culture, many philosophers and theologians defended orthodox positions against their Kantian critics by naively adopting Kantian principles and using Kantian terms to clarify what were originally Thomistic and Augustinian positions and distorting them in the process.[314]

One such philosopher theologian was Antonio Rosmini Serbati (1797-1855). Rosmini, in trying to defend and articulate a Thomistic epistemology of our knowledge of transcendent reality, conceded too much to Kantian principles, arguing that as knowledge consists in more than the apprehension of particular things, empirically given to the senses, the human subject brings to his apprehension of them the *a priori* and universal idea of being. This *a priori* idea enables the mind to transform the sense data of individual things into universal truths. But the idea of being

---

[312] Cf. J. Weisheipl, O.P., "The Revival of Thomism: An Historical Survey", published online at http://www.domcentral.org/study/default.htm .
[313] Cf. *ibid.*, 69.
[314] Cf. *ibid.*, 70.

is not formed like all other ideas, by abstraction from what the mind empirically receives; rather it is presented to the mind by God acting upon the mind.[315]

The argument bears, however, an essentially Kantian character and is contrary to Thomistic realism, fundamental to which is that our idea of being, the *ratio entis*, results from the existing object itself acting primarily upon the passive subject after which begins the mind's activity in the apprehension of necessary and universal truths.[316] Our knowledge of reality then begins in sensation by which the knower comes into contact with self-manifestly real things. Thus it is from real things and our sensible experience of them, from their acting upon us as real things, that the mind derives its primary abstract concepts (abstract because they are *abtracted* from real things). This includes concepts of transcendental reality, and not the other way around as Kant concluded. By employing a Kantian argument, Rosmini failed both philosophically and theologically: it was neither consistently Kantian nor theistic. As MacIntyre has pointed

---

[315] Cf. *ibid.*

[316] Modern Thomists dispute among themselves the precise definition of being. But I have presented here the view of what is called Existential Thomism (expounded by notables such as Gilson and Maritain) as distinct from the two other schools, Aristotelian Thomism and Transcendental Thomism. The difference between the Aristotelian Thomism and Existential Thomism is comparatively insignificant, so far as the question of modernity is concerned, in that they both follow an *a posteriori* epistemology in that both posit that knowledge begins with the knower's contact in sensation with self-manifestly real things; but the difference between both and Transcendental Thomism is profound considering that it follows an *a priori* post-Kantian epistemology. (Cf., "John Knasas on Thomist Metaphysics Past, Present, and Future: an Interview" at www.innerexplorations.com/index.html)

out, Kant rightly understood that within the cognitive structures of the mind no *true* knowledge of God could obtain. So, identifying God with the universal being apprehended *a priori* by the mind was only another kind of pantheism.[317] Rosmini's failure was inevitable; for the standards of Catholic thought and the standards of modernity are at bottom mutually exclusive. His mistaken use of Kant to render Catholic theology acceptable to modern thought presaged the same mistake made by much of early twentieth-century modernism and Catholic thought since Vatican II, whether it is Blondel's use of Bergson or Rahner's use of Heidegger.

Rosmini was not the only influential Catholic theologian in the first half of the 19th century to owe so much to Kant and post-Kantian idealism. There were others, like Vincento Gioberti, Anton Günther, and George Hermes, who together had a tremendous influence within Catholic ecclesiastical and educational institutions.[318] Hermes, for one, was the most distinguished and influential Catholic thinker in Germany, who "demonstrated" the truth of Catholicism from within the Kantian system as it was the prevailing philosophy in Germany at the time. Hermes' theological rationalism was finally condemned as subversive of the Catholic faith and placed on the index by Pope Gregory in 1835. Günther (1783-1863), rejected Scholasticism and attempted to demonstrate the transcendence of God by

---

[317] Cf., *ibid.*, 70-71.
[318] Cf., *ibid.*, 72

means of Hegelian forms of thought, against the Hegelian pantheism that was spreading in Germany and taking the place of Kantian idealism. Günther's Christian-Hegelianism became a broad movement in mid-nineteenth-century Germany, carrying with it many very distinguished Catholics. It was taught in nearly all the German universities.[319] Günther's system too was eventually placed on the Index, in 1857. But by then the damage was done. Günther himself, a devout and pious priest, willingly submitted to the censure of the Holy Office under Pius the IX, but his many followers did not comply.

With Leo XIII's mandate in *Aeterni Patris*, to give St. Thomas the signal position in Catholic theological studies, the expectation was that, by reestablishing Thomism, the post-Kantian and Hegelian[320] influences in Catholic theological culture would be quashed. Leo XIII was well informed about the serious errors that these zealous but philosophically ill-prepared apologists had been spreading in the Church and understood better than most the need for a sound Christian philosophy to meet the challenge of modernity. But the influence of Kantian structures of thought already introduced through Rosmini *et alis* in the first half of the century had rendered the intellectual soil in the second half a deficient culture for Thomism to flourish

---

[319] Cf. Weisheipl, p.5.
[320] Some believe that rather than post- Kantianism, it was the Hegelian influence in the Church through the work of scholars like Günther that was largely responsible for modernism. But I have here adopted the opinion of those, such as Kranak, Knasas, and MacIntyre, who favor the view that Kantian epistemology is the root cause.

in. While there was no little willingness to obey the pope's mandate, it had become impossible to interpret St. Thomas consistently.

The difficulty, then, was not the rejection of Thomism, as happened later, but the generation of a variety of rival Thomisms.[321] Out of the soil fertilized with a Kantian epistemology grew not one but many "Thomisms" and what resulted was not a unified theological culture but one in which modernism could, it seems, only flower.

---

[321] See A. MacIntyre, *ibid*, *p. 73 et seq.* for a thorough treatment of this phenomenon on which I have based mytreatment of the subject.

IX

St. Thomas and Catholic Tradition

ore even than the influence of Rosmini and
company in insinuating in many Catholic
theologians a certain post-Kantian epistemological
outlook --though still *in defense* of Catholic orthodoxy -- was
the influence of Joseph Kleutgen (1811-1883) on the way in
which St. Thomas was understood. He was "the single most
important influence upon the drafting of *Aeterni Patris*".[322]
But, as MacIntyre explains, the effect of Kleutgen's
interpretation of St. Thomas was more significant in the way
Leo's encyclical was read and implemented than in the text
itself.[323]

Kleutgen was a Thomist who understood better than most
men of his time that a rift had occurred in the history of
philosophical thought, dividing modern thought from all
that preceded it in ancient and medieval civilization. He

---

[322] MacIntyre, *ibid*, 73.
[323] Ibid.

locates the rift where anyone would look for it, in the philosophy of Descartes. That is where it is most obvious and (to Catholics) least controversial. But the rift came earlier and much more subtly with late scholasticism and particularly with those Jesuit interpreters of St. Thomas. Led by Suarez, these interpreters, who were some of Thomas' immediate successors in the scholastic tradition, failed to appreciate the ways in which St. Thomas' thought "transcended the limitations" of the Aristotelian and Augustinian traditions in which he worked[324] (it is a mark of Thomas' extraordinary genius that he could work in several traditions at once, one might say he worked *above* them). Kleutgen, who was, like Suarez, a Jesuit, supposed an almost complete identity between Suarez's thought and that of Thomas, but he had grossly overrated the disciple's indebtedness to the actual thought of the master. Suarez wanted a theology that could meet the reformers on their own ground and was thus lead to mix the metaphysics of St. Thomas with non-Thomistic principles. That confusion of Thomistic realism and non-realist principles made Suarez's thought in some ways more akin to the late twentieth-century analytical metaphysicians than to the Thomism Leo XIII enjoined the Church to embrace.[325] So, Kleutgen blindly

---

[324] Ibid. St. Thomas was in dispute with two groups: the Augustinians, on the one hand, represented by the Franciscans and secular teachers; and, on the other, radical Aristotelian naturalists, whose teachings were very difficult if not impossible to reconcile with Christian orthodoxy. But Thomas did not merely ignore these traditions and then proceed around them, but found a position that made peace with both. See John Haldane, "Thomism and the Future of Catholic Philosophy", *New Blackfriars* 80 (938), 1999
[325] Cf. J. Haldane, *op. cit.*, p. 4.

followed Suarez, thinking him a faithful guide to an understanding of St. Thomas. Consequently, brilliant as Kleutgen was, his was a seriously uncritical use of tradition.

The problem for later Catholic theology and for the effectiveness of *Aeterni Patris*, was that Suarez "both in his preoccupations and in his methods, was already a distinctively modern thinker, perhaps more authentically than Descartes, the founder of modern philosophy".[326] Descartes was, after all, trained by Jesuits who had been influenced by Suarez.[327] Suarez taught that the proper object of metaphysics was the objective concept of being, which to him meant the thing (which may or may not exist) *as conceived in the mind* rather than the thing in itself.[328] His doctrine is understood to be "a bridge between scholastic and modern philosophy", a further step (after Ockham's nominalism) toward the subjectivization of metaphysics which culminated in Kantian idealism.

Suarez's rendering of St. Thomas, as MacIntyre explains, was such that it seemed to Kleutgen helpful to apply Cartesian principles to understand Thomas's supposed theory of knowledge. But Thomas had no theory of knowledge as such. Thomas' purpose was not to come to epistemological conclusions, but to describe and clarify concepts and to analyze problems that occur within the

---

[326] MacIntyre, *ibid.*, 73.
[327] Ibid., 75.
[328] Cf., "Suárez, Francisco (1548-1617)" in *A Companion to Epistemology*, eds. Jonathan Dancy and Ernst Sosa, (Cambridge, Mass: Blackwell Reference) 1992.

Aristotelian and Augustinian traditions of explaining how the mind moves to the achievement of truth. One can come at a Thomistic epistemology only indirectly, that is by way of his metaphysics (which is where any epistemology must begin), with which it is inextricably interwoven. All knowledge, according to Thomas, begins necessarily with being (*esse*), with what is, not with mental concepts which, for knowledge to be possible, must originate with the mind's direct apprehension of real objects.

It is worth noting here that scholastic Thomism's disregard for the subjective in human experience renders that theory, in the view of modern philosophy, an ineffectual instrument. But if St. Thomas, or any other scholastic philosopher, did not regard the subjective, it was because subjectivity was inherently irrelevant to his theological project which was the elucidation of the *objective* reality of God, His creation, and particularly man's relation to Him. The field of modern philosophy called Epistemology would lead us to suppose that our subjectivity is very important indeed, but epistemology is a peculiarly modern preoccupation, if it is not an obsession. Descartes' dualism of mind/body gave birth to "subjectivity" a philosophical problem. But it is a problem, as are many problems, created by an error. Medieval philosophers didn't reject or ignore the subjective because they failed to see the "I" of the subject, but because the supposed dichotomy between subject and object had yet to be invented and so the question of subjectivity had little or no interest to them. Their preoccupation was with *objective* reality. Modern man is caught in the trap of subjectivity because he has disregarded the philosophical premises upon which alone reality can be *known*. If he is to be helped out of his dilemma, it will not do for Catholic thought to dismiss those premises.

Kleutgen, influenced as he was by Suarez, misidentified Thomas' real focus and concern with respect to the mind's knowing and then constructed arguments (which had no place in Thomas's own scheme of thought) in answer to questions modern post-Kantians were asking, but which Thomas himself never did. The result was that Thomism appeared to be just another (unsatisfactory) way of addressing the concerns of Cartesian and post-Cartesian epistemology, which rejected the metaphysical realism that was the essence of Thomas' understanding of knowledge.[329]

The effect of Kleutgen's error does not occur in *Aeterni Patris* itself, in which nowhere are epistemological questions adverted to, for it cites, not Suarez, but the other of St. Thomas' great commentators, Cajetan, a Dominican and, whereas Cajetan's own interpretation of St. Thomas is, as we have noted, very possibly flawed, his mistakes were not epistemological. But Kleutgen's' mistake had led those who followed him to make epistemological concerns central in their understanding and use of Thomism and in so doing, "doomed Thomism to the fate of all philosophies which give priority to epistemological questions: the indefinite

---

[329] Cf., *ibid.*, 75

multiplication of disagreement."[330] And thus, by being made to run on the slippery modern ground of epistemological bafflement, Thomism falls into the same irresolvable contentiousness that has afflicted modern philosophy since Descartes parted ways entirely with realist metaphysics.

Epistemology is a characteristically modern mode of philosophical inquiry. It is a preoccupation that results when metaphysical realism, which is rooted in theism, is abandoned and knowledge becomes not merely a matter of description of the mind's encounter with being, but a problem to be solved or, rather, to be endlessly debated. There is no solution to the "problem" of knowing, which modern philosophy has invented for itself, because there is no possibility of *knowing* the solution if it were presented, for the actual problem is the mind doubting its own ability to apprehend reality. Epistemology, as treated in modern philosophy, is like taking out your eyes to look at them and then concluding that they must be defective. By inventing the problem of epistemology and the mode of inquiry to address it, modern philosophy destroyed philosophy as a science, that is, as a way of knowledge and understanding of reality and so as a way of wisdom.

Making Thomism just another ingredient in the stew that is modern philosophy had not only frustrated the efficacy of *Aeterni Patris* in engendering theological unity, but made it an unwitting agent of the philosophical and theological

---

[330] MacIntyre, *ibid.*

confusion it was meant to redress. But Leo XIII's encyclical was not to be wholly ineffectual or only the occasion of trouble. It was responsible for generating among Thomists projects which over time have retrieved an historical (as distinct from historicist, *a la* Chenu) understanding of what St. Thomas himself said, wrote, and did, and thus correcting a defective tradition.[331] For 20th century Catholic theology, there was a very significant difference between those scholars, such as Etienne Gilson and Martin Grabbman, who were attentive to the historical dimensions of Thomas' thought without abrogating the scholastic tradition, and those like Maréchal, Rousselot, and even (on occasion and uncharacteristically) Maritain,[332] who tried to make Thomas all things to all men. They constructed Thomisms custom-made for the epistemological (or political in Maritain's case) positions they were confronting. And it must be said that the work of those historical scholars of neo-Thomism were also a corrective to those Thomists who, following Suarez, ignored the historical aspect altogether and treated Thomas' thought as a "finished system", and not as the culmination of a tradition which continues nevertheless to be an "ongoing enterprise of enquiry".[333] It was a tradition that was *open-ended* because it was, as St. Thomas worked in it, a living tradition to which both classical writers as well as the Fathers of the Church contributed, and to all of whom was St. Thomas indebted. He did not stand independent of them,

---

[331] Cf., *ibid.*, p. 77.
[332] Cf., *ibid.* p. 76.
[333] *Ibid.*, p. 74.

as Suarez and Kleutgen supposed, but worked *within* the Aristotelian and Augustinian traditions; his accomplishment was otherwise impossible.[334]

If Thomism is to address the profound problems and questions of modernity, as *Aeterni Patris* intended it, it can only do so by being itself unencumbered by the confusions that beset modern thought and by being a mode of inquiry that itself does not formulate dogma but uses the revealed truths, both natural and supernatural, to give an intelligible account of reality and from that account deduce what is man's moral duty.

The kind of pluralism that has dominated Catholic thought for the last 40 years is founded on a primary assumption expressed in Karl Rahner's dictum, "There is no getting beyond Kant" (*Nicht hinter Kant zurück*). It has been assumed that what Descartes began, by wiping away the entire philosophical tradition since Plato and starting over again, and what was completed by Kant in the abrogation of metaphysics, was *necessary*. Hence, the problems peculiar to modern philosophy, problems which are irresolvable because they undermine the very foundations of knowledge and so of philosophy itself, are the ineluctable result of a supposedly *correct* accounting of reality. But from Descartes on there has been absolutely no agreement on any given accounting. What has driven philosophical inquiry for 400 years has been profound disagreement about the

---

[334] Cf., *ibid.*, pp. 74, 75.

fundamental questions of being and knowing. The only continuity in modern philosophy has been, broadly speaking, a general agreement that Descartes' rejection of the Aristotelian tradition and the realism inherent in it was necessary.

Some theologians, like Henri de Lubac and Hans Urs von Balthasar, have parted ways with Kant and particularly the likes of Rahner who tried to merge Kant's epistemology with St. Thomas' theology of grace and with such cross breeding gave us his "supernatural existential", a kind of theological freak.[335] But even de Lubac and Balthasar were largely reacting against scholasticism and neo-Thomism, which carried on the tradition into the 20th century. They renounced the scholastic tradition, to which they thought themselves superior; but this only distorted their own understanding of St. Thomas whom they claimed to follow. At very least, de Lubac and Balthasar could not have judged their own interpretations of the Common Doctor's theology except by working, as did Thomas himself, within the scholastic tradition rather than by rivaling it or undermining it. They and Gilson[336] may have been right that Cajetan was wrong in his interpretation of St. Thomas, but to admit so much is not to declare Cajetan and the entire neo-Thomist

---

[335] Cf., Edward T. Oakes, S.J. *First Things* (October, 2007) in Letters to Editor.
[336] Ibid. "Etienne Gilson . . . claimed of Cajetan's commentary on the *Summa* that 'as much remained [of Thomas' doctrine on being and the natural desire for God] as remains of a watch when the spring has been taken out.' He further claimed that Cajetan never brought to bear 'any disinterested historical curiosity' and that 'the distinctions he introduced so skillfully are not directed to making St. Thomas's thought clearer but to substituting his own.'"

tradition *irrelevant*. Although Gilson did not make this mistake, De Lubac and Balthasar, not content to merely correct him, turned Cajetan *against* Thomas. This is not the way to practice something as inherently traditionary as theology.

As long as there persists the general belief among Catholic theologians that there is no way out of modern philosophical problems and that the only way to preserve faith and to elicit it in the modern world is to turn inward, to make our subjectivity the primary source of faith in a transcendent reality, there will be no escape from modernism and the other debilitating effects of modernity upon the Church. It was the premise of *Aeterni Patris* that there is a way out of the prison of modern thought and that St. Thomas and the metaphysical realism of the scholastic tradition is that way of escape. But don't let us fool ourselves. Modernity is a rebellion against God by a civilization that *prefers* its pretended autonomy in addition to a philosophical mistake. The return to God and the restoration of faith must be then, an act of the will as well as an act of reason, and not only for the philosopher but for everyman. Faith must be sustained by reason, which need not be abstract and learned ratiocination, for man is by nature rational and so the act of faith is at once rational and volitional.

Let no one suppose that Europe forsook Christianity because of a philosophical error. Nothing about Descartes' thinking was compelling; there was no necessity in his forsaking a tradition of metaphysics 2000 years old.

Whatever were his reasons and his motivations (and pride doubtless played no small part), when all is said and done, he *wanted* to be done with Aristotle and Scholasticism. So did his successors, who would not return to that tradition, and even those who found Descartes' own system unconvincing. To say that scholasticism had seemed to discredit itself tells only half the story and that with some distortion. Certainly, Scholasticism was already in some confusion by the 16th century, but what drove it into exile and irrelevance was a violent revolution of thought directed against it (and to some extent within it). A tradition, when it grows rigid and mechanical, cannot be reduced entirely to that state for it is in the nature of tradition to retain its living past, especially in a literate culture. The memory lives, even when the tradition does not. There is never an excuse then for wholly and uncritically abandoning a tradition in need of reform, when it has within itself and, equally important, has external to it (but not in contradiction with it) that which can be used to restore it to life. This is precisely what St. Thomas did for scholasticism when he used the conflicting Aristotelian and Augustinian schools to forge a new understanding of Catholic thought that jibed with both.

But if modern philosophy is a prison the doors are locked on the *inside*. Many Catholic intellectuals suppose that modern philosophy is the progressive development of philosophical inquiry since antiquity, Descartes being the great watershed after medieval philosophy broke down under the weight of an insupportable skepticism. The disunity of modern philosophy is called "pluralism" and is considered necessary to the fulfillment of the modern philosophical enterprise which is itself necessarily open-ended (in a different sense than the Thomist tradition), since truth and reality are no longer objects of philosophical inquiry.

The trouble, then, is not just getting "beyond Kant", which can only be preliminary, but going back to the Thomas of the scholastic tradition and thus to the tradition itself. Admittedly, some responsible orthodox theologians have used Kantian forms of thought in subtle and complex ways to render their thought more palatable to the modern intellect; de Lubac was one of these. I am not interested here in untangling that web, but the danger should be plain to see in explaining Catholic truth, by playing, however cautiously, to the prejudices of those who profoundly reject that truth. Gilson has warned us in *Methodical Realism* that it is fatal to attempt to argue with an idealist on his own terms.[337] Yet the principal question is not how to use Kant or Bergson or Wittgenstein, but how to understand and use St Thomas *in the teeth of* these thinkers and their philosophies. It was, after all, the rejection of scholasticism that made modern philosophy the problem that it has become. Hence, it is a false dilemma that the Catholic intellectual feels himself to be on the horns of: the choice between an "irrelevant" orthodoxy and the insoluble problems of modern thought.

---

[337] E. Gilson, *Methodical Realism*, (Front Royal: Christendom Press, 1996), p.98.

The operable but untenable solution has been an indiscriminate philosophical and theological pluralism; but such a "separate but equal" arrangement is no more that an expedient for "dialogue". Apart from the supreme usefulness of understanding the enemy, the beneficial uses of modern philosophy will be clear only after we have learned our philosophy over again, metaphysics in particular, from the Common Doctor and the larger Catholic tradition. But, of course, that cannot happen until we first understand who *is* our enemy, that it is not and never has been scholasticism but modernity. It will then be plain to see which of the two is truly irrelevant.

It is almost paradoxical that error is so often the unintended consequence of reform, especially when reform is proposed as necessarily involving the destruction of tradition, even, as in the case of the *Ressourcement* movement of the mid-20th century, when it is proposed with the aim of restoring an older tradition. That movement, begun by Jesuit theologians, Jean Daniélou, Henri de Lubac, and Henri Bouillard, called for the return of Catholic theology to it's Scriptural and patristic *fons et origo*. Reviving the tradition of patristic theology with its profound attention to Scripture was a laudable goal and those who carefully guarded Catholic theology from modernism, such as Garrigou-LaGrange and Michel Labourdette praised the effort. It was not the positive aims of the movement that those guardians set themselves against, but its negative and destructive aims and the underlying rationale of the project which was to break neo-scholasticism's hold on Catholic theology by utterly discrediting it.

Alarming indeed was these new theologians' claim that the Latin and Greek Fathers exhibited certain affinities or corollaries to modern thought that were absent in scholastic theology. Whether such an unlikely reading of the Fathers was well-founded is certainly questionable. Understandably, one would suspect that they saw in the Fathers what they wanted to see, allowing their endearment to certain modern ideas and modes of thought as well as, perhaps especially, their fierce antipathy to scholasticism to lead them away from a just interpretation.[338] And seeming to confirm such suspicions were statements like Bouillard's that "a theology that does not belong to the present (*actuelle*) is false."[339]

It would not have occurred to these theologians that in abandoning the scholastic tradition it was ignoring an essential source of Catholic theology – whatever its faults – that has been at the heart of the development of Catholic thought from the 12th to the 20th century. They would not acknowledge, because they would not see, the certain continuity of medieval scholasticism and the Fathers. They believed that neo-Thomism as rendered by scholasticism was incapable of speaking to contemporary man or, better, the contemporary *intellectual*. They were also convinced that

---

[338] Cf. Peddicord, *loc. cit.*, 142-150.

[339] Admittedly, Bouillard and others went farther toward modernism than Daniélou or de Lubac were inclined to for in their work they completely revised or "updated" the dogmatic formulations of the Council of Trent (Cf. Peddicord, *ibid.*, 152-4).

only that those forms of thought could speak to contemporary man that were informed by the modern principles of historicity and subjectivity, to which they were themselves endeared. That these principles obtain in, say, the writings of St. Augustine is undeniable; but that they, therefore, render Augustine more acceptable or even more intelligible to the modern mind and modern intellectual prejudice is almost fanciful. That historical consciousness and subjectivity are important to modernity as well as to Christianity no one denies. But because modernity makes these principles fundamental conditions of truth and meaning, they have in modern thought significance so utterly different from what obtains in perennial Catholic thought that they are almost alien concepts.

That mere historical consciousness, for instance, cannot answer for objective truth, is evident in Machiavelli, that patriarch of modernity, who rejected Aristotle's metaphysically and ethically founded political principles for a well-ordered polis, in favor of the study of historical origins. There he found by careful selection that city-states had been founded and regimes changed by violent conspiracies and accordingly defined political life as being normatively violent and unjust, thus regarding the "good" of politics as being founded in evil.[340] Machiavelli could only have reached this conclusion by substituting historical origins of political order for its end or finality, which Aristotle and the Church taught to be justice.

---

[340] Cf. P. Manent, *loc. cit.*, 14

The dangers of subjectivity to theological inquiry are perhaps obvious to anyone already wary of the problems with Kantian epistemology. But it is worth noting here that it is, of course, necessary to distinguish between our experience of God through faith (*fides qua*) and the Faith of the Church handed down from the Apostles (*fides quae*), that is, *what* is to be believed. While that may be an obvious distinction, the essence of it has been ignored or repudiated by modernists. For the essence of that distinction is, I suggest, that between the "map" one is following (to borrow an analogy from C.S. Lewis) and knows to be accurate and the actual terrain through which the map is guiding him. If the Church has given us the theological map, the Deposit of Faith and her magisterial reflection on it over millennia under the auspices of the Holy Spirit, then there can be no radical autonomy of theology from revelation as the objective data of the faith and which our experience must follow (or we must lose our way). To suppose that the traveler draws the map as he goes according to his experience of the actual terrain is absurd, for only the map can tell him where to go and is provided not to show him the contours of the land, hills, lakes, valleys, and mountains, etc., for those things he will see inevitably, but to mark the way *through* them to another country, which cannot be reached without it.

The obligation of those who find a tradition inadequate to accommodate a different but valuable tradition of thought is to accommodate the new to the old and vice versa rather than destroy the old to adopt the new. The problem with the Ressourcement movement in Catholic theology is that in its desire to return to the ancient sources of the Church, it ignores the Middle Ages (except as a subject of purely historical interest) in which scholasticism grew up and thus, by design, eliminates a tradition it finds unpalatable. It is as though scholasticism were at odds with and a disruption of the ancient tradition of the Church (of the Western Church at least) rather than an accommodation of it. It is possible if not probable that the Ressourcement movement would have born more and better fruit if it had occurred at a different period in the Church's history. But it occurred at a time when modernism had become a strong, though still underground, current in the Church.

Neo-scholasticism (particularly, its dominant school, neo-Thomism), the new theology's immediate bugbear, was the direct descendant of the scholastic tradition. Whatever its deficiencies and however badly it may have been rendered in many (by no means all) the manuals of theology, particularly moral theology, it was a valuable resource of Catholic theology. But its modernist detractors see or wish to see only its deficiencies. To the fair-minded critic, it must be said, even the "deficiencies" had the virtue of being theologically true, if somewhat naïve psychologically.

Even sound theologians like de Lubac were modernist in at least one sense: they were revolutionaries with respect to their particular *bête noire* of neo-scholasticism, which had become perhaps a bit too precious to them. And so it was ironic, at least in de Lubac's case, who was a great student of the Middle Ages and had a great appreciation for medieval expression, that the scholastic tradition should have been rejected without remainder. It is typical of revolutionaries to prefer to destroy than to reform. With de Lubac, its wholesale destruction may have been unintentional, but such was the ineluctable effect of his kind of opposition when given its head. In the epigraph of his controversial book, *Surnaturel*, he says: "Buried under five centuries of deposits, ignorance of itself is the most serious ill from which Scholasticism is suffering. To cure it, let us listen to the counsel of history." De Lubac would have history judge tradition, and presumably condemn it. But if tradition is anything, it is the past living (sometimes barely) in the present, as T.S. Eliot well understood. It is *history* that is "dead" in so far as it is a mere abstraction, the mere idea of the past rather than its living effects. So, de Lubac had it upside down and backward, which is why he and his movement were willing to do something as paradoxical as destroy a tradition to revive the past.

Of all that can be said to define theological modernism, it is a rejection of or inattention to the principles of metaphysical realism. This was Blondel's error of substituting his Kantian principle of *conformitas mentis et vitae* for the Thomistic and scholastic principle of *adaequatio rei et intellectus*. But there can be no adequate substitution of the mind for reality as there is no substituting (I don't say *preferring*) something imagined for something true. While

Kant's philosophical system as a whole has gone the way of all modern philosophical systems, his epistemology or idealism has become the foundation of all modern thought, thus making what was once a conscious rejection in the western mind of Catholic principles into an unconscious habit. Idealism is a kind of philosophical blindness; it is like shining the flashlight into one's own eyes to see -- or better: like *closing* one's eyes to see.

The very fact that the new theologians could not see the fundamental problem with Kant's epistemology, and especially with Blondel's use of it, for any possible orthodox understanding of Catholic theology indicated their fundamental incompetence to pronounce judgment on neo-scholasticism which could see the fundamental problem (while it may be admitted that many neo-scholastics did not understand it as clearly as could be desired). They who thought themselves best suited philosophically and theologically to engage the modern world were in fact the least qualified. They insisted on demonstrating either that Catholic dogma was both rationally and historically admissible as true by modern intellectual criteria or, despairing of those criteria to demonstrate anything as true, they wished to show merely that Catholic dogma could be rendered *meaningful* to modern western culture at an almost purely subjective level. Without ignoring the subjective dimension of religious experience, theology must elucidate the truth *as received*.

The purpose of theology, even speculative theology, is to illuminate the teachings of the Church under her auspices as the visible presence of Christ in the world, Who speaks to the world through her. That is at once a rational and a mystical, or supra-rational enterprise, a collaboration of reason and faith. Such collaboration, however mystical or rational, cannot be conducted independently of the Church's divine authority. In so far as theology is mystical (as scholastics had always to be reminded), because of the mystery of grace's operation through nature (in this case the intellect to illuminate it), the truths of the faith cannot be rendered with mathematical or compelling certitude; if they could be, the act of faith would be unnecessary. Theology is not revelation; it is not the perfect articulation of revealed truth. The fullness of truth will always be greater than theology can render it and so will always be in a somewhat paradoxical relationship to the act of faith, because although faith depends on its making revealed truth intelligible, faith is nevertheless anterior and superior to it as a cause is to its effect. But in so far as theology is a rational endeavor, because it would otherwise be unintelligible, it proceeds by rational argument, which depends necessarily on the general principles of rational discourse. If we accept the Aristotelian and not the eliminative or exclusive modern definition of science, we must acknowledge that theology *is* a science, that it effects real knowledge, because it intends to determine the nature and properties of the articles of the Christian faith.[341] Like all sciences, the practice of theology is

---

[341] This conforms to Aristotle's definition: "scire est cognoscere causam

to draw conclusions from principles by which it arrives at certain knowledge. But it is a peculiar science; because theology's formal principles are divinely revealed.

In so far as theology is dependent upon rational principles and is necessarily interested in the nature of reality, it is the Thomistic contention that metaphysics is indispensable to the task of theology. After all, philosophically, God is Primary Being, Absolute Uncontingent Reality. The one thing to be absolutely taken for granted in all thinking is the fact of being, the sheer existence of things. Reality – what is – is nothing less than astonishing and to account for it is the first task of philosophy, for, as Aristotle said, philosophy begins in wonder. But theology is the higher science because, as it is concerned with Absolute Uncontingent Reality, it subsumes philosophy. The philosophical enterprise is inherently speculative because it relies upon reason alone to understand the real. But it is not so with theology, which, while necessarily rational, relies primarily upon revelation, a Source of truth beyond reason. There is, then, a healthy skepticism that obtains in philosophy that cannot in theology.

Yet even in philosophy there is no place for the radical skepticism that extends to first principles, which is inherent in modern philosophical inquiry. Since the death of philosophy as a science, as a way of knowledge of reality, certitude has shifted to empirical science where it has been

---

propter quam res est et non potest aliter se habere" (*Posterior Analytics*, 1. I, lect. 4). See Peddicord, *loc. cit.*, p.141.

given exclusive rights to that name. But modernism in theology turns the proper relation of philosophy to empirical science and both to theology on its head. It is rather empirical science that is subordinate to philosophy, because it depends (even when it denies any dependence outside its own method) on the metaphysical assurance of being which its own method cannot provide. All scientific investigation necessarily but tacitly assumes that the thing under investigation *exists*. If empirical science did not assume the objective existence of the material world, *it* could not exist. Modern science does not bother itself with the question of existence, nor does it take its realist assumptions seriously, because philosophy has resigned its position as a science and so denies any possible knowledge of reality. Yet, paradoxically, modernist theology claims modern philosophy indispensable to theology's project, viz., the illumination of ultimate or transcendent reality, which modern philosophy has explicitly rejected any knowledge of. The contradiction would be tolerable but for the modernist theologian's acceptance of philosophy's rejection of the scholastic metaphysical tradition and the Aristotelian principles of especially formal and final causation that inform it. They are like co-dependent brother and sister in a dysfunctional family -- call it modernity, because both philosopher and theologian insist on that fundamental autonomy to make of reality what they wish. By accepting the premises of modern philosophy, the modernist theologian yields willy-nilly to the claims of empirical science -- if he chooses to acknowledge them at all. For those claims become insuperable, and theology becomes like philosophy, an aimless skepticism.

Pius IX in his *Syllabus* declared that Catholicism is incompatible with modern civilization. And St. Pius X in *Lamentabili* declares Catholicism is compatible with science. Although the Church values knowledge, she abhors its counterfeit: mendacity and presumption. Between modern thought and real knowledge, the fruit of genuine science, there is an unbridgeable gulf. Because modern philosophy has repudiated realist metaphysics by its rejection of Aristotle and the scholastic tradition, it is dangerous to Catholic thought which is rooted in that intellectual tradition and which she regards as inalienable.

Whether in theology or philosophy, the principles at the core of the complex tradition of scholasticism are, for reasons that have been discussed in this book, alien to the modern view of reality and from which the whole of the modern world is estranged. Among the most fundamental are *essentialism*, that everything possesses a substantial form which is its fixed essence (what we mean when we say tautologically, "It is what it is" or "A rose is a rose by any other name"), and *finality* or *teleology*, that the intelligible order of existence is based on a specific finality or final cause of everything in existence, that in the natural order everything has an end or purpose that is independent of any human participation or interest. These metaphysical ideas of final cause and substantial form run directly counter to modernity's exclusively empiricist or idealist view of reality, which had long ago rejected these ideas (along with everything else in scholastic thought) as indemonstrable. The very notions, then, of purpose and causation according to final causes and fixed essences in a given natural order, which are fundamental to every aspect of rational thought, and so to Catholic principle, from ethics to economics. They form no part of modern thought. Not only do they form no part of the intellectual tenets of modernity, they are rejected with a *hostile* prejudice. Coming to terms with modernity has meant making peace with it. But modernity has written the terms of that "peace" and will accept no others. To conciliate the modern world to the Church and her message is, as we have witnessed in the post-conciliar era, a one-way street.

I think it is only fair to introduce the distinction here between modern philosophical inquiry that is possibly useful to Catholic thought (but dangerous because it goes unexamined by a Catholic intellectual tradition in desuetude) and modern thought that is *inherently inimical to* it. Modern philosophy is not inimical to the Catholic tradition for being "modern", merely in the neutral sense of that word; it is inimical only in so far as it excludes principles on which rational thought and therefore Catholic thought is possible. In the order of the intellect, the ultimate sources of modernity are, as we have seen, specific philosophical errors and the conclusions they lead to, but it does not follow that *every* philosophical endeavor since Descartes is to be rejected a priori.

Certain entirely new philosophical lines of inquiry in the last 400 years can and have rewarded Catholic teaching with deeper insights into human nature and behavior. One of these is Edmund Husserl's phenomenology. The philosophical work of Karol Wojtyla and his pontificate as Pope John Paul II made better understood the relation between Phenomenology and Catholic doctrine and particularly its compatibility with Thomistic metaphysics (though its compatibility has I think been overstated even by the philosopher Wojtyla[342]). Of course, in the hands of some if not many theologians, modern methods like phenomenology have not deepened or clarified Catholic teaching. But even these potentially useful modern philosophers remain dangerous; we need only recall how dangerous was Aristotelian philosophy in the hands of the likes of Siger of Brabant or even Peter Abelard.

But if Catholic theologians are to use, positively or negatively, modern philosophy safely, there must already be firmly established a tradition from which to make such speculative sorties. Without a tradition, the inquiry has no context and no purpose, no definite finality, because it has no received body of thought to make the inquiry itself intelligible. It becomes mere speculation for its own sake. If you were to change the way chess is played, you would have first to accept and understand thoroughly the rules and nature of the game. Otherwise, what would be the point? The very standard of inquiry that makes inquiry purposeful

---

[342] See *Faith and Reason*, Spring. Vol. XXXI, no. 1 pp.65-109.

is provided by the tradition itself. The Church has already set the standard of Catholic thought in the work (and not merely the "method") of St. Thomas. But, we must be reminded, that is only an endorsement, though a solemn and uncompromising one, not a dogmatic requirement of faith.

Theology is a science and as such its principles are concerned with knowledge of objective reality and, therefore, it is not a mode of rational inquiry into a purely subjective experience. It follows that the range of theological speculation is inherently circumscribed by those very scientific principles. Unlike art, theological inquiry has little or no place for innovation and originality. While art is free to invent meaning by imaginative creation, theology must discover meaning rationally in truth both revealed and ascertained. Originality as an intellectual principle has little value to the Catholic mind. Catholic thought, if it is anything, is rooted in tradition, that is, in an inherited body of thought and principle. And thus the substance of Catholic thought is more like an heirloom that is preserved and cared for than a blank canvas on which to make something new each time. But, of course, it is also unlike an heirloom in that it is not hermetically sealed from *all change.* Catholic tradition is not immutable. It changes but only according to its own principles, which are immutable.

Now, because art is at liberty to make meaning and to broadly interpret human experience to use it as the raw material in its creative endeavor, art may be useful to theological speculation *ad experimentum* without danger of formal error. Perhaps, what some modernist theologians sought in their speculations was very much like or analogous to what the artist or poet seeks (or used to seek) in artistic creation, viz., that which is inexpressible by any other means. In so far as the modernist theologian genuinely adheres to Catholic truth, but believes Scholasticism (or strict Thomism) is incapable of accounting for and articulating the whole range of religious experience especially of modern man, he may find in artistic, particularly literary and visual, expression of what is still theological truth the freedom denied him in discursive theology.

Of course, such a project is more easily accomplished in a Christian culture like that of the high Middle Ages where the literary forms for religious art are already available and well developed. It may be that the literary imagination is precisely the medium for the kind and degree of theological speculation to which the believing modernist theologian is most given. One might site the religious transformation of the secular romantic tradition of literature and the 12th-century development of the new sophisticated and exotic courtly epic and lyric poetry that was entirely lacking in any religious inspiration, and the "deliberate attempt" in the 13th century "to moralize the courtly tradition and to infuse an element of religious idealism into the secular romanticism of the courtly epic".[343] The Grail Legend was perhaps the culmination of this Christianization by the religious imagination of a thoroughly secular form of literature and from it a highly developed literary imagination merged. We may recall too that theology itself once enjoyed a distinct literary quality in the Augustinian tradition before the advent of scholasticism whose developed, rigorous, and precise method of inquiry supplanted Augustinianism as an analytical instrument for the definition of Christian truth.

If my suggestion seems impracticable, as it certainly must be for most theologians of any stamp, its value may lie less in its practicality than in what it implies about the proper place of the modernist project. If the modernist wants to examine religious experience in the modern world with all of its ambiguities and perplexities (rather than in terms of strict theological orthodoxy with its certitudes and authority), it is in the order of the literary and visual arts and not in theology per se where he belongs. There he can avoid hardening his speculations into abstract assertions which can lead others (and himself) astray of the truth. Literature is also a very – perhaps the most -- effective means (by the well-intended modernist's own reckoning) of penetrating the modern consciousness with Catholic truth. The writings of T.S. Eliot, C.S. Lewis, J.R.R. Tolkien, Walker Percy, and Flannery O'Conner are excellent examples in literature of the possibilities. For this reason among others, Frederick

---

[343] C. Dawson, *Medieval Essays*, New York: Sheed & Ward, 1954, p. 177

Wilhelmsen has called art "the instrument of evangelization."[344]

I have indicated how culture is the necessary medium of any communication of Catholic truth to a secularized and desacralized culture. *Gaudium et spes* addresses the matter of secular culture but fails to explore the inevitable and deleterious effect of secular culture as a medium for the communication of the Gospel. Marshall McLuhan's principle, "the medium is the message", is especially true (notwithstanding his particular concern with specifically electronic media) when it is a case of a culture, estranged from Christianity and all Christian principle, becoming the medium of the Christian message. This is much like using wood as the medium for conducting electricity. Yet, even at this late date, it would be rash to say that western culture is altogether the same thing as the culture of modernity. The old western tradition (which was culturally Christian and which we still admire even if we will not embrace it), though moribund, is not quite dead. There is still scholarly attention to it as well as vestiges of it in architecture, literature, and a number institutions, the greatest of which is the Church. All of these, but especially the labors of the Church, help keep at least our memory of the old western tradition alive. Nevertheless, modernity is at best an inept medium of a message for which it has no symbolic or otherwise imaginative means of representing. Hence, there is the

---

[344] "Art and Religion: Felicitous Tension or Conflict?" in *The Intercollegiate Review*, Spring, 1975, 94.

necessity to re-sacralize culture. In the post-Christian west today, there is already developing a real competition between a number of religions besides Christianity to do just that. For the spiritual vacuum will be filled – by one thing or another.

What modernity had first rejected intellectually, then excluded politically and socially it is now incapable of comprehending – let alone expressing – culturally. The culture of death, though it might quibble over it as a legal issue, does not argue the moral questions of abortion and contraception (which even most professing Christians don't acknowledge) it just goes on doing uncritically, even thoughtlessly, what is now habitual to it. The traditions in literature, sculpture, painting, and music which were capable of expressing and in many instances bore the Christian message are no longer widely taught and are taught and learned with less and less comprehension. At least 100 years of modernism in literature, sculpture, painting, and music have gutted these art forms of meaning, having deracinated them from all that is natural as well as supernatural and making them incapable of expressing anything human or divine. But having been gutted of meaning and significance, they can be refilled. It is the critical task of Catholic participation in western culture and the Church's necessary fostering of that participation. Yet it is, admittedly, all against the grain. And while there have been some successes in literature and film and architecture, these are as yet only the flashes of a strobe light in what is otherwise total darkness. These remarkable but all too rare glimpses of the embodiment of Christian truth by the Christian imagination do not constitute a sufficient influence to draw modern man to Goodness, Beauty, and Truth.

I have already asked the question what is to be done in such a dilemma; the answer is the conversion of culture. This cannot be done by a naïve reception of the prevailing culture of modernity but quietly and prudently opposing it, by fostering the remnants of the western tradition, reconstructing it from them, not in order to restore the past which cannot be restored, but to make within the Christian tradition a culture and civilization that is at once old and new. The reconstruction (or perhaps it will only be a rehabilitation) will have to be done one way or the other. The commercial and political order that is the modern world is already bowing under the enormities of its own vices. When it collapses, assuming the end of the world is not yet, the Church must be prepared spiritually and intellectually to lead men into a new civilized order. The foundation of that order has always been in our possession in the great and perennial of Catholic thought founded as it is in her Sacred Tradition. It is only from that intellectual tradition that a truly civilized order can arise from the ashes of the present order. Should that tradition be allowed to die, the new order will then be a new paganism and like the possessed man to whom our Lord compared his own generation, who, having been delivered of one demon, invites seven more, will be in a far worse state than before.[345]

Theology bears a tremendous responsibility in the Church's mission to impress Christian truth upon society. Only under its auspices can the Catholic mind renew the culture to make art, political and institutional life once again at least formally cooperative with the spiritual aims of the Church. But it is no part of the Church's mission to render society or the culture sacred. The Church has always, at least implicitly, recognized long before even St. Augustine articulated it as doctrine in his *City of God*, the existence of the two distinct orders of reality, the temporal and the spiritual. The doctrine makes clear that the temporal order is necessarily profane as distinct from the sacred and that the spiritual order while above it is not unrelated to it. They are not wholly separate orders, nor equal; for it is in the nature of the higher order to subsume and act upon the lower. The spiritual order cannot make the temporal order sacred, but it can and does manifest itself in the lower order. That manifestation occurs at the level of culture. It is not identification. In this case, the medium is not the message; it is only the purely natural and therefore oblique incidence of (non-sanctifying) grace.

---

[345] Mt. 12:43-45: "And when an unclean spirit is gone out of a man he walks through dry places seeking rest, and finds none. Then he says: I will return into my house from whence I came out. And coming he finds it empty, swept, and garnished. Then he goes, and takes with him seven other spirits more wicked than himself, and they enter in and dwell there: and the last state of that man is made worse than the first. So shall it be also to this wicked generation."

The last forty years have witnessed the effects of theological ambiguity and confusion. Some have paradoxically argued with an almost child-like naiveté that the rapid secularization of society and its alienation from all things Christian in the post-conciliar era was the cause of the Church's crisis and not the effect of the theological effort to accommodate the Church to the modernity. It was supposed that the Church should cease to attack modernity and to try to understand it and make her peace with it. The truth is that the Church opposed modernity because she understood it better than modernity understood itself. In the early days of the Syllabus and the fight against modernism, the Church's actions which were easily mistaken as unprovoked attacks on the modern world, as liberalism was "nobly" was shaking off the "chains" of the old ideas of freedom and authority. But her critics who would make accommodation with modernity in the Church failed to understand that she was acting *in defense* of the perennial truths of the Catholic faith, which were being threatened on every side as well as from within, not lashing out fearfully at what she didn't understand. The Church's critics also failed to understand that she was protecting more than just her authority, but an entire civilization, which depended on her for its moral and spiritual direction and social well-being. For under her auspices civilization in the west developed and matured as the first (and perhaps the last) Christian civilization.

At the heart of the modernist's incomprehension of the Church's wisdom in her rejection of modernity is a profound confusion of the orders of love and truth and a failure to philosophically acknowledge the essence of things (a kind of philosophical practice supposed to belong to a dead and discredited tradition). Love is thought to be prior to truth just as it is supposed to be prior to law as well. But Truth is prior to both. It is prior to law because law is impossible without truth. And love is impossible without the moral law, which is necessary to an act of the will and love is essentially any act of will (in scholastic terms, the moral law is the formal cause of love).[346] This is why our Lord *commands* us to love God and our neighbor.

Attempting to reach modern man with the truths of the Gospel is of course an act of charity, but charity must be ordered to truth which is necessarily prior. It is this truth that Pope Benedict XVI has profoundly reflected on in his encyclical, *Caritas in veritatae.* Accommodating modernity in any of its essential modes of thought, to the end that modern civilization would again embrace Christianity, can only be called a fool's errand, because it is *a priori* impossible to achieve. Somewhere St. Thomas says *"omni virtus moralis debet esse prudens",* that all virtue is necessarily prudent, because prudence is the virtue of seeing things *as they are.*[347] The Catholic modernist's project is imprudent not because

---

[346] Cf. Romano Amerio, *Iota Unum,* Kansas City, MO: Sartor House, 1996, pp. 388-89.
[347] Cf. Pieper, *The Four Cardinal Virtues,* (New York: Harcourt, Brace & World, 1964), pp. 50 *et seq.*

the end is a perfection impossible to achieve in this world, but because its end is imperfect or defective, because it supposes the union of contradictory things, Christianity and modernity.

That profoundly flawed supposition is at the heart of the Catholic modernist error, but behind that error is modernity's still more profound error of the rejection of the realist principle that the Catholic modernist has uncritically accepted as true but which is fundamental to all of Christian thought. This is the truth that the True (and the Good) is convertible with being. There is no finally escaping this principle. Modernity can run but it cannot hide from reality; it can deny or ignore the truth by simply thinking what it wishes but as everyone knows who has ignored, say, a bill past due, reality has a way of finding you out. The scholastic habit of thought made it difficult to deny or ignore the truth of a thing, its essence. To ignore or deny the essence of anything is to fail to understand it and perceive it for what it is. Modernity, refusing any truck with such realist principles, prefers to make its own reality. That to do so is a metaphysical impossibility never occurs to modernists. They prefer – like children in a game -- not to think along those lines, persuading themselves that it is the outlandish stuff of a dead scholasticism with its metaphysical preoccupations and rigorous logic and linguistic exactitude, all of which rather spoil the fun and creativity of making your own reality. What is truly outlandish is things like the perverse jurisprudence of the majority of our supreme court justices, which would find the justification of the murder of innocents in a principle such as "At the heart of liberty is the right to define one's own concept of existence, of meaning, of the universe, and of the mystery of human life".[348]

The Church can only relate to the modern world by being what she is, a spiritual society divinely ordained and inspired. And in so far as her relation is one of charity and justice, she must necessarily reject modernity. Of course, to reject is not to ignore. If she is to evangelize modern man effectively, she must not fail to understand modernity. It is very difficult to distinguish the culture of modernity from the civilization it informs. But if it can be done; it will require a pre-modern tradition of thought. The Church has already wisely determined that through St. Thomas, the scholastic tradition fits the bill, but not to the exclusion of other pre-modern traditions. Scholasticism, when directed by a sound Thomism clarified by the elimination of those elements of modern thought alien to it, particularly a Kantian epistemology, possesses the precision and versatility needed to address every concern of contemporary man. If we are to have for the sake of answering those concerns an epistemological Thomism, then, as any scholastic would know, the substantive must govern the qualifier, not the other way round (the scholastic knows that even grammar is rooted in metaphysics). If modern man is to hear and learn the truth, it must come from an intellectual tradition that has

---

[348] Justice Anthony Kennedy in *Planned Parenthood v. Casey*, 505 U.S. 833.

been ordered to truth. Modern man must not, for his own sake, be allowed to have the discussion of truth, the truth of his existence no less than the truth of his redemption, *on his own terms.* Modernity has failed him utterly and corrupted his thought and his civilization beyond even what the failure of classical paganism had wrought upon Graeco-Roman civilization. Modern man can never discover the reality of his own condition. Only the Church by a genuine evangelism rooted in her profoundest intellectual traditions can lead him to it and beyond that reality to the Source of all being, He Who is "I AM".

The Church and the Culture of Modernity

A Bibliography of Recommended Readings

Adler, Mortimer. *Ten Philosophical Mistakes*. New York: Touchstone Books, 1997.

Amerio, Romano. *Iota Unum*, tr., Fr. John P. Parsons, Kansas City, Missouri: Sarto House, 1996.

Aquinas, St. Thomas. Fathers of the English Dominican Province, trans. *The Summa theologica*. 2d, rev. ed. 22 vols. London: Burns, Oates & Washbourne, 1912–36; reprinted in 5 vols., Westminster, MD: Christian Classics, 1981.

------------------ Pegis, Anton C., James F. Anderson, Vernon J. Bourke, and Charles J. O'Neil, trans. *On the Truth of the Catholic Faith (Summa Contra Gentiles)*. 5 vols. New York: Doubleday, 1955–57.

Augustine, Saint. *The City of God*. Marcus Dods, trans. New York: Random House, 1950.

Benedict XVI, Pope. *Caritas in Veritate* (2009).

Berger, Peter L. *The Sacred Canopy, Elements of a Sociological Theory of Religion*. New York: Doubleday Anchor Books, 1969.

Cochrane, Charles Norris. *Christianity and Classical Culture*, New York: Oxford Galaxy Books, 1957.

Craycraft, Jr., Kenneth R. *The American Myth of Religious Freedom*. Dallas: Spence Publishing Co., 1999.

Dawson, Christopher. *Christianity and European Culture, Selections from the Work of Christopher Dawson*, ed. Gerald J. Russello. Washington, DC: Catholic University of America Press, 1998.

Ferrara, Christopher A. *The Church and the Libertarian*. Minnesota: The Remnant Press. 2010

------------------- *The Judgment of Nations*, New York: Sheed & Ward. 1937

------------------- *The Formation of Christendom*, New York: Sheed & Ward, 1967.

------------------- *Progress and Religion: An Historical Inquiry*, London: Sheed & Ward, 1931.

------------------- *The Crisis of Western Education*, New York: Sheed & Ward, 1961.

------------------- *Medieval Essays*, New York: Sheed & Ward, 1954.

------------------- *Christianity and European Culture: Selections from the Work of Christopher Dawson*. ed. by Gerald J.

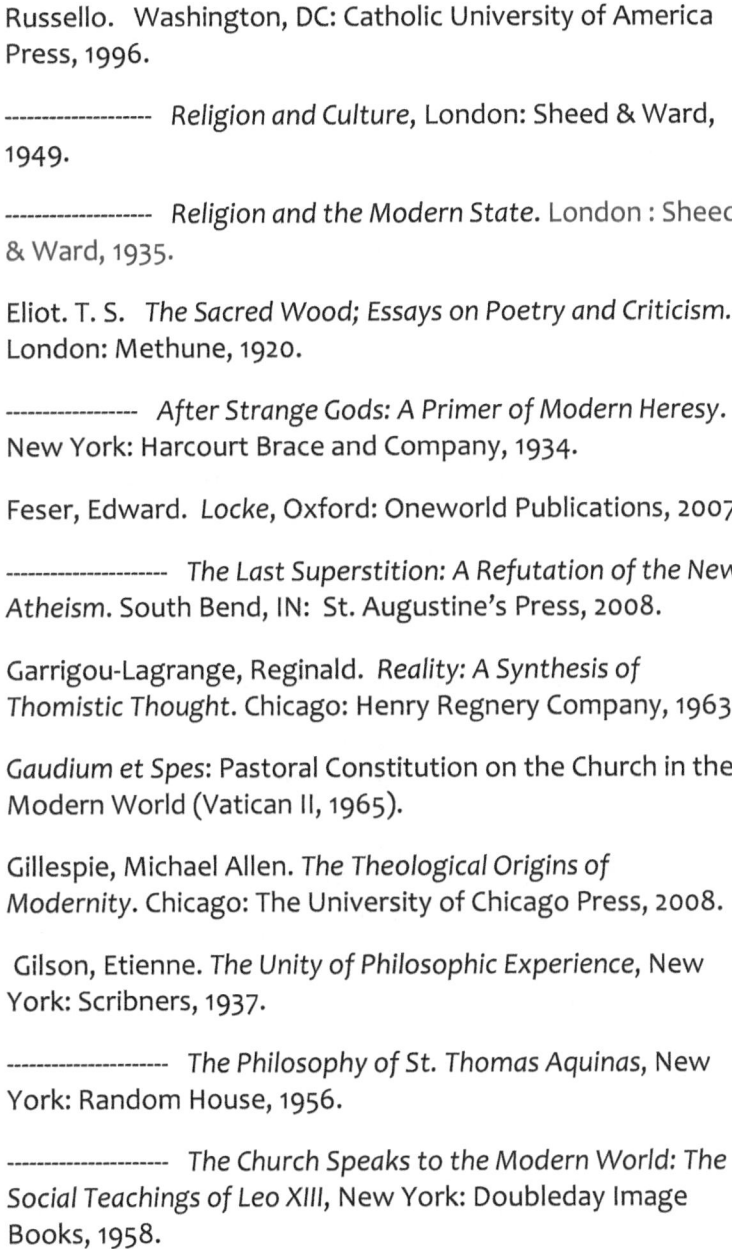

Russello. Washington, DC: Catholic University of America Press, 1996.

-------------------- *Religion and Culture*, London: Sheed & Ward, 1949.

-------------------- *Religion and the Modern State.* London : Sheed & Ward, 1935.

Eliot. T. S. *The Sacred Wood; Essays on Poetry and Criticism.* London: Methune, 1920.

---------------- *After Strange Gods: A Primer of Modern Heresy.* New York: Harcourt Brace and Company, 1934.

Feser, Edward. *Locke*, Oxford: Oneworld Publications, 2007.

--------------------- *The Last Superstition: A Refutation of the New Atheism.* South Bend, IN: St. Augustine's Press, 2008.

Garrigou-Lagrange, Reginald. *Reality: A Synthesis of Thomistic Thought.* Chicago: Henry Regnery Company, 1963.

Gaudium et Spes: Pastoral Constitution on the Church in the Modern World (Vatican II, 1965).

Gillespie, Michael Allen. *The Theological Origins of Modernity.* Chicago: The University of Chicago Press, 2008.

Gilson, Etienne. *The Unity of Philosophic Experience*, New York: Scribners, 1937.

--------------------- *The Philosophy of St. Thomas Aquinas*, New York: Random House, 1956.

-------------------- *The Church Speaks to the Modern World: The Social Teachings of Leo XIII*, New York: Doubleday Image Books, 1958.

Guardini, Romano. *Letters from Lake Como Explorations in Technology and the Human Race.* Trans. Geoffrey W. Bromiley. Grand Rapids, MI: Eerdmans Publishing Co., 1994.

---------------------- *The End of the Modern World.* Wilmington, DE: ISI Books, 1998.

Haldane, J. "Thomism and the Future of Catholic Philosophy", *New Blackfriars* 80 (938), 1999.

Hayles, E.E.Y. *Pope John and His Revolution*, London: Eyre & Spottiswood, 1985.

Hazard, Paul. *European Thought in the Eighteenth Century from Montesquieu to Lessing*, London: Hollis & Carter, 1954.

Hittenger, Russell. "Christopher Dawson on Technology and the Demise of Liberalism" at www.catholiceducation.org.

John Paul II, Pope. *Fides et Ratio* (1998).

---------------------- *Motu Proprio*, History and Aim of the Pontifical Academy of Social Sciences (1994).

Kalb, James. *The Tyranny of Liberalism: Understanding and Overcoming Adninistered Freedom , Inquisitorial Tolerance, and Equality by Command.* Wilmington, DE: ISI Books, 2008.

Kelly, Tony. "*Gaudium et Spes*: Too much Joy and Too Much Hope?" in *The Australian EJournal of Theology*, August 2003.

Kerr, Fergus . *Twentieth-Century Catholic Theologians: From Neoscholasticism to Nuptial Mysticism.* Oxford: Blackwell, 2007.

Kraynak, Robert. *Christian Faith and Modern Democracy.* Notre Dame, IN: University of Notre Dame Press, 2001.

Leclercq, Jean ,O.S.B. *The Love of Learning and the Desire for God, A Study of Monastic Culture,* New York: Fordham University Press, 1961.

Lewis, C. S. *Studies in Words,* Cambridge: Cambridge University Press, 1964.

de Lubac, Henri. *The Drama of Atheist Humanism,* San Francisco: Ignatius Press, 1995.

Leo XIII, Pope. *Aeterne Patris* (1879).

Lockerd, Benjamin G. "Nature and Religion in the Cultural Criticism of T.S. Eliot" in Modern Studies in English Language and Literature, vol. 51, no. 1.

MacIntyre, Alasdair. *Edith Stein: A Philosophical Prologue 1913-1922,* Rowman & Littlefield Publishers, 2005.

---------------------- *Whose Justice? Which Rationality?* (Notre Dame: University of Notre Dame Press) 1988.

-------------------- *Three Rival Versions of Moral Inquiry,* (Notre Dame: University of Notre Dame Press) 1989.

-------------------- *After Virtue: A Study in Moral Theory* (University of Notre Dame Press, 1984.

Manent, Pierre . *An Intellectual History of Liberalism,* tr., Rebecca Belinski. Princeton: Princeton University Press, 1994.

Maritain, Jacques. *Integral Humanism.* Notre Dame, Indiana: Univ. of Notre Dame Press, 1973.

---------------------- *Man and the State.* University of Chicago Press, Chicago, ILL, 1951.

---------------------- *The Peasant of the Garonne, An Old Layman Questions Himself about the Present Time,* trans. Michael

Cuddihy and Elizabeth Hughes, Holt, Rinehart and Winston, NY, 1968.

Mercier, Cardinal, ed. *A Manual of Scholastic Philosophy.* 2 vols. Reprint. Whitefish, MT: Kessinger Publishing Company, 1922.

Mitchell, Mark T. "Michael Polanyi, Alasdair MacIntyre, and the Role of Tradition" in *Humanitas* 19, 1-2, Spring-Fall 2006.

Molnar, Thomas. *The Emerging Atlantic Culture.* New Brunswick, N.J. : Transaction, 1994.

Newman, John Henry. *Sermons Preached on Various Occasions.* London: Longmans, Green & Co., 1908.

Paul VI, Pope. *Optatam Totius* (1965).

Peddicord, Richard, O.P. *The Sacred Monster of Thomism: An Introduction to the Life and Legacy of Reginald Garrigou-Lagrange, O.P.* South Bend, IN: St. Augustine's Press, 2005.

Pieper, Josef. *Happiness and Contemplation",* tr. Richard and Clara Winston, Chicago: Henry Regnery Co., Logos Books, 1958.

-------------------- *The Perennial Scope of Philosophy,* trans. by Ralph Manheim, New York: Philosophical Library, 1949.

-------------------- *Belief and Faith A Philosophical Tract,* Chicago: Regnery 1965.

-------------------- *The Four Cardinal Virtues,* (New York: Harcourt, Brace & World, 1965)

Pius IX, Pope. *Syllabus of Errors* (1864).

-------------------- *Quanta Cura* (1864).

Pius X, Pope St. *Pascendi dominici gregis* (1907).

Reno, R.R. "Theology After the Revolution", a review of *Twentieth-Century Catholic Theologians: From Chenu to Ratzinger* by Fergus Kerr in *First Things*, May 2007.

Rizzi, Anthony. *The Science Before Science*. Baton Rouge: IAP Press, 2004.

Rowland, Tracey. *Culture and the Thomist Tradition*, London: Routledge, 2003.

Schama, Simon. *Citizens, a Chronicle of the French Revolution*, New York: Alfred A. Knoff, 1989.

Senior, John. *The Death of Christian Culture*. Repr., 1978 ed., Norfolk, VA: IHS Press, 2007.

Sullivan, Daniel J. *Introduction to Philosophy: The Perennial Principles of the Classical Realist Tradition*. Charlotte, NC: TAN Books, 1992.

Wilhelmsen, Frederick. "Faith, Sign, and Society" in *Faith & Reason*, Summer, 1994.

------------------ *Christianity and Political Philosophy*, Athens: Univ. of Georgia Pr., 1978.

ABOUT THE AUTHOR

Richard Divozzo is a librarian and writer living with his wife and their four children in Grand Rapids, Michigan

www.ingramcontent.com/pod-product-compliance
Lightning Source LLC
Chambersburg PA
CBHW061333280526
45784CB00001B/5